BEFORE THE WALL CAME DOWN

Soviet and East European Filmmakers Working in the West

Edited by

Graham Petrie
McMaster University

Ruth Dwyer
McMaster University

UNIVERSITY
PRESS OF
AMERICA

Lanham • New York • London

"A Dissenting View of Milos Forman's *Amadeus*" © 1990
by George Lellis

"Patterns of Spirituality in Tarkovsky's Later Films" © 1990
by Alexandra Heidi Karriker

Proceedings of a conference held at McMaster University,
Hamilton Ontario on March 10-11, 1989, under the auspices of
McMaster University's Inter-Departmental Committee on
Communist and East European Affairs, with funding from
McMaster University and the Social Sciences and Humanities
Research Council of Canada.

Library of Congress Cataloging-in-Publication Data

Before the Wall came down : Soviet and East European filmmakers
working in the West / edited by Graham Petrie and Ruth Dwyer.
p. cm.
"Proceedings of a conference held at McMaster Universtiy, Hamilton
Ontario on March 10-11, 1989, under the auspices of McMaster University's
Inter-Departmental Committee on Communist and East European Affairs"—
Verso t.p. 1. Motion pictures—Europe, Eastern—Congresses. 2. Motion
pictures—Soviet Union—Congresses. 3. Motion pictures—United States—
Foreign influences—Congresses. I. Petrie, Graham. II. Dwyer, Ruth.
PN1993.5.E82B44 1990 791.43'0947—dc20 90–39188 CIP

ISBN 0–8191–7858–6 (alk. paper)
ISBN 0–8191–7859–4 (pbk. : alk. paper)

Table of Contents

Session Four: Yugoslav Cinema

Session Five: Soviet Cinema (Andrei Tarkovsky)

Appendix

Notes on Participants

through the system, and even relatively well-known figures like Renoir were forced to make do with what the studios were prepared to offer them rather than having the degree of choice initially accorded to Lubitsch, Sjöström or Murnau.

Leaving aside such perennial immigrants as directors and actors from Great Britain, Canada and, more recently, Australia, the third wave, starting in the mid-1960s, combines features of both the earlier ones. On the one hand are Swedish, French, German or Italian directors lured to Hollywood after one of their films has enjoyed some commercial success in the States, but rarely staying longer than to make one or two, often poorly-received films there (Jan Troell, Bo Widerberg, Michelangelo Antonioni and Lina Wertmuller come to mind here.) On the other are the directors from East or Central Europe who leave their own countries for political reasons and, having drifted around Western Europe or Britain for a time, generally end up in the United States, rarely with much of an advance reputation and even more rarely with contracts, and with little prospect of "going home" if things work out badly for them there.

The fate of these latter resembles more that of the post-World War I immigrants than that of the later generation. A few, notably Miloš Forman and Roman Polanski, have achieved both critical and commercial success; but, for the majority, there has either been an exhausting and eventually futile struggle to obtain a foothold or, as with Ivan Passer, a promising beginning fading into almost complete obscurity. (The analogues in the 1920s would be with the dazzling success of Ernst Lubitsch, contrasted with the increasing frustration of Murnau, Sjöström and Mauritz Stiller, and the eventual departure of the last two.)

One way of looking at the similarities and differences between these three waves of immigration might be to connect them with, respectively, the consolidation, the heyday, and the crumbling of the Hollywood studio system. Those, like Lubitsch, Sjöström and Murnau, who arrived around 1923-25, entered a system still receptive to innovation and prepared to tolerate mavericks and inde-

Introduction

Graham Petrie
McMaster University

As several of the contributors to this volume point out, there have so far been three major influxes of European film making talent into the Hollywood system. The first, lasting from 1923 to around 1930, was dominated by Germans, Swedes, Danes and Hungarians, and brought such figures as Ernst Lubitsch, F.W. Murnau, Greta Garbo, Alexander Korda, Michael Curtiz and Victor Sjöström to the United States. Except in the case of the Hungarians, political motives played no significant role in the decision to come to America: financial incentives, curiosity, and the ambition to prove themselves on a wider stage than that provided by their native countries were the major factors.

The second wave, from the mid-1930s to the early 1940s, was, by contrast, almost exclusively political and brought refugees from Germany, Austria and France fleeing, first of all from Nazi Germany, and later from Nazi-occupied Europe. They included, a-mong the directors, Billy Wilder, Jean Renoir, Fritz Lang, Otto Preminger, René Clair and Max Ophuls and, though several re-turned to Europe after the end of the War, others stayed to continue their careers in the United States. Whereas those arriving in the 1920s came almost exclusively by invitation and had already sign-ed contracts with major studios or producers in advance, the war-time immigrants came to America on their own initiative and usually as virtual unknowns who had to work their way slowly artistic identity that results only in unmade films?

Another variant of the problem, explored in some of the papers and discussions, looks at it from a reverse angle: is there any place any longer, even in Poland, Hungary or Czechoslovakia, for films that put artistic requirements ahead of commercial ones? All these countries, and even the Soviet Union, need desperately to sell their films abroad if their industries are to survive; some, like Hungary and the U.S.S.R., are now turning to a free-enterprise model that makes commercial success at least as important as artistic quality or political orthodoxy. One increasingly favoured solution is co-production, with a West European nation or even the United States, yet this seems to result too often in films that have no particular identity and exist in a cultural vacuum that satisfies no one. The most promising path, and one that may be taken more often now that film makers in Poland, Hungary and the Soviet Union may no longer need to emigrate in order to express themselves freely,[3] is the one described by Andrew Horton in his paper, where the film makers do not emigrate, do not attempt to strike a big-budget deal with a major studio, and instead make their own films, in their own time and their own way, on a realistic budget that does not make them dependent on a large commercial success — and then go back home to continue their careers.

....

The two opening papers of the conference, on Soviet directors, raise most of the basic issues summarised above. Alexander Batchan's interview with Slava Tsukerman, director of the cult hit *Liquid Sky*, illustrates many of the choices and problems faced by a totally unknown Soviet director who preferred to work independently and to keep his distance from the lure of Hollywood. His training in the Soviet Union gave him a wide technical mastery far superior to that of most beginning American directors, yet left him totally unprepared for the "budgetary and human shortages" that he had to cope with in making his film. He was able, however, to work with subject matter that would have been totally forbidden in the Soviet Union of the time (the early 1980s) — though, as a symptom of the rapid changes taking place that are, for good or ill, "internationalising" film making everywhere, the film has now been shown and acclaimed in his home country. Freedom of expression, in this case, has to be balanced against lack of resources and a lengthy and tedious struggle to get the film made, and then released.

Andrei Konchalovsky, by contrast, as Vida Johnson argues in her paper, has chosen to try to crack the Hollywood system on its own terms and has been prepared to make compromises on the artistic and personal level in order to do so. He has been helped in this, she suggests, by the fact that, even in the Soviet Union, he was more commercially oriented than most of his fellow directors and was already working, in *Siberiade*, on a scale, and with a type of narrative structure, that could be easily adapted to Hollywood's requirements. Konchalovsky has understood that a successful American film has to be centred round action and strongly delineated characters; his ability to produce these, especially in *Runaway Train*, has got him off to a good start in America, though he has not yet totally consolidated this and his future prospects are still somewhat problematic.

....

The second session, covering aspects of Hungarian, Czech and Soviet cinema, began with George Lellis' detailed analysis of Milos Forman's Academy Award winning *Amadeus*. While acknowledging Forman's intelligence and skill as a film maker, Lellis suggests that the film avoids most of the stylistic and thematic challenges present in Peter Shaffer's play and that its vast popular appeal can perhaps be linked with what he calls its "ambivalence" and its "indirect and non-threatening confrontation with questions relating sexual identity to cultural expression." It is essentially, he claims, a film that "mistrusts" the power and potential of its own medium and, though Lellis does not cover Forman's American career as a whole, his argument would tend to support those who feel that it has increasingly avoided taking the risks, both in style and subject matter, that made his Czech films so fresh and exciting.

Like Konchalovsky, Forman seems to have preferred to adapt and compromise, but perhaps at greater cost to his own integrity as an artist.

Catherine Portuges' paper, on the Hungarian Márta Mészáros, presents yet another option: a film maker who has not yet worked in America, though her films are known and respected there, but who has attempted to escape some of the restrictions involved in working in Hungary by making co-productions, in particular with French companies. In her case the restrictions were not so much political as sexual: though not considering herself as a feminist, she found the viewpoint she took, as a woman, towards Hungarian society led to her work being resented or ignored there. Faced ultimately with the prospect however, of having to continue to work in the West and so cutting herself off from her national and cultural roots, she chose to re-establish herself in her homeland and to make the kind of film — her projected autobiographical trilogy — that it would be impossible for her to make anywhere else. In her case, "departure [has led] to return, and to a deepening, rather than neutralization, of artistic and political vision."

John Twomey introduces a lesser-known yet fascinating figure from an earlier generation of immigrants, the set designer Nikolai Soloviov, who made important contributions to Eisenstein's *Alexander Nevsky* and *Ivan the Terrible, Part I*. His later career in Canadian television, and the number of "firsts" with which he was associated in the heyday of CBC drama production, suggest that he may be representative of many other relatively unknown artists whose achievements deserve further examination and acknowledgement.

··················

The session on Polish cinema began with Peter Christensen's examination of Jerzy Skolimowski's *The Lightship*, not so much as an adaptation of Siegfried Lenz's novel, but as a reworking of the main themes of Joseph Conrad's *Victory*. Skolimowski's chequered career in the West has involved some dubious and unsuccessful enterprises but, Christensen argues, in this film, he found a way of assimilating some of the main themes of his earlier work with the "Conradian philosophy" of another Polish exile living and working abroad. Christensen traces in particular "the representation of temptation in connection with both the common fallen state of mankind and male homosexual attraction" as being the two crucial themes that link Skolimowski with Conrad and perhaps give this film a more personal and deeply-felt edge than his more anonymous adaptations of such writers as Vladimir Nabokov and Sir Arthur Conan Doyle.

In "Exile and Identity" Paul Coates takes up, in a Polish context, some of the questions of national identity raised earlier by Catherine Portuges. After discussing the "problematic options" available to Polish directors until fairly recently — the "director of integrity will be compelled to go into exile," like Skolimowski or Polanski, or at least do some work abroad; or, if staying or returning home, he or she should do a co-production — Coates examines in some detail Krzysztof Zanussi's *The Year of the Quiet Sun* and Agnieszka Holland's *To Kill a Priest*. Finding that both of them fall between two cultural stools, Coates argues that, paradoxically, it is their contemporary, Krzystof Kieslowski, all of whose films have been made in Poland and who has never worked abroad, who is both "the most Polish of directors" and also "the most Western". Through a commentary on Kieslowski's *Blind Chance* that compares it to the work of Bernardo Bertolucci, Coates claims that his analysis of the theme of power is typical of what "renders East European cinema so bewitchingly accurate a mirror of our era" and makes this film truly international in its scope.

Agnieszka Holland's script for the American-made *Anna* is given kinder treatment by Natasa Durovicova, who suggests that this somewhat hybrid film (combining Polish, Czech and American elements) deserves rather more serious and favourable attention than was granted on its release. The film in fact raises the question (also picked up by Patrick MacFadden in his discussant's comments after this panel) as to why we should expect East European film makers to act as a moral conscience or guide in an otherwise crassly commercial industry. In *Anna* Durovicova argues, the film makers have used formulaic generic devices for their own purposes, and the deliberate banality of these aspects is carefully interwoven into a complex mix of fiction, history and biography. Critics who saw only the banality, the deliberate conforming to generic expectations, saw merely a betrayal of the dedication to high art presumed to be inherent in East European film making, and failed to understand the strategies employed by the film as a whole.

A different perspective to the academic analyses up to this point was provided by the documentary film maker Slawomir Grunberg, whose first-hand account of the problems faced by an unknown, Polish-trained film director attempting to establish himself in an alien environment complemented some of the remarks made in the interview with Slava Tsukerman. His list of the elements of "culture shock" that he and his fellow exiles had to cope with is particularly instructive and heart-felt.

....

Much of the session on Yugoslav cinema centred round its most notorious and controversial figure, Dusan Makavejev, who, like Andrei Tarkovsky, is something of a touchstone for the ability of a serious and talented director to retain a personal artistic identity in a bewildering variety of different settings — in Makavejev's case Yugoslavia, the United States, Canada, Sweden and Australia. Daniel Goulding maintains that, contrary to received critical opinion, Makavejev's most recent films continue to display his characteristic "predilection for bizarre plots, surrealistic images and sharp social and political satire," even if, perhaps reflecting a worldwide retreat from stylistic experimentation, they are more conventional in structure than his earlier works and pay less attention to "discontinuous narrative structure and multiple levels of montage associations." His quirky, nonconformist temperament enables him to occupy a creative space that "intersects East and West, but belongs to neither" — though, as with others, he has perhaps paid the penalty of refusing to conform to either side by a relatively small filmography and a continuous and exhausting search for funding.

Another personal perspective came from Andrew Horton, who spoke of his experiences in scriptwriting co-productions with Yugoslav film makers, most notably with Srdjan Karanovic for *Something in Between*. Horton sees Yugoslav film makers, like Hungarians and now perhaps Poles, as occupying an "in-between" situation in which they can always go home if they fail to establish themselves abroad. They are thus perhaps unwilling or unable to make the kind of compromises accepted by a Forman or a Konchalovsky, or to seek to understand the secret of Hollywood narrative technique, preferring to continue to try to make "Yugoslav" films in an alien and inhospitable setting. The solution may be to exploit this "in-between" position by making use of what both Belgrade and Beverly Hills have to offer: to by-pass the usual Hollywood channels by finding independent sources of funding and to use Yugoslav techniques and expertise to make films that utilise American settings and characters and have an appeal to both worlds.

A further reverse angle to the topic came from Gerald Peary, reporting, not on Yugoslav film makers attempting to break into Hollywood, but on the Yugoslav obsession with Hollywood and its pervasive influence on the country's film culture. His account of some of the cultural misperceptions and misunderstandings involved in this helps both to complement and explain the kinds of difficulties experienced by Yugoslav and other East/Central European film makers who try to adapt to a world that they know more as a myth than as a reality.

....

The final conference session dealt exclusively with the work of the late Andrei Tarkovsky. While his death renders futile speculations on whether he could have continued to make films in the West on his own intransigent and uncompromising terms, or whether, under *glasnost*, he would now be enjoying privileged and honoured status as the leading film maker in his native land, there is little doubt that his career presents the conflict between the two systems in its starkest form. On the one hand is a system that respects artistic values and serious intellectual purpose, and shelters the artist from budgetary and other economic problems, but, in return, restricts his or her intellectual and political freedom; and, on the other, a system that leaves the film maker theoretically "free" to say or do what he or she wants — provided only that he or she can raise the money required and that the result satisfies the two primary demands of entertainment and box office success.

It can be argued that, for all his well-publicised problems in the Soviet Union, Tarkovsky was temperamentally better suited to working there than to attempting to survive in the free-enterprise jungle of the West, even when it manifested itself at its mildest in the form of the Swedish Film Institute and RAI Television in Italy. Some such argument may lie behind Paul Coates's comments in the post-panel discussion that Tarkovsky's two "Western" films are little more than a tired reworking of themes that he had already come close to exhausting in the Soviet Union. None of the panellists, however, saw things quite that way. Heidi Karriker argues for a consistency of theme, style and imagery in Tarkovsky's work that manifests itself just as strongly and effectively in *The Sacrifice* as in an earlier masterpiece such as *Mirror*; she sees his spiritual and philosophical concerns as deepening and refining themselves in his final films.

James Leach, in a paper centred round *The Sacrifice*, studies Tarkovsky's representational strategies as they explore the problems of "wholeness" and "fragmentation" in modern cultural experience and question whether the modern artist can any longer strive for or attain the "higher and communal idea" achieved in the work of Bach or Leonardo (both referred to throughout the film). Anna Makolkina also examines the "theme of the fragmented world", but in relation to *Nostalgia* and in the context of the meaning of that word to a Russian audience to whom it suggests a general longing for unity and harmony rather than the mere homesickness or desire to return to an idealized past that the word conveys to a Western audience (though this element too is present in the film).

* * *

Though the conference was designed to raise rather than to solve problems, certain, sometimes conflicting, conclusions seemed to emerge from the papers and from the subsequent discussions. With a changing artistic (and economic) climate in the Soviet Union, Poland, Hungary and Yugoslavia (and now, since the conference took place, in Czechoslovakia), East European film makers may no longer be faced with having to make the agonizing decision to leave their homelands, perhaps for good, if they wish to work free of overt political or ideological constraints. Like French, British, Italian or Dutch film makers, they will come to America if they want to take on the challenges and rewards that it offers them: some may wish to break into big-budget, overtly commercial film making, and will be prepared to accept all the restrictions and limitations involved in this; others may prefer to safeguard their artistic independence, and also retain the right to say what they want to say, in their own way, by accepting lower budgets, fewer technical facilities and a more specialised and restricted form of distribution. They may also come, as a result of changes taking place in their native film industries, far better equipped to deal with the problems of raising and administering budgets and with a more realistic sense of the difficulties of casting and maintaining shooting schedules than has been the case so far. Whether this last development will be to the advantage of cinema as a whole, however, remains to be seen: at its worst it could lead to the elimination of the few protected environments in which endangered species like Tarkovsky and Miklós Jancsó have so far been able to survive and even flourish.

In a rather unexpected way, then, the conference perhaps found itself considering a phenomenon which, in its classic form, is already coming to an end. Though it is far too late to reclaim all the careers damaged, destroyed or warped in the process, and though there is a genuine and increasing danger that "East" and "West" cinema may eventually merge in some bland and innocuous soup in which the individual ingredients have been homogenised out of all recognition, there is nevertheless also the prospect that talented film makers may come to find their own niche in the new pattern that is evolving and that fewer of them than in the past will be reduced to frustrated and lonely silence.

ENDNOTES

1. For a fuller account of this "first wave" see my *Hollywood Destinies: European Directors in America, 1922-1931* (London: Routledge & Kegan Paul, 1985).

2. The use of the overall term "East European" to cover Poles, Czechs, Hungarians and Yugoslavs was, rightly, questioned several times during the conference. It was agreed to retain it, however, as a convenience rather than as an accurate title for the whole area under examination.

3. Even under the "old" conditions, however, many film makers had to cope with the paradox that American producers, distributors and audiences were rarely interested in the kind of serious intellectual debate that they were accustomed to conducting by means of film in their homeland, and that the requirement to produce acceptable commercial entertainment was, in the long run, just as confining and soul-destroying.

EDITORIAL NOTE

The papers are published in the form finally chosen and submitted by the participants themselves. Some delivered formal papers that, with minor changes, appear exactly as they were read. Others were more informal and colloquial in their presentation and have chosen to retain some of this informality in their final version. Bart Testa, who chaired the Tarkovsky session, later submitted a paper on Makavejev that is printed here as an Appendix. Editorial changes have been confined mainly to minor stylistic matters and to rationalisation of aspects of format and presentation, though, as some of the speakers were American and some Canadian, I have left variations between "American" and "British" spelling as they stood in the original. The system of reference and annotation employed by each contributor has been retained, provided that it corresponded to one of the generally recognized standards, such as the *MLA Handbook* or the *Chicago Manual of Style*.

ACKNOWLEDGEMENTS

The editors would like to express grateful thanks to Dr. Hans Schulte of McMaster University for generously making available his Ventura Desk-top Publishing System in the preparation of this volume.

The "Alienation" of Slava Tsukerman

Alexander Batchan
Columbia University

Two years ago in a piece on new developments in the Soviet cinema written for *Film Comment* I mentioned the authorities' belated rehabilitation of Andrei Tarkovsky. At that time it looked like the renowned emigré director's untimely death in Paris at the end of 1986 was the main explanation for his triumphant rehabilitation in the Soviet Union, *glasnost* and *perestroika* notwithstanding. Yet, since then quite a few articles arguing for lifting the ban from the work of other emigré film directors, screen writers, cameramen, and actors — now, rather than upon their deaths, have appeared in the Soviet press. Names like Vasily Aksenov, Iuri Liubimov, Mikhail Bogin, Mikhail and Ilya Suslov, Mikhail Kalik, Savely Kramarov, Boris Sichkin have been mentioned in this regard and some of their shelved films released. In fact, it has not been such a difficult thing for the authorities to do. For all those pictures, no matter how different they could be one from another, undeniably belong to the Russian and Soviet cultural tradition. The same is also true for Tarkovsky's and Andrei Konchalovsky's films made in the West, now becoming available to the Soviet audiences.

However, as I wrote in the aforementioned article, "another film made by emigré director Slava Tsukerman, *Liquid Sky*, which had become a cult classic in the West, has almost no chance of being shown in the Soviet Union in the near future. *Liquid Sky*[1] might look too shocking for puritanical Soviet tastes." ("Mad Russian"

49) Now, as I am delivering this paper, Slava Tsukerman is being lionized in Moscow where his film has just been shown at a dozen prestigious locations including *Dom Kino*, and *VGIK*, the main Soviet film school from which he graduated in 1966 after studying directing under the venerable Lev Kuleshov. (Incidentally, *Liquid Sky*'s director of photography Yuri Neyman as well as associate producer and co-scriptwriter Nina Kerova, Tsukerman's wife, also graduated from VGIK.) Yet at the time the film was shot (the day of its US release — April 15th, 1983, as Tsukerman told me, coincided with the tenth anniversary of their emigration from Russia) hardly anybody could predict such a turn of events.

Liquid Sky is the first Western-made movie since the twenties in which Russian emigré filmmakers play a leading role. Altogether there are ten recent Soviet emigrés listed in the credits of *Liquid Sky*, and their success has almost equalled that of their predecessors who had worked in the French and German cinema and contributed to such silent classics as *Raskolnikoff, Kean, Michel Strogoff, Le Brasier Ardent, Casanova*, and *Napoleon*. But unlike Grigory Khmara, Ivan Mozhukhin, Aleksandr Volkov, Viacheslav Turjansky, or Dmitry Bukhovetsky, *Liquid Sky*'s creators were hardly known in the West. (In this respect they rather resemble another group of the Russian-born European and American filmmakers, whose careers developed only after emigration: Dmitry Kirsanoff, Boris Kaufman, Anatole Litvak, Rouben Mamoulian.) Also, their project was much more unusual, especially for people who grew up in Soviet society and left well into their thirties: not an avant-garde film, a respectable literary adaptation, or a costume epic, but an offbeat movie commenting on a relatively obscure phenomenon of the seventies' New York scene — the downtown life-style.

According to Michael Musto, who writes the weekly nightlife column in *The Village Voice*:

> Downtown parties are exercises in sensory stimulation. A rat put in a hot club instead of a Skinner box would probably go borderline psychotic from all the fabulous stimuli. Club regulars have seen it all, and want more. Just dancing is boring... But dancing with video

and live bands and fashion shows and art installations might hold some people's attention . . . The clubs, with all these elements thrown together, are a microcosm of the whole outlandish mishmash that is downtown, a best-of-the-wildest vaudeville revue that starts at midnight and ends when everybody feels like it. (4)

Yet "downtown" has been known not only as a particular area of Manhattan but also as a definitely provocative state of mind. So even when downtown trend setters are not able to afford any longer the ever rising rents and have to move elsewhere, they do not change their "downtown" life-style, where life, art, and hype are inseparable. This trend in music, visual arts, and fashion is called "post punk" or "new wave". The new wavers, Musto writes, (*Downtown*, p. 15), took punk's rebellious anger and made it more aesthetically pleasant. The pioneer of the new wave clubs was the Mudd Club which after a five-year existence folded in 1982. It seems, nonetheless, that *Liquid Sky*, which was being shot at the time, was not just an attempt to pay a homage to Mudd Club and its regulars. And here lies the difference between Tsukerman's picture and a few other low budget movies coming out of downtown in the early eighties, which dwell on downtown myths and the new wave mentality. True, *Liquid Sky* also deals with those myths and tries to recreate the Mudd Club-like atmosphere but not to tell a story of the new wave. In a radically stylized manner the film uses a new wave subject to make a broader (and heavily moralistic) statement on the precarious state of Western mass culture and society in general. *Liquid Sky* also deals with topics which have already appeared in Tsukerman's earlier films: such as issues of freedom of the will and personal responsibility for one's deeds, which were already present in his Soviet-made and shelved fiction short *Night of Decision* (1972),[2] where not unlike in *Liquid Sky* the lead character (Innokenty Smoktunovsky) plays a scientist and his double.

The universality of *Liquid Sky*'s appeal has led to its popularity not only in the American big cities but in Europe and Australia as well. It won major prizes at the Montreal, Sydney and Brussels film festivals and is considered a cult classic among young New Yorkers, Berliners, and now, perhaps, the Muscovites. As I have been told by visiting Soviet artists, the underground videocassettes of *Liquid Sky* had reached the USSR prior to Tsukerman's visit as well as the LP with its mesmerizing music. Yet most of those Russians who have seen *Liquid Sky* on a cassette have had difficulties in comprehending its contents since the characters speak a very specific downtown slang which is hardly understood even in uptown Manhattan. So, before embarking on his trip to Moscow Tsukerman had been busy translating his film into Russian. Luckily, he found some time to answer my questions about his career in the West and his work on *Liquid Sky*.

Q. The first question asked by many people who have read that *Liquid Sky* was a low-budget production is: how on earth did you manage to spend on it less than half a million dollars? For it looks like it cost you at least several million. Does it have anything to do with your experiences as a Soviet filmmaker?

A. No. It is rather a peculiarity of my personal biography. In fact I was one of the first Soviet film amateurs and was used to doing everything with my own two hands. Consequently, in film school I turned out to be the only student who had made movies before. As a result I was trusted by the school management as an experienced filmmaker. I spent days and nights in our training studio and managed to make professional films with very poor equipment. The Soviets do not have the word "producer", but I did serve as a producer for other students' films. I was assigned to supervise their projects and was made responsible for the budget and scheduling. That's how I learned to work with a limited amount of money under time pressure but still making decent movies. Upon graduation I was given a job at the Central Studio of Scientific Films (*Tsentrnauchfilm*) where I was producing fiction shorts — again with low budget and lousy technical base. Thus, all the time while making films in the USSR I had to design some schemes to achieve what I wanted and quite unintentionally was preparing myself for a career as independent producer in the US. Many a Soviet film director with a "normal" biography does not know even how to work with a camera. The division of labor in the Soviet film industry is ordinarily very strong. In contrast, I can do almost anything, although while in America it still took me years to make a final decision: to become an independent producer. I knew that I wanted it but I was afraid. I remember when the money came to the bank and I withdrew the first five thousand in order to pay the bills, I was shivering from fear. I know, for example, that a great Polish filmmaker Zbiegnew Rybchinski several days after he arrived in this country opened his own company to produce music videos. Recently I visited him and he complained that he had bought two million worth of equipment, that the profits are scarce, yet each month he has to write checks for seventy-five thousand dollars . . . I cannot imagine a talented film director emigrating from the Soviet Union capable of starting a business immediately upon arrival without a fear of paying such high expenses. I know some Russian emigrés who have lived here for twenty years, but each time they begin talking to me they ask the same question: at what studio do you work? The idea that one can do something on his/her own seems to them inferior. It never crosses their minds that it could be better than working for somebody else. For they are used to working for the state.

Q. I think that this notion comes from a general assumption of a Soviet person that it is shameful, dishonest, to be a small businessman, a NEP-man. At least that had been a part of official ideology until Gorbachev came to power, and even now the idea of a private enterprise seems despicable to many a Soviet citizen.

A. Exactly. For a Soviet intellectual is used to believe that it is indecent even to think about money. Let those "smart dealers" discuss financial issues. An artist should be beyond them. Mind you, the Soviet film directors are quite sincere in this conviction because working in the Soviet studios they can afford not to think about such matters. And not only directors. When I arrived in this country everybody who saw my *Night of Decision*, asked me how many shooting days I was given, because this is a very complex film with special effects. Naturally, Americans asked that kind of question. I did not remember that. Nobody counts shooting days in the Soviet film industry . . .

Q. Well, now they will have to, won't they? Since the studios are supposed to turn into self-financing, profitable enterprises.

A. I am not sure that it will be possible. The whole structure of the filming process over there won't allow them to do it. They are always lacking something. Always dependent upon some deficit materials. O.K. Suppose I, as a director, could not care less about those shooting days. But I have some emigré friends who were employed as the "director of the film" in the Soviet Union, which is like a production manager over here. At least they have got to remember how many days it takes to shoot a movie in the USSR. Yet not one of them is able to recollect the figure . . .

Q. We have been discussing technical aspects of the filmmaking process so far. How about the creative process? Is it also different in the Soviet Union?

A. Actually, I think that creative aspects are almost the same everywhere. There is one distinction though: American pictures differ from all other films in the world in their structure. This is a real difference: in style, rhythm, tempo which clearly distinguishes American cinema as a whole. European and Soviet films presuppose a great stylistic diversity depending on the personal styles of directors, scriptwriters, cameramen and others. American film guarantees a certain high level of industrial quality. Individual differences are not so significant. It is like an automobile. You can treat it as a shortcoming, or as a merit. Interestingly enough, most of the European directors, while admiring Hollywood cinema (people like Truffaut, who promoted American films in Europe) would, I doubt, have gone to Hollywood to make a movie. A famous German director Wim Wenders spent many years in Hollywood trying to make an "American film", yet on his own terms. He failed and ended up returning to Germany and making a quintessential European picture *Wings of Desire*. You cannot force Americans to accept your standards, and you cannot afford to ignore theirs: once you fail nobody would give you money for your next film. Look what happened to Billy Wilder . . . There is one spectacular exception though — Louis Malle, who makes films in Europe and in this country. Once he was asked what he would have done if he could do anything he wanted. I am doing just that, Malle answered. The secret here is that he is very rich. He has inherited a large sum of money and can afford to experiment and make mistakes. His American picture *My Dinner With André* does not look like anything coming out of Hollywood . . .

Q. How about Milos Forman?

A. Forman . . . I have a theory about his career. I cannot guarantee though that he would corroborate it. Forman came here at a very good time. His two films *Loves of a Blonde* and *The Firemen's Ball* were nominated for Oscars and he was known here as a genius. Also at that time, twenty years ago foreign filmmakers in general were treated with greater respect. The old German emigré directors who made a great contribution to Hollywood cinema were still alive and nobody cared that they were foreigners. Besides, living in Czechoslovakia in the sixties was not the same as living in the Soviet Union at the time. Forman's ties with America were quite strong. He used to come here before, he knew the language, he had some contacts. Yet, as it turned out even he had to go through tremendous hardships, and his film *Taking Off* was made eventually with an independent low-budget producer. The film had a modest commercial success and some good reviews. However, after this picture for several years he had no offers, which was a shock for him. So, when he was given an opportunity to make *Cuckoo's Nest*, Forman, being a very talented and smart man, probably decided not to take any more chances and to start making regular American films. Since then he stopped being an experimental director. Quite recently his producer was making an adaptation of a brilliant Kundera novel *The Unbearable Lightness of Being*. It was directed not by a Czech, Forman, but by an American director. Of course, Forman could have done it better, but he would not tackle a film dealing with politics or any other subject that might seem not very attractive to mass audiences. In my film *Liquid Sky* I kind of cheated on the viewers. The film does have both European and Russian elements but packed in a form palatable for the American viewers. That is, it has American tempo and irony which were partially responsible for its success amongst certain audiences, although in Hollywood it was still perceived as an "alien creature", not unlike Forman's *Taking Off*. Alas, if you are a mediocrity your chances for getting a job in Hollywood are better because they know what to expect from you, and they are not afraid to entrust you with the script. But nobody wants to deal with mavericks: Orson Welles, Polanski, Kubrick . . . they all had to leave . . .

Q. So what is the way out for a creative American filmmaker: to go to Europe?

A. No, this is not a solution. For there is almost no cinema nowadays in Europe. Although I have to admit that in both Western and Eastern Europe film directors are treated with greater respect than in America. True, here nobody will fire a director or violate his other rights specified in the contract. Yet at the same time there is no such thing as creative copyright. In Russia, for example, if the director won't compromise on some sequences, the film will be shelved (as happened to Aleksandr Askoldov's *Commissar*, for instance, banned for twenty years due to the director's unwillingness to delete a Holocaust episode — A.B.). In America nobody will do that. The film has to be released no matter what, otherwise the investors might lose money. In Russia though such considerations don't count. The art and the artist are treated very seriously over there. You can be shot or decorated for your art, depending on your luck . . .

Q. So, with all your knowledge of both systems, if you were given a chance to start a new life would you stay in the USSR and by submitting to certain political compromises try to work in the Soviet film industry? Do you think that you could have made more films in Russia than in the West?

A. I am all for capitalism. So I never even ask myself such questions. No, I do not like the Soviet regime. I'd rather suffer from certain difficulties here than make films there. True, Soviet directors are given a lot. But since it's a country with arbitrary rule, it's like easy come, easy go. Anyway, to compare the two systems is quite difficult. I'd just say that the profession of film director is very hard no matter under what system you work. On one hand it's art, on the other hand it depends on money, industry, people, and even weather. In the same vein I often hear: why don't you go to Europe? I know for sure than in Europe it would have been easier for me to make unconventional movies. Europeans respect that kind of filmmaking. But I don't want to go anywhere. I would like to live in New York.

Q. Lately, the Soviet filmmakers have begun coming to the West, and we hear every now and then about the new co-productions. What is in your opinion the most important thing Soviet directors should know about Western film industries to be more prepared to work here?

A. I think to teach this is hopeless. To understand what is going on in the US, in its film world, one has to live here for some years. For the systems are so different. And here lies the main reason of failed American co-productions with the Soviet Union. For example, I have this book *The Touch* written by a renowned Soviet screen writer and director Rustam Ibragimbekov. He is the only Soviet filmmaker so far who has really begun working on a co-production with the Americans, which is much more difficult than having a Soviet-European co-production, for example. The short annotation on the front page of this book states that Ibragimbekov's characters are "irreconciled to philistine ways of life, to money-grubbing, and to careerism." If you translate these three things into English, they would mean family values, making money, and career making. Most Americans would see nothing wrong in all this. But if you admit publicly in the Soviet Union that you want to make a career, you will be called a scoundrel, whereas here if you do not want to succeed you are considered a failure. This is just one example of the difference in values. That's why such co-productions would seem to me strange hybrids. So far those Soviet film directors who work abroad have made European-like art films with very limited circulation in this country.

Q. And what happened to your film when it was released in 1983? Was it successful at the box office? I know that *Liquid Sky* was eventually included in encyclopedias of science fiction and cult films; praised in Musto's trendy *Downtown*, who does not even mention that this is a film made by a recent Soviet emigré; and cited in a treatise on new developments in American arts as an examplary punk movie; and your star and co-scriptwriter Anne Carlisle was widely admired (*Playboy* even named her a cult star of the year). Also, the critics pointed to the superb cinematography of Yuri Neyman and the inventive new wave costumes and art design by Marina Levikova, his wife. Even the Soviets finally decided to bow to *Liquid Sky*'s international acclaim and allowed it to be shown in Moscow. But has *Liquid Sky* been successful commercially as well?

A. My film had a sufficient commercial success. I cannot complain. The public loved it and I know some people who saw it eighteen times in a row.

Q. I bet when you finished *Liquid Sky* you must have felt twenty years younger, especially with all this sudden fame?

A. No. I felt exhausted for two years and dreamt of leaving for some quiet place for a rest. I have been always amazed by the people who tell me: "Oh, you probably had a lot of fun making this film". Actually, *Liquid Sky* was a very intense experience for me, both mentally and physically. To make on a half a million budget something that requires fifteen million is not a joke. Now when I visit the offices of my colleagues I sometimes see crowds of people working on some low-low budget film. And the producer keeps saying how he is ashamed to show me his office which looks so poor. But all the work made by fifteen people in his film, in my film was made by a single person. Every one of us was working like fifteen people. Nobody wants to work like this any more. My wife, for example. Now, seven years later I think I would have done it again, and I would pay twice as much as I did on *Liquid Sky* but it won't help to find a crew. We were at that time in a very unique situation. The nucleus of the crew consisted of our two families who had to break into the American film business. Now my cameraman Neyman is quite successful and he does not need to go through that ordeal once more.

Q. Yuri Neyman told me how he was helped in his work here by some of his Soviet experiences. He was also a film amateur first and he even remembers how both of you were members of the board of the Moscow society of film amateurs. Yet, upon graduation from *VGIK* with distinction Neyman could not find a permanent job. The personnel employees hinted to him that it was due to his Jewish origins, and eventually this situation led to his emigration. However, for a while he was able to work on a temporary basis at various Soviet studios doing cinematography and visual effects. At one of the studios in Kiev he became aware of the system of color solarization implemented by a cameraman called Shekhter. Later Neyman did it electronically for *Liquid Sky*, and you were able to save money without sacrificing the quality.

A. Still it was very difficult to create images the way we wanted them to be considering our budgetary and human shortages. Another difficulty was emotional. Our subject led to a lot of tension and psychological pressure. Eventually, Anne Carlisle had to leave her studio where we were shooting *Liquid Sky*. She was afraid she could kill herself.

Q. You insist that you dealt in this picture with basic problems of contemporary civilization. Yet most American critics have emphasized that you are a foreigner, an alien, and this is an eccentric view of New York as seen by a stranger. Jim Hoberman of *The Village Voice* even points out that your flying saucer is an old Cold War metaphor for Russian invasion.

A. Critics are also people. When they get a press-release mentioning that the director is a Russian emigré, this fact begins to dominate their perception of *Liquid Sky* where after all you do encounter aliens: the German scientist and the UFO. I must emphasize though that while working on the film I never thought in such terms. But not all of the viewers get these press-releases and those who don't could never guess my origins from the picture. Moreover, all Hollywood, including its educated segment, was sure prior to meeting me that *Liquid Sky* was made by a twenty-year old American. One critic even thought that Tsukerman was a young woman . . . As to the fifties' sci-fi movies, I did not see them at that time. But perhaps, the fact that I picked up those aliens for my picture indicates that I felt something, albeit unconsciously, in that vein. Hoberman mentions another thing, that *Liquid Sky* contains everything I could not do in Russia, which was perhaps done on an unconscious level as well. I can suggest the third unconscious motive: to make a film which would be impossible to show in Russia at the time and thus to strike out the past. Of course, all these are post-factum speculations. I can talk with certainty only about what was consciously running through my mind during the filming of *Liquid Sky*.

Q. So, would you mind naming a few conscious motives for your choosing, of all possible subjects, the one that had led you to *Liquid Sky*?

A. No matter what I do in my life (I used to make scientific films) I base it on some kind of research, even when the subject has nothing to do with science. Hence, when I started working on *Liquid Sky* it was natural for me to spend years studying this type of life and people. I was curious about it for many reasons even before this project. And one of them was that before *Liquid Sky* we were involved in other project named *Sweet Sixteen*. As a matter of fact, I met Anne Carlisle during the casting of that film, which didn't come through. At that time I made friends with Adele, a very good rock singer who became a prototype for Adrian. She was Anne's lover and what you have in the film is a stylized, cartoon-like story of their relationship. The papers reported correctly that when Anne had read the script she said that this is new wave. But I never responded to that, as some of the papers reported: what is it? By that time I was aware of new wave's existence and the person who took me for the first time to the CBGB club was a Russian emigré artist Vitaly Komar, and I became very interested in the

New York art and club scene apart from *Liquid Sky*. It is very close to my mentality. The thing is that I am fond of the Russian avant-garde art of the twenties and Brecht's epic theater. Surely, American pop art and new wave continue this trend. A miniature punk rock singer Adele Bertei who comes from a working class neighborhood of Cleveland knew who Mayakovsky was, and I was amazed that we had so much in common. So it was natural for me to get interested in such things upon arrival in America. Myself, Nina, Yuri and Marina never missed a single new wave art exhibit. We saw the first shows of the most famous American artists. We were even going to collaborate with Keith Haring on *Liquid Sky*. He was supposed to paint a wall in my loft where we were going to shoot a scene at the bathroom, but only on one condition: nobody would ever touch this wall. At that time I was working like crazy, sleeping two hours a day, and I did not want my bathroom to become an art gallery. Haring still cannot forgive me that . . . But my main source of inspiration for the film was Brecht's *The Threepenny Opera*. I was obsessed by the structure of one of the songs in it — "Pirate Jenny":

> *Gentlemen, today you see me washing glasses*
> *And I make all the beds each morning . . .*

And then a ship "with fifty great cannon" arrives and she kills all who humiliated her. My idea was to create a situation of an American woman, an anti-Cinderella type who cannot find her prince in contemporary society. The only "prince" she does find comes from outer space and takes revenge on all who did unjustice to her. I decided that the heroine should be a new wave model, yet not at once. In another version she was a Jewish girl from Brooklyn. But finally I realized that for an alien from the cosmos, new wave would be a more attractive thing, being kind of "outlandish". Another thing is that since *Liquid Sky* is related to Brecht and pop art the characters should not be regarded just as persons. They rather have to embody certain myths of their society. But the main myths of mass culture at that time were drugs, sex, alien creatures. I worked hard to tie all those myths together by one plot. I did not suspect then that it would be a social prophecy: that the AIDS virus would emerge and start killing people. By the way, in the first draft of the script I had a lot of philosophical talks with explanations of various intellectual allusions made in *Liquid Sky*. Moreover, there was a scene where the alien turns human for a short while to make a long explanatory monologue. The Brechtian parallel is the only intellectual parallel left in the final script. One should not explain anything in a movie. My favorite film is Eisenstein's *Ivan the Terrible*. Recently I was rereading its script and comparing it to the movie. I noticed among other differences between the two that Eisenstein consistently eliminated from the film everything that revealed hidden meanings in the script. The film should be simple like a story, a straightforward narrative.

Q. Since you've mentioned Eisenstein I would like to ask you: *Liquid Sky*, not unlike Eisenstein's movies or Meyerhold's theater productions, influences the spectators in a variety of ways: by its images, music, tempo, rhythm, words, ideas. Isn't it an old German idea of *Gesamtkunstwerk* (a total work of art) you were after in *Liquid Sky*?

A. Absolutely. I have a theory which I use more and more in my work. It deals with cinematic counterpoint. If a work of art has only one meaning it will stay this way — a simple linear piece. If you put into it two meanings, people would definitely find the third, and, perhaps, the fourth one. But if you have five meanings they are going to interact in many ways, some of them unpredicted by the artist himself. Eisenstein would have a minimum of three meanings in his cine-metaphors which is a traditional Russian form of art. I try to load my films maximally, and not only by additional intellectual meanings, but also by other significant components: sets, costumes, make-up, music — and make each of them tell its own story.

Q. That's how Eisenstein wanted his art to work, and because he could not achieve this effect in the theater at the beginning of his career he moved into cinema.

A. And yet his last film *Ivan the Terrible* turned out to be an extremely theatrical work, which amused the director himself.

Q. Your *Liquid Sky* is also very theatrical, stylized, especially in acting.

A. The subject of the new wave was picked up partially because of its theatricality. But this theatricality is not just aesthetic: beautiful costumes and a lot of make-up. It is rather ideological. And here comes the kinship with *The Threepenny Opera*. The punks made a "threepenny opera" out of their lives. The brilliance of Brecht was that he managed to show relations amongst criminals as normal bourgeois relationships. Thus the estrangement (Brechtian *Verfremdungseffekt* — A.B.) took place which led to the spectators' revision of their values: the modern world was suddenly perceived as criminal. The new wavers projected the violence of surrounding milieux onto their lives. By pushing these three major themes of mass culture: sex, drugs, and cruelty *ad absurdum* they made a bloody spectacle out of their existence in order to demonstrate the absurdity of the contemporary world. The theatricality of this demonstration attracted me very much. By reproducing this kind of behavior by means of theatrical, stylized performance and by filming it I achieve a triple theater in *Liquid Sky*. I am fascinated by the Brechtian tradition in modern cinema. I've been thinking about it a lot and was really surprised when I recently read a book by a Moscow film critic Maya Turovskaya dealing with all these issues. [*Brecht i kino* (Moscow: Iskusstvo, 1985)] Some American films of the sixties and seventies, Altman's, for example, or Paul Morrissey's, were very Brechtian. Nicholas Roeg is also an important figure of the seventies in this respect. Now this trend is not so popular although it has some followers such as Alan Rudolph. In Europe one could still mention Godard and a Belgian filmmaker Chantal Akerman who develops Godardian aesthetics. In the seventies, of course, there was a heavily Brechtian cinema of Fassbinder, and to a lesser degree of Herzog and Schlöndorff. Among the Soviet films in this vein I can name only Aleksei Gherman's *My Friend Ivan Lapshin*. I haven't seen too many recent Soviet pictures though. I was told that Soloviev's *Assa* resembles my *Liquid Sky*.

Q. You've mentioned Morrissey, who used to work with Warhol. How about the films Warhol made himself, and his art of the last decade which, as his recent retrospective at M.O.M.A. has confirmed, was very much in tune with new wave? I have been thinking of Warhol while watching *Liquid Sky* also because the loft where the two heroines live, have sex, take drugs, and run fashion shows, looks like a pastiche of Warhol's legendary Factory.

A. Andy Warhol is my favorite American artist. Of course, there is an allusion to him in the film. I am sure Warhol saw it. However, he avoided conversations about the film. I think though *Liquid Sky* had some impact on him. There was a certain challenge in it for Andy Warhol. I was always thinking why his art became world famous but his cinema never achieved similar status. Warhol himself was puzzled by this fact. He was waiting for an invitation from Hollywood, which never came. I think that his films, such as *Chelsea Girls* are great, better than Godard's; they are purer, less commercial. At the same time his art is the best commercial art one can imagine. So I decided to express by means of cinema what Warhol was expressing in his art. I think that nobody has ever done it before. Warhol's art represents a fusion of the cold, intellectual Brechtian element, which he implemented in the most radical way, and the hot, emotional, rock-n-roll, psychedelic element coming from the sixties' culture. This fusion is what attracts me most to Warhol. And that is what I wanted to achieve in *Liquid Sky*. Hence some people find the film cold, whereas the others think it is hot. This ambiguity is quite conscious and I believe it has worked to the film's benefit. When I came to America for the first time in 1975 I talked to many people in the industry and tried to convince them to start making science fiction movies. But they all said to me that this genre could not be commercially successful. Yet soon *Star Wars* triumphed and they changed their opinion. Yet the success was due not to the fact that *Star Wars* was a sci-fi film. It was a new type of science fiction picture which attracted huge young audiences to the screening rooms after a period of stagnation in Hollywood. In order to do that one had to change the style of the movies, to adjust to teenagers' sensibilities, who at that time were into rock. *Star Wars* updated the cinema of the seventies which was still lagging behind painting and music by furnishing it with one element of modernity which was born in the sixties. I call it "rock-n-rollism". It means not only rock but this new principle of fusion of cold and hot elements, of estrangement and energy. Plus the comic strip. So the cinema after *Star Wars* began to change. Not because rock songs hadn't been performed in the movies before. That was done in the sixties and did not change anything. Only when the whole structure and rhythm of the movies started changing one could see the difference. Yet not all elements of that "rock" mentality were implemented successfully. One of them, very important for rock, was self-consciousness. Before rock-n-roll nobody sang songs about other songs. This self-irony, a mirror-imaging of oneself which comes from rock-n-roll attracts to *Liquid Sky* enthusiastic audiences. As a matter of fact, *Liquid Sky* has beaten all the records of cult film screenings at the Waverly movie theater in Greenwich Village and, as I was told, the students in Yale film classes want to write their papers not on film classics but rather on *Liquid Sky*.

Q. Could we call it camp?

A. You could, but in general I don't like it when my film is called camp. Camp is more of an amateurish art where a joke is a final purpose. In *Liquid Sky* elements of camp are the aesthetic elements built into others. Many people do not understand that. And here is where I'll mention Andy Warhol's art again. Because this Hollywood slickness of *Liquid Sky* is combined with camp. Camp by itself oughtn't to be aesthetically perfect. It should rather be clumsy in performance. It is not the case of my film: it is more than camp. The public especially loved it when the characters' words could be perceived not only as parts of filmic dialogue but also as their comments on the film itself. Yet I was told at the scriptwriting stage that it is impossible to plan a cult film in advance, that all existing cult films obtain that status quite unpredictably. But I turned out to be right. That's why I am amused when people tell me that the funniest things in *Liquid Sky* were unintentional, and also when they ask me to what extent the film was improvisation. There was no improvisation at all. Each word was a thousand times thought over and rehearsed.

Q. That was exactly my impression after the first screening: that this film is based on a well calculated formula. It is like a machine...Yet one thing is kind of loose: the genre.

A. I mix genres also quite consciously. As I was also told, it is all very interesting but films made at the intersection of genres could not become profitable. There is some truth in it if we speak about big commercial success. The mixed genre films appeal mostly to a sophisticated public and never become real blockbusters. Take Ken Russell's films as an example of this mixture. The same is true for *Liquid Sky.* It is impossible to define its genre. There are elements of sci-fi, of comedy, of tragedy, of a parable. It is a parable more than anything else — a modern fairy-tale.

Q. Now as you are going to Moscow to show *Liquid Sky* to Soviet audiences, how do you feel about it?

A. My return is quite a mystical event for me. In my youth I never thought of emigration. In general, I was a very conservative person and those who knew me as a young man would be shocked to see *Liquid Sky.* Nevertheless, when I was taking my entrance exams to *VGIK* and, working under time pressure, was supposed to write a short story (I had felt tremendous pressure also because for me at that time nothing could be more important in life than getting into film school), I wrote about a Russian emigré who stayed for a long time in the West and now comes back and visits the house he used to live in as a young man. I couldn't imagine a more inappropriate and strange subject for the entrance exam and couldn't explain why on earth this idea came to me. Now I've understood that in the most critical moment of my life my unconscious prompted me about what would happen to me in the future.

Q. May I suggest that the role America played in your life was to liberate your unconscious in a similar way which resulted in your making of *Liquid Sky*?

A. Yes, you may look at it this way, but there is more to that. When my old friend Vladimir Matlin, who wrote the script of *Night of Decision* and then also emigrated, saw *Liquid Sky* he asked me: "What's happened to you? Over there you were making films about scientists and here you come up with a picture on punks. Why?" I answered him that I don't see any discrepancy in such a thematic shift. In Russia I was interested in the most active group of society at that time, the scientists, who defined the dynamics of social processes; and here I am also interested in the most dynamic group: the new wave crowd.

March, 1989
New York City

ENDNOTES

1. *Synopsis*: An alien ship with creatures who take sustenance from heroin is attracted by the high concentration of drugs at the lower East Side rock clubs and invades Manhattan. Landing on the roof of a penthouse where Margaret, a bisexual new wave model (Anne Carlisle) and her lover — a heroin dealer and punk rock singer Adrian (Paula Sheppard) live — the aliens realize that a euphoria-inducing substance produced during earthlings' orgasms is even better than drugs. At the same time the UFO "falls in love" with the model and starts killing all men who happen to have sex with her, thus achieving two purposes: getting revenge and getting high. Upon realizing her new powers Margaret also begins to kill those who wronged her by causing their orgasms, including her double, the obnoxious gay model Jimmy, played by Carlisle as well. A weird German UFO-logist Johann (Otto von Wernherr) who comes to New York from Berlin to study the intergalactic visitors fails to save Margaret from imminent danger. When he explains to her what has attracted the aliens to her penthouse and shows her where her "prince" has been hiding she kills the German and then quickly shoots heroin to prevent the UFO from leaving. Margaret approaches the flying saucer and then in the presence of the two astounded women — one of her victims' lovers and a Jewish TV producer who happened to see the murder of Johann through the telescope he set in her apartment to watch the UfO — vanishes into space. It is not clear whether the departing aliens killed her or took her with them.

2. *Night of Decision* was awarded a prize at the Los Angeles International Film

Festival in 1975.

WORKS CITED

Batchan, Alexander. "Mad Russian", *Film Comment*, June 1987: 48-51.
Musto, Michael. *Downtown*. New York: Vintage Books, 1986.

The Films of Andrei Konchalovsky

Vida T. Johnson
Tufts University

From the point of view of Soviet filmmaking this is a propitious moment to take a look at EASTERN EUROPEAN DIRECTORS WORKING IN THE WEST. Co-productions between the Soviet Union and Western Europe are becoming more and more frequent, with such critically acclaimed and commercially successful films as Nikita Mikhalkov's *Dark Eyes* and Otar Ioseliani's *Favorites of the Moon*. In the political liberalization and economic restructuring of the Gorbachev era the Soviet cinema industry has demonstrated its eagerness both to work in the West and to export more Soviet-made films. The most commonly asked question of Western film scholars and critics is: what would make Soviet films commercially viable in the West, especially in the United States? But the Soviets are generally ill-prepared to compete in the Western arena, since they really have had no tradition of film making in the West.

Unlike other East Europeans, until very recently, few Soviet directors have had the opportunity to make films abroad. Of those who were not emigrés, only two come to mind: Sergei Eisenstein in the early 1930s and Andrei Konchalovsky in the 1980s. Although Eisenstein was recognized as one of the greatest directors of his time and became a Hollywood celebrity in the early 1930s, his scripts were repeatedly turned down by the American producers because they were too experimental, too far ahead of their time. Not surprisingly, his *Que Viva Mexico*, the first attempt by a Soviet

filmmaker to make a film in Hollywood, became a financial quag-
mire and was never completed. A disheartened Eisenstein returned
to the Soviet Union without the Western acclaim which he and the
Soviet film industry had so eagerly sought and which Eisenstein
so richly deserved.

In the 1980s Andrei Konchalovsky was to succeed where Eisenstein had failed. He completed not one, but four films in only five
years in Hollywood. Sceptics might argue that Konchalovsky was
not hampered in his artistic quest either by Eisenstein's genius or
by his commitment to cinematic experimentation. They might also
point out that all these films were made for Cannon, a film company notorious for producing mediocre films on extremely tight
budgets and limited shooting schedules. In a recent interview published in the Soviet journal *Ogonyok*, Konchalovsky admits that
working for Cannon was far from starting at the top, yet he is also
proud of the fact that he was the first serious filmmaker hired by
that company and that since then Cannon has signed many foreign
directors such as Godard, Zeffirelli and Passer (18). Whatever the
artistic merit or commercial success of his films in the West, the
undeniable fact remains that Andrei Konchalovsky is that rare
Soviet filmmaker who is successfully *working* in the West. In fact,
one could argue that Konchalovsky was well-prepared for a foray
into the more commercial Western filmmaking both by his artistic
temperament and by the technical expertise that he demonstrated
in his Soviet films.

Before he moved to the West (not as an emigré, but legally
because he was married to a foreign national), Konchalovsky was
a successful Soviet director. He had scripted and/or directed a
number of impressive films in the Soviet Union. His best-known
script was an early collaboration with Andrei Tarkovsky on the
latter's monumental film, *Andrei Rublev* (1966). His directorial debut in 1962 was a short, *The Boy and the Pigeon* which won the
Bronze Lion, the Grand Prix of the International Film Festival for
Children in Venice. His first two feature-length films, *First Teacher*
(1965) and *Asya's Happiness* (1966) have been highly praised for

avoiding schematic socialist realist plots and characters and presenting genuine human conflicts and rich characterizations. The latter film was shelved for twenty years because of its unflinching, honest look at realities of contemporary rural life in the Soviet Union. Already in these films Konchalovsky showed himself to be a director with strong visual and narrative orientations and an ability to present emotionally engaging characters who are closely linked to a specific, often exotic, physical and social environment.

These first two films were among the best produced at the end of the liberal "Thaw" period and identified Konchalovsky as a major talent in a new generation of young directors. So despite the banning of *Asya's Happiness*, he continued to be offered work by Goskino. Although many of his proposed projects were rejected - when he suggested a film on Che Guevara, he was asked if he were a provocateur (*Ogonyok* 17), he finally settled on a screen adaptation of a nineteenth century classic of Russian literature, Turgenev's novel *The Nest of Gentry*. As did many of the best Soviet directors, in the late 1960s and the 1970s, Konchalovsky also turned to the safety of the literary classics. *The Nest of Gentry* (1969) was quickly followed by a screen adaptation of Anton Chekhov's *Uncle Vanya* (1970). In their survey of East European cinema Mira and Antonin Liehm call the latter film "easily the best film version of the Chekhov play: The sorrow, the nostalgia and the hopelessness of the Russian intelligentsia had found a true poet even in Soviet film" (309). In the next decade, during what is now called "the period of stagnation," Konchalovsky wrote scripts and shot only two films: *In Love* (1974), "a true model of well polished conformism for the seventies," (Liehm 310) and finally his biggest, longest, most ambitious, and certainly most popular Soviet film: *Siberiade* (1979).

Once again Konchalovsky came into conflict with the censors and the picture was not released. Konchalovsky's poetic style and visual symbolism, the sex scenes (tame by Western but not by official puritanical Soviet standards) even the film's length were all probable causes for his being told that the picture "must be reshot" (*Ogonyok* 17). In order to save the film he accepted many cuts (from

4 1/2 to 3 1/4 hours) including a sequence on Stalin's death. After a year of "fiddling", and only after the film received the Special Jury Prize at Cannes and became a European sensation, was *Siberiade* finally distributed (*Ogonyok* 17). It became a great box-office success. The 70 million tickets that Konchalovsky said were sold by 1982 (*Christian Science Monitor* interview of Sept. 23, 1982) had grown to 100 million by the time of his interview with *Boston Globe* in 1986 (January 11, 1986).

The cut version, which Konchalovsky likes even though he feels the original was more powerful (*Ogonyok* 17), was relatively conservative ideologically. Although the hero is Siberia itself (as the land or nature often is in Konchalovsky's films), the film is the saga of the coming of the revolution and the establishment of Soviet power in Siberia from the beginning of the twentieth century to the 1960s. But all the historical upheavals are recorded through the lives, the loves and hates of two village families, a rich and a poor one. As always for Konchalovsky historical, political and social changes are recorded only through believable, complex individual characters. As in all his films, his ability to cast roles and evoke excellent acting, and thus to create memorable characters was once again demonstrated here. The technical expertise, the sheer difficulty of the task of filming and successfully projecting a visceral feeling for the Siberian vastness, especially the magnificent explosions of the oil gusher, revealed Konchalovsky's readiness for Hollywood. Thus before he left for the West, Konchalovsky was an established and experienced film maker, technically sophisticated, a good storyteller capable of mesmerizing the audience with larger than life characters and settings, which are always intriguing, and at times, even profound.

Even after the impressive European success of *Siberiade*, Konchalovsky found it impossible to get directing work in Paris, where he had moved to join his wife. Not being an emigré, he was suspected of being a spy. According to him, when he proposed a film for Simone Signoret, she first agreed and then recanted when she heard rumors that this would ruin her career. Konchalovsky notes that other directors from Eastern Europe, Forman, Passer, Polanski, all tried fruitlessly to begin their Western careers in Paris. But Konchalovsky had found a friend and admirer in the American actor Jon Voight who invited him to Hollywood and arranged scriptwriting contracts with Universal and then with Columbia (*Ogonyok* 17). He spent a year teaching film, and writing scripts, all of which were rejected, and generally being an unknown. His Soviet and European fame meant nothing in Hollywood. No one there had heard of this director: "is he from Turkey? Afghanistan?" (*Ogonyok* 17).

Just as in the Soviet Union he was able to make the necessary cuts, choose a different subject, or adapt to existing conditions in order to keep working, he now accepted work under the restrictive conditions of Cannon Films (budgets of 2-3 million, 6-8 weeks for shooting.) He didn't care about Cannon's reputation or his own. As he himself said, he was tired of teaching and wanted to make films under any conditions. Setting himself in contrast with Andrei Tarkovsky, the other major Russian filmmaker working in the West, he admits to being an adaptable man, not pursued by one unified artistic vision, but a man who craves work, who takes on a variety of projects, often lightheartedly, with only the restriction that he must make films "about characters he likes" (*Ogonyok* 18). Thus Konchalovsky himself provides the reason why he has managed to break into Western film making with four films in half-a dozen years: *Maria's Lovers* (1984), *Runaway Train* (1985), *Duet for One* (1986) and *Shy People* (1988). A personable man who quickly made friends with Hollywood celebrities such as Shirley McLaine and Jack Nicholson, he attracted an impressive group of actors for his films: Nastassia Kinski, Jon Voight, Julie Andrews, Alan Bates, Max von Sydow, Jill Clayburgh, Barbara Hershey......

Clearly Konchalovsky's personality, attitude to work and adaptability helped him to make the first step into Western filmmaking. But even more importantly, he did not attempt to change drastically either his cinematic style or thematics. While primarily setting his stories in America — "In America you must make films about

This is just as true of *Siberiade* and *Uncle Vanya* as it is of *Maria's Lovers*, *Duet for One, Runaway Train* and *Shy People*. In fact, it is quite amazing how little Konchalovsky's films abroad really differ from the last films he made in the Soviet Union. *Runaway Train* and *Shy People* owe much to *Siberiade* and *Duet for One* harkens back to *Uncle Vanya*.

In *Runaway Train* and in *Shy People*, just as in *Siberiade* the strikingly beautiful cinematography of monumental, mysterious, awe-inspiring nature is based on careful framing and contrasting extreme close-ups and extreme long-shots. (Not much on the comfortable mid range in this film.) In America Konchalovsky even finds familiar landscapes. After all, it was a train trip over the vast American continent that first gave him the idea of Siberiade, because of the similarity which he saw between the two landscapes. The rugged winter setting in the Rockies found in *Runaway Train* is reminiscent of the Siberian winter in *Siberiade*, while the foggy, mysterious bayous of Louisiana in *Shy People* harken back to the summer hazy swamps of Siberia in thaw in *Siberiade*.

In all three films the characters' lives are organically and inextricably intertwined with the land. In *Siberiade* the family feud between the rich Solomins and the poor Ustuzhanins, despite wars and revolutions, is played out in Siberia itself. The two heroes, Nikolai and his son Aleksei, are drawn away from the village, the former to fight a revolution, the latter to fight a war, only to be drawn back and to die at home. In *Runaway Train* the fury of nature and the fury of the escaped prisoners are merged in the train rushing headlong to destruction. (Konchalovsky gives many close-ups of the train itself, using beautiful imagery and framing, as well as extreme long shots.) The characters are shot in disconcerting close-up, especially Manny's (Jon Voight's) gleaming metal tooth and facial scars as he leers, scoffs and rages, thus helping to create a larger-than-life figure of this desperate man, who cannot live by society's rules, and chooses death as the ultimate act of his freedom. Konchalovsky's most successful film in the West, *Runaway Train* is a powerful film which earned good critical reviews and even modest commercial success (if not in the original run, on cable television!) and an Oscar nomination for best and facial scars as he leers, scoffs and rages, thus helping to create a larger-than-life figure of this desperate man, who cannot live by society's rules, and chooses death as the ultimate act of his freedom. Konchalovsky's most successful film in the West, *Runaway Train* is a powerful film which earned good critical reviews and even modest commercial success (if not in the original run, on cable television!) and an Oscar nomination for best actor for Voight. In addition to demonstrating technical expertise, Konchalovsky shows himself , as in *Siberiade*, to be an excellent storyteller — as few Soviet directors really are. The Soviet sense of narration and action in films is generally so different from Western, and especially American films, that most are seen as slow. *Runaway Train*, however, is a gripping story and better edited than *Siberiade*, perhaps because of the latter film's somewhat problematic length. And what Konchalovsky can do with nature: fire, water, snow are all visually spectacular!

In *Shy People* too, he is drawn to the dramatic primeval beauty of nature: in the bayous, with giant trees standing in water, in a land that time forgot. He even uses electronic music similar to that in *Siberiade* as well as an almost identical setting: the swamp scenes in both films are very similar. *Shy People*, like *Siberiade* presents characters as emanations of this landscape, completely and majestically created by it, while the destruction of that nature and the old way of life is also present in both films. In each case oil is the culprit. In *Siberiade* the oil had some redeeming significance, revealed in a fabulous drilling sequence and a love of machinery worthy of Eisenstein. But now in *Shy People* there are only decaying remains of the machines in the swamps, and the filthy, rusty harbors, with a two headed pet turtle as a symbol of what has gone wrong. Konchalovsky's thematics in his Western films seem to focus more on the nature of freedom and control of self and others, but presented on an individual level, and often within the context of the family. Though this too had its beginnings in *Siberiade*, it was overshadowed there by more obvious themes with broader social significance.

Besides improving his storytelling ability, honing his technical expertise, and creating splendid visuals, Konchalovsky in his Western films presents us with some wonderful characters, as he had done in *Uncle Vanya* and *Siberiade* - though there he had Chekhov, among others to thank for this. He has continued to write, or at least collaborate on the scripts for almost all his Western films, except for *Runaway Train*. Although in *Shy People* the story of an educated, upper class New Yorker and her poor, southern relative from which she has much to learn about life comes close to being clichéd, it is rescued from mediocrity by two wonderful roles and actresses: Jill Clayburgh and Barbara Hershey, especially Hershey.

A general danger in Konchalovsky's Western films, in fact, is his tendency toward clichéd presentation of social types whom he knows only on a rather superficial level. That's why in *Duet for One* Alan Bates, as the long-haired conductor and composer, and Julie Andrews (who was better) as a famous violinist with multiple sclerosis, just weren't convincing. The characters surrounding the failure of the career and the break-up of the family seemed out of Chekhov and misplaced here. Konchalovsky is best when his tendency toward monumentalization of characters is justified on narrative and psychological planes, and when the actors are able to cope with this, as in the case of Voight in *Runaway Train* and Barbara Hershey in *Shy People*.

Despite the real, though modest, success of his American films to date, Konchalovsky may still encounter problems in pursuing his career in the West. [Since this paper was delivered, Konchalovsky has made two more Hollywood films: *Tango and Cash* (1989) and *Homer and Eddie* (1990) —ed.] Although he has demonstrated his box-office potential with some visually spectacular films that, at their best, have the strong narrative drive so essential for popular acclaim in the United States, he remains in danger of stereotyping and over-sentimentalizing his characters. Critical opinion on his films remains sharply divided, panned by many and yet, as with *Shy People*, occasionally ending up on a well-known critic's list of Ten Best Films of the Year.

WORKS CITED

Liehm, Antonin and Mira. *The Most Important Art: Soviet and East European Film After 1945.* Berkeley: U of California P, 1977.

Ogonyok 51 (December 1988).

Discussion and Responses

Session One

Andrew Horton, as discussant, remarked that there are two categories of East European filmmakers who work in the West:

1) those who come already trained, who "have an established identity, and then switch gears" and 2) those who begin abroad.

Konchalovsky came from a system that gave him almost unlimited resources to make a film like *Siberiade*, an ideal shooting schedule in ideal working conditions. What is remarkable about his switch is that he was working for Cannon films in the US. Cannon philosophy is this: a budget maximum of $2 million; get it in on time; not a penny over $2 million; a very, very tight shooting schedule with a maximum of six weeks, and trying to use non-union people as much as possible. That's a hell of a switch. He was a nobody for two years, has paid his dues, none of his films has been a popular success, just enough to get the next film done. He is still in danger, he knows that. Perhaps his return to the USSR is a positive thing, keeping a foothold in the two worlds. He still has to make THE American commercial film.

Andrew Horton felt that both Alexander Batchan and Vida Johnson were apologetic about commercial cinema and wondered why they should be so.

If filmmakers want to work in America they have to understand the commercial market; there is nothing wrong with selling millions of tickets. Wanting to sell tickets AND to keep some integrity has always been a difficult balancing act in Hollywood. It is possible but difficult. *Liquid Sky* can afford to be more pure and avoids the compromises imposed by Cannon film.

With reference to Vida Johnson's paper he remarked:

It is possible to see Soviet influence in Konchalovsky's films, and to
see the bayous through Soviet eyes is interesting. Apparently a
mixed Cajun-New Orleans audience was extremely puzzled by the
film. It DID capture atmosphere; the trademark of wedding nature
to character was definitely there.

Most Soviet directors are interested in doing co-productions but
were warned by David Putnam in Tbilisi they must understand
American narrative mentality first. "If you can't tell a film in an
American narrative structure, it won't work". *Liquid Sky* offers a different picture...very clearly an auteur film, the work of an individual talent, an act of love, a cult film.

Andrew Horton asked Alexander Batchan how the film did
commercially, and Batchan replied that the film did well for other
people, not for Tsukerman.

Andrew Horton:

Changes in the Soviet Union are giving rise to films like *Assa*, which
has a good deal in common with *Liquid Sky*—sex, drugs, and rock
and roll.

There is the danger that everybody will try to make American films,
and end up with a huge mishmash somewhere in the middle that
pleases nobody. Yet the door is open for all sorts of experimentation.

John Mosier:

There is an unfamiliar visual perspective brought by foreign directors to what is taken for granted by Americans themselves and this
is more important than minor mistakes in understanding the culture.

Vida Johnson disagreed that mistakes in understanding culture
are unimportant:

There are moments in Konchalovsky's work that make Americans
squirm: it rings false. Why? One is occasionally wrenched out of an
understanding of the characters. He breaks the emotional bond with
the character by excessive elements or a false-sounding note. The
result is cliché and melodrama.

Ruth Dwyer asked whether such excessive elements as jangling
bracelets were not used consciously as distancing devices. Vida

Johnson replied that yes, there are elements of parody.

Gerald Peary noted:

> We tend to categorize all East European directors in America as great artists, lost creatures trying to find the key to Hollywood. But we have to see each of them differently. Some like Forman are comfortable and happy in this jet-set world; others like Passer really *are* lost. The recognition of an Academy Award would mean so much more to Forman than to Passer, because Forman is so much more a "Hollywood" person.

Alexander Batchan, when asked how Tsukerman could be procapitalist when he is a victim of a system which allows him to make one film and then no more, replied:

> It is Tsukerman's intention to expose this world. He prefers the American system to other systems. The choice is relative. He wants to achieve success. He has escaped the dilemma of being an art filmmaker vs. a Hollywood filmmaker. His formula is to make American films by inserting in a hidden way a Russian and European sensibility. Irony is one of the means by which he accomplishes this. There is always the danger that such a formula will not work.

Anna Makolkina asked Alexander Batchan about the tyranny of genre. He replied that Tsukerman mixes genres purposely and yet is aware that the films made at the "intersection of genres" are rarely successful commercially.

Misplaced Mistrust:

A Dissenting View of Milos Forman's *Amadeus*

George Lellis
Coker College

We are all aware of how Milos Forman's *Amadeus* is one of the most honoured films of the 1980's. The work won eight Academy Awards, for best film, actor, director, adapted screenplay, sound, art direction, costumes and makeup. The Los Angeles film critics gave it awards for best picture, director, screenplay and actor. In France, where the movie was one of only four films to sell over one million tickets in 1984 (Zimmer 67), it similarly won the César award for best foreign film. The Italians included *Amadeus* in their David Di Donatello Awards with prizes for best foreign film, foreign director, and foreign actor. Although it was not universally praised by critics, it ended up on a number of "ten best" lists for the year and as of December 1988 had grossed over $22.8 million in the United States and Canada alone ("All Time Film Rental Champs").[1]

Much has been made, by both the film's admirers and the film-makers themselves, of the significant number of supposedly beneficial changes Forman, working with screenwriter Peter Shaffer, made in adapting Shaffer's own play for the screen (Kakutani). Although we would all acknowledge Forman's extraordinary skill and intelligence as a filmmaker, let me propose a point of view dissenting from this fully positive tone. I would suggest that Forman and Shaffer's artistic strategies implicitly show a dual and contradictory mistrust, both of the potentialities of film as a medium for adapting stage material, and for cinema as an independent medium in its own right.

My comments on this misplaced mistrust will centre around three distinct areas: Shaffer and Forman's use of the aged Salieri as narrator; Forman's *mise en scène* and editing—and particularly his handling of those scenes in which Mozart and Salieri interact verbally; and what I take to be the premises underlying both the production of the film *Amadeus* and the critical and popular acclaim it has received. In the process I will discuss as well two aspects of *Amadeus* that have been more or less overlooked by its commentators: its high cutting rate, and the film's fairly obvious homosexual subtext.

My goal will be to treat the film less as an adaptation than as an independent work in itself, and I will not even broach the question of whether *Amadeus* is a good or bad play to begin with, or better or worse in its film version. In at least some cases reference back to Shaffer's source material may prove enlightening and pertinent, but in the end I will argue that what makes *Amadeus* interesting, and probably most appealing to a mass audience, are exactly the aspects of the Mozart character that subvert the movie's evident high-culture aspirations. The film is richest and most ambiguous when it is most vulgar.

One can note immediately that *Amadeus'* subject matter is by its nature long on talk and ideas and short on action. *Amadeus* is faced with the dramatic problem common to all film biographies of composers, and one standardly commented on by their critics: that unlike careers in law enforcement, the military, athletics, crime or prostitution, the profession of being a composer offers little of inherent visual dramatic interest. For all of Forman and Shaffer's attempts to enrich the film visually through period spectacle and interpolated excerpts from Mozart's operas, the film's action consists fundamentally of dialogue. And for all of Shaffer's building new suspense elements into the screenplay—in the housekeeper

Salieri hires to spy on Mozart, in the insistent physical presence of the figure of Mozart's father, in the question of whether Mozart will be justly paid for the vaudeville production of *The Magic Flute*—the conflicts of the drama remain internal and psychological rather than physical.

One of Forman and Shaffer's most fundamental innovations was to rework Salieri's theatrical monologues by means of a framing device whereby Salieri, years later in a mental hospital, recounts his story to a priest who has come to hear his confession. Material in the play that was in the form of stylized soliloquy is spoken to the priest and becomes a voice-over narration for the film as a whole.

In her recent book, *Invisible Storytellers: Voice-Over Narration in American Fiction Film*, Sarah Kozloff does an impressive job of articulating and debunking the standard critical biases against voice-over narration as a screenwriting device. These standard biases are the arguments that voice-over narration involves verbal communication in a primarily visual medium, that it involves "telling" rather than the preferable "showing" of material, that it is excessively literary, that it is redundant, and that it is the last resort of the incompetent filmmaker who cannot visualize his material by other means (8-22). Although I agree absolutely with Kozloff's conclusion that "our assessment of the merits of a film's narration...should depend upon the case, not on a priori legislation" (22), I must ultimately assert that in the specific case of *Amadeus* virtually all of the above arguments apply.

Although the framing voice-over narration does give structure to an otherwise episodic story, the device often results in a flat redundancy between word and image. Salieri tells us he was in love, or at least in lust, with the singer Katherina Cavalieri right after his face and manner have already indicated exactly these feelings. Comments about how beautiful Mozart's music is reduplicate the unsettled but ecstatic looks on Salieri's face, looks that in turn become all but completely redundant because we can hear the evident brilliance of Mozart's music on the soundtrack. It is not enough to see Salieri's face begin to break into a smile when the emperor yawns at the performance of *The Marriage of Figaro*; Salieri's voice also has to describe to us these same perverse feelings of glee. In short, Shaffer's script continually "tells" what has already been shown.

Forman seems to mistrust the strength of his own imagery. Rather than let his burial scene speak for itself about Mozart's mortality and God's supposed capriciousness in letting Salieri survive to a ripe old age, the filmmakers immediately have Salieri explain it all to us in a way that reduces rather than expands the range of possible meanings of the imagery. Similarly, the filmmakers use a strong image of Salieri throwing a crucifix into the fire to substitute for a long monologue at the end of Act I (46-48), only to retain enough of the spoken explanation to pin the meaning of the gesture down to a single interpretation. In the play the monologue has the evocativeness of words without images as Salieri describes his anger and withdrawal from God, yet the filmmakers forgo the chance to let the reverse technique be similarly evocative, since the single image says it all.

Unlike the use of voice-over narration in the films of Stanley Kubrick, where the spoken text is so often a couple of provocative steps out of synch with the image, or in Robert Bresson, where redundancy becomes purposefully banal to emphasize the seeming meaninglessness of everyday life, Shaffer's words too often render Forman's images as mere illustrations. This tactic gives *Amadeus* a very definite clarity and comprehensibility, which the filmmakers may have deemed necessary to reach a mass audience, but at the expense of a specifically cinematic richness.

At least one report of the Shaffer-Forman collaboration describes Forman as determinedly trying to rid the filmscript of all vestiges of theatricality (Kakutani 20). What I find both peculiar and questionable is the way in which this disdain for the theatrical extends to *Amadeus'* patterns of *mise en scène* and editing. A fundamental tactic of stage *mise en scène* is to partition the space of the playing area to make it a visual analogue to whatever power struggles are going on in the script. Characters claim physical space and dominant position as they claim power. Similarly, the physical distance between characters becomes a physical analogue to their psychological closeness or distance. This analogic use of space is fundamental to much film *mise en scène* as well.

Amadeus is striking for Forman's all but systematic avoidance of such techniques. Scene after scene in Forman's movie is constructed around a physically static speaking situation in which Forman uses a rapid cutting rate rather than composition to shift attention and emphasis. By and large, Forman avoids lateral compositions in which characters face off at opposite sides of the screen, just as he avoids two-shots in which two characters share the frame as they talk.

One of the oddities of the reception of *Amadeus* has been a lack of discussion of the director's high cutting rate. By my own rough estimate, one based on fourteen 45-second samples taken at regular intervals throughout the film, Forman uses an average shot length of less than 4.5 seconds. Quantitative researchers in film, and I cite here in particular the work of Barry Salt, have proposed that the average shot length for Hollywood movies from 1929 to 1960 was between ten and eleven seconds, a figure that admittedly drops to 7.5 seconds in the late 1960s (345). Forman thus cuts more than twice as fast as a traditional Hollywood filmmaker would, using a rate far more comparable to that of the silent era (Bordwell, Staiger and Thompson, 60-62). Where the classical Hollywood sound film has some 200 to 500 shots per hour, *Amadeus* has over 800 for the same time.

Although rapid cutting rates have become all the more common in recent years, *Amadeus'* cutting rate seems somewhat odd for a work that emphasizes dialogue over physical action. Not surprisingly, Forman in *Amadeus* most frequently treats two-person conversations using a pattern of alternating shots and reverse angle shots. Group discussions involve cutting to each participant as he speaks, with occasional reaction shots. Consider, for example, the scene in which the Emperor and members of his court debate the merits of the German language opera as opposed to Italian language opera. A filmmaker like Otto Preminger might have grouped each faction on separate sides of the CinemaScope screen, allowed the Emperor or Salieri to move between them in the course of the debate, and thus graphically underlined the displacements and shiftings of allegiance during the conversation. Forman simply cuts among the different participants. He abandons, in effect, two major cinematic techniques—movement of the subject and movement of the camera—to rely solely on editing to provide for visual interest and variety. With a lack of long shots to orient them, unwary viewers may in fact lose track of the spatial geography within such a scene, forgetting, if they are not attentive, who is standing where.

Forman uses this combination of rapid cutting, spatial disorientation, and single shots of faces to advantage in the scene in which Mozart, his wife and his father all go to the masked party. At the party, Salieri watches Mozart play musical chairs and do a vulgar parody of the lesser composer's own work. As the scene progresses, we completely lose touch with the relative physical location of each of the characters, but we see through editing how wife, father and rival all watch Mozart's actions, each with his or her own agenda toward them. The scene works not only because the spatial confusion of the scene reflects the emotional and subjective instabilities of the characters, but also because, apart from the funeral, it is the one scene in the film in which action wholeheartedly takes over from dialogue, with a visual style to match.

I do not mean to suggest in an academically prescriptive way that Preminger's mode of *mise en scène* is right and Forman's is wrong, but I find it odd that in adapting a play to the screen Forman should mistrust the one visual strategy that the stage has most in common with the screen. If, as communication theorists argue, human speech always serves to mark the power relationships and emotional closeness or distance of conversational participants, why, in a drama that puts primary emphasis on dialogue, would a director avoid using the one visual tactic that articulates most directly power relationships and emotional closeness between speakers?

What is most strange in this regard is that Mozart and Salieri rarely appear in the same frame together, even in those scenes where the two converse. Out of an estimated 2,125 shots in *Amadeus*, I have counted only 54 in which Mozart and Salieri are co-present in the frame. Three of these are long shots in which both men are part of larger groups of people, four involve the sequence in which Salieri has the unconscious Mozart carried to Mozart's apartment, and 44 are either reverse angle shots or shots in which one of the pair has his back to the camera, putting the emphasis in the shot on the other. This leaves only three shots in which the two men are together in the frame on an equal footing, and all three of these are fleeting takes, lasting only a few seconds. Two of these are in the scene in which Mozart comes to Salieri to seek his help over the censorship of the ballet in *The Marriage of Figaro*; the third I will discuss shortly.

Consider the group of shots in which Salieri helps Mozart write the requiem mass. Out of 134 shots that cover this action, one of them is that third two-shot of the two composers together, which occurs the first time Salieri hands to Mozart the manuscript so that the dying composer can check what Salieri has written down for him. All 133 of the others are shots of the individual men. The uneasy rapport that develops between the two is not spatialized; it exists on a verbal level only. When Mozart's wife Constanze returns and finds Salieri asleep in Mozart's room, the preceding scene acquires a clear homosexual subtext: she behaves as though she were interrupting her husband with a lover. Yet this subtext makes no sense visually, since Forman has almost never joined the men in his *mise en scène*. Indeed, one thing conspicuously absent from *Amadeus* is the kind of eroticism that may be a fundamental mechanism for much audience identification and desire in both theater and movies. One can see Forman's as a de-eroticized editing style in that he rarely allows characters the physical proximity needed to sexually charge the space between them.

One might well contrast here the movie's approach to that of the play. A repeated visual pattern in Shaffer's play is to construct an interlocking series of scenes which begins with several characters on the stage. In time the other characters leave, until only Mozart and Salieri are left. Issues, ideologies, and feelings repeatedly reduce themselves to the core opposition between the two men, an opposition physically represented by the two men on stage. It is curious that as the play and film respectively develop, it becomes the film in which this opposition is developed more in verbal terms, through Salieri's narration, while on a fundamental level the enacted play embodies it physically. If one is going to remove from a play the erotic, theatrically charged space of the theater, why bother at all to adapt the play to film, a medium based in the dynamics of voyeurism and scopophilia?

Consider, by extension, the scene in which Constanze brings to Salieri some of Mozart's manuscripts without her husband's knowledge. The scene is a rich one precisely because of the erotic possibilities inherent in Constanze's somewhat indiscreet assertiveness in coming alone to visit Salieri. Salieri even offers her a confection known as Nipples of Venus, and asks her to stop calling him "Your Excellency", since, in his words, "It keeps us at such a distance". Yet Forman's staging of the scene all but undercuts the erotic tension. He slips into his usual pattern of sequenced reverse angle medium shots, with Salieri and Constanze seated at a table. What becomes in stage productions a seductive dance of approach and retreat is actually rendered less visual, more verbal, more literarily theatrical.

How then does one account for *Amadeus'* popularity? Part of *Amadeus'* success has been in its ability to ride the high-status, high-culture coattails of both the Broadway stage and the classical music establishment, both cultural institutions whose continuing artistic validity and relevance can at least be questioned. Despite some attempts at subversiveness, *Amadeus* is basically a variant on the standard pious biography of the great composer, complete with the obligatory scene portraying the ecstasy of musical composition. I will not be the first to note that it certainly provided members of the Academy of Motion Picture Arts and Sciences with a chance to show how cultivated they are.

Yet beneath *Amadeus'* success may be an ultimate irony. In *Amadeus*, Mozart, in describing *The Marriage of Figaro* to the king, rails against the "elevated themes" and "dead legends" that dominated the artistically respectable operas of his time. Is not *Amadeus*, with its own elevated themes and dead legend, exactly the cinematic equivalent of the kind of opera Mozart was reacting against—an elitist subject of historical and highbrow pedigree, detached from the dynamics of authentic popular culture? Perhaps. Yet if *Amadeus* represents only a cinema of elevated themes and dead legends, why has it been so relatively popular with a mass audience? I would argue: precisely because it expresses such ambivalence about its own status as a presumably educational, edifying, culturally significant film.

I have a colleague who once argued to me that *E.T.* and *Gandhi*, both released in 1982, were essentially the same movie. Both featured bald, physically unimposing, soft-spoken, other-worldly heroes battling the spiritual ills of the modern world.[2] Recognizing that it was the supposedly uplifting *Gandhi*, and not *E.T.*, that won the Oscar for Best Motion Picture, I'd like to propose a similar analogy between *Amadeus* and Pee-wee Herman. Both Tom Hulce's Mozart and Pee-wee Herman represent characters who are infantile, sexually ambiguous, loud, impolite, spontaneous and imaginative. Both create or surround themselves with objects that are colourful, playful and potentially offensive to refined sensibilities—Pee-wee in his playhouse, Mozart at the opera house. Both associate with women who are strong-willed and assertive. Both appeal to, and simultaneously court the rejection of, mass audiences. Both use emblematic, childlike laughs. Both are adult children.

Henry Jenkins III has argued that the appeal of *Pee-wee's Playhouse* for children lies exactly in its providing children with a diametric opposite of educational television, with free form play and pleasure detached from purpose and social restraint (175-77). So it is also with the Mozart character in *Amadeus*, who represents the playful child-genius who creates for self-gratification and pleasure, who rejects the constraints and goal-oriented structures imposed by standard socialization. Like Pee-wee, this Mozart is simultaneously loveable and threatening, and therein lies his uneasy appeal.

Yet there is a fundamental difference between *Pee-wee's Playhouse* and *Amadeus*. Several commentators have noted how the Pee-wee Herman character is continually surrounded by men who are hypermasculine in character, macho even to the point of embodying icons of gay pornography—the sailor, the cowboy, the lifeguard (Penley 145-6; Balfour 156-7). By contrast, with the very important exception of his father, the Mozart of *Amadeus* is by and large surrounded by wimps—the inept, half-wit Emperor; the petty, pompous, physically repulsive Kappellmeister and opera director; the delicate-looking priest who comes to hear the confession; and not the least Salieri himself. If Pee-wee Herman's approach to confronting the child's emerging sexuality has been to contrast Pee-wee with hypermasculine characters, *Amadeus* does just the opposite to its main character.

I have established earlier how Forman's *mise en scène* tends to de-eroticize several scenes in which sexual elements are either latent or obvious. Shaffer's adaptation of his own play also softens several of the play's overt heterosexual references. Although it is not a speaking part, there is a role for Salieri's wife in the play, but none in the film. One can also compare the two speeches early in both film and play in which Salieri describes his childhood prayers to God to make him a great composer. In the play, Salieri says:

"In return, I will live with virtue. I will strive to better the lot of my fellows. And I will honour You with much music all the days of my life" (8).

In the film, by contrast, Salieri says: "I will give You my chastity, my industry, my deepest humility, every hour of my life." The latter version, to the extent that it suggests a vow of celibacy, also suggests a repression of sexuality.

In the next scene of the play, Salieri describes his feelings toward his singing pupil Katherina Cavalieri:

"I was very much in love with Katherina—or at least in lust. But because of my vow to God I was entirely faithful to my wife" (10).

The line makes clear the relation between the first promise and this later comment, rendering all the more meaningful the second act appearance of Katherina, now as Salieri's mistress, at the premiere of *The Magic Flute*. For the film version, Shaffer follows the line about love and lust with a line of denial (in point of fact a paraphrase of a later line from the play), "But I swear to you I never laid a finger on her."[3] Given the absence of Salieri's wife from the film, and of all references to Katherina's becoming Salieri's mistress, the line seems like one more implication of a flight from heterosexual expression.

More importantly, consider the previously mentioned scene in which Mozart's wife visits Salieri. In the play, Salieri actively sets out to seduce Constanze. When she comes to visit him in Mozart's behalf, he is expecting her, and has purposefully ordered his cook to prepare the confection known as Nipples of Venus for her benefit. Constanze later returns and offers herself sexually to Salieri. Although Salieri rejects her advances, he explains to the audience that it was because his quarrel had become with God, not Mozart, and immediately describes his seduction of Katherina Cavalieri the following day: "So much for my vow of sexual virtue" (51). Forman's Constanze, by contrast, first takes Salieri by surprise. The Nipples of Venus are there by chance, and while there is a flirtation between Salieri and Constanze, the emphasis in the scene shifts markedly to Salieri's realization that Mozart writes his music in single drafts, without having to make corrections. If anything, Salieri seems bothered by the woman's interruption, and she never returns to give Salieri sexual favours.

If one accepts the implicit homoeroticism of Mozart and Salieri's final scenes together, the two characters come to embody what may be the homosexual's two social options—to flout, as Mozart does, the conventions of society, to be outrageous, blatant and liberated; or to be discreet, polite, conforming, and upwardly mobile, like Salieri. Certainly the performances of both actors can be read as encoding gay stereotypes. Tom Hulce's cuteness, giggling and falsetto laugh, and F. Murray Abraham's refinement and catty articulateness become two sides of the same coin. And in both cases the composers flee identification with their fathers—Salieri in wishing his father's death, Mozart in defying his father's standards for propriety. By cloaking these gay icons in the unfamiliar exoticism of eighteenth century court behaviour, and by depriving the viewer of contrasting figures who would embody conventional images of masculinity, Forman and Shaffer, consciously or not, cushion the audience against potential discomfort. Given our society that has traditionally associated both classical music and the theater with homosexuality and sissified culture, this cushion allows for an indirect and non-threatening confrontation with questions relating sexual identity to cultural expression.

Amadeus thus becomes a movie which links an ambivalence toward theater with an ambivalence toward sexuality with an ambivalence toward gentility and social politeness, and it is in this network of associations that the work becomes culturally significant. *Amadeus*'s very peculiarities—from its high cutting rate to its virtual effacement of the traditional Hollywood iconography of masculinity—make it a film of potential provocation. Indeed, if one follows the debatable dictum of Pascal Bonitzer (8-10) that all editing can be seen as symbolic castration, cutting rate and iconography may well be related. There are surely positive arguments to be made for *Amadeus*'s resistance to being a filmed play, its decisive visual style, its ambitious reaching out to a mass audience without compromising its philosophically abstract subject matter. But underlying the film is a tone of essential mistrust: mistrust for the ability of film and theater to coexist on the screen, mistrust in the fundamental eroticism of motion pictures, mistrust in the power of the unedited and verbally unexplained image.

NOTES

1. An advertisement in the *New York Times* (4 Jan. 1985: C7) for *Amadeus* indicates that it was included in lists of ten best films for 1984 by *People*, Judith Crist of WOR-TV, Gene Siskel and Roger Ebert of *At the Movies*, Bob Thomas of the Associated Press, and Jack Mathews of *USA Today*.

2. I wish to thank James K. Chalmers for this observation.

3. In the play, in Act I, Scene 7, Salieri says, "I had kept my hands off Katherina. Yes! But I could not bear to think of anyone else's upon her" (25). In effect, Shaffer in the film script collapses these lines with the previously mentioned line about love and lust, which in the play occurs several scenes earlier.

WORKS CITED

"All Time Film Rental Champs." *Variety* 11-17 Jan. 1989: 28+.

Amadeus. Dir. Milos Forman. Orion, 1984.

Balfour, Ian. "The Playhouse of the Signifier: Reading Pee-wee Herman." *Camera Obscura* 17 (1988): 155-68.

Bonitzer, Pascal. "Fétichisme de la technique: La notion de plan." *Cahiers du cinéma* 233 (1971): 4-10.

Bordwell, David, Janet Staiger and Kristin Thompson. *The Classical Hollywood Cinema: Film Style and Mode of Production to 1960.* New York: Columbia U P, 1985.

Jenkins, Henry III. "'Going Bonkers!': Children, Play and Pee-wee." *Camera Obscura* 17 (1988): 169-92.

Kakutani, Michiko. "How 'Amadeus' was Translated from Play to Film." *New York Times* 16 Sept. 1984, Sec. 2: 1+.

Kozloff, Sarah. *Invisible Storytellers: Voice-Over Narration in American Fiction Film.* Berkeley: U of California P, 1988.

Penley, Constance. "The Cabinet of Dr. Pee-wee: Consumerism

and Sexual Terror." *Camera Obscura* 17 (1988): 133-154.

Salt, Barry. *Film Style and Technology: History and Analysis*. London: Starword, 1983.

Shaffer, Peter. *Amadeus*. New York: Harper and Row, 1981.

Zimmer, Jacques. "Exploitation: 8 ans de box-office." *La revue du cinéma* 442 (1988): 66-77.

Between Worlds: Re-Placing Hungarian Cinema

Catherine Portuges
University of Massachusetts, Amherst

"We are increasingly becoming a world of migrants, made up of bits and fragments from here, there. We are here, and we have never really left anywhere we have been."—Salman Rushdie, quoted in *The New York Times*, 2/23/89

When Graham Petrie invited me recently to offer a presentation on Hungarian cinema for this conference, I was at once pleased and dismayed: delighted by the opportunity to participate in such an exciting occasion, yet concerned at the absence of a designated space for Hungarian cinema. In retrospect, however, its very absence from the original program affords us a moment to reflect upon a tradition peculiar to its cultural history with regard to film. For the operative question of the conference: "Did Soviet and East European directors sacrifice artistic freedom in exchange for Western political and financial benefits?" recalls the fact that Hungarian film artists have, in fact, been working in the West for many decades.

Growing up in Hollywood in an Austro-Hungarian family, I was keenly aware of the presence of a dynamic community of Hungarian artists whose contributions helped to shape what we think of as "Hollywood," perhaps more substantially than is commonly recognized. Korda and Kertész, Balázs, Rózsa and Fejös were among those who emigrated, crossing cultural boundaries, languages, and intellectual traditions and enduring the difficulties of exile. It was well known that many were never truly at ease or at home outside of Hungary, as Otto Preminger testified when haranguing his fellow Central Europeans to the effect that, in order to succeed in Hollywood, they would have to do more than speak Hungarian.

That world, obviously, has changed, and the current wave of boundary crossing indeed displays other characteristic features, other motivations. Aspects of that experience, however, shared as it is by so many who are dispossessed of language and identity—through departures either chosen or forced, or both—are, I think, more than pertinent today. The retrospective preoccupation of many East European artists, for example, bears eloquent witness to the pull of the past, the need to uncover repressed individual and national consciousness of the Stalinist and post-Stalinist eras, the double impetus of memory and forgetfulness. Torn by the desire to leave and the equally insistent prompting to remain or to return, Hungarian filmmakers are not alone in experiencing doubt and ambivalence with regard to the West and its representations. And I think it important to bear this in mind as we consider the specificities of the Hungarian national cinema within the framework of the Soviet Union and Eastern Europe, for their differences are both instructive and perplexing.

Under Stalinism, Hungarian filmmakers remained at home; they worked in relative isolation, representing themes such as the plight of a recently collectivized peasantry and the lives of the working class. It was not until the late 1960s that such isolation was penetrated by Miklós Jancsó, who achieved celebrity in international festivals for films including *The Round-up* (1965) and *The Red and the White* (1967).

Not long thereafter, Prague Spring flowered, in 1968, heralding a new epoch for East European cinema, about which we shall be hearing more today, particularly with regard to Czechoslovakia and Poland. Encouraged by the greater freedom resulting from the economic transformations then underway in Hungary, Jancsó went on to make several films in Italy, where he lived for some time. Yet even within an intellectual climate traditionally favorable to lives conducted in more than one sphere, Miklós Jancsó's visibility was extraordinary. The films he made abroad—*La Pacifista* (1970), *Technique and Rite* (1971), *Rome Wants Another Caesar* (1973), and *Private Vices, Public Virtues* (1976) however, were often thought to lack the power and originality of those for which he had first been hailed, and it was not until his return to Hungary in the mid-1980s that the director regained the momentum and vision evident in his earlier work. Since then, even under the constraints of the current economic crisis, he has produced a new film each year, the most recent of which is his *Season of Monsters* (1988).

Jancsó's experience paved the way for others, as attested by the sustained popularity enjoyed by István Szabó's co-productions *Mephisto* (1981) and *Colonel Redl* (1984), both available at local video stores (at least at mine). Despite the occasional co-production with other East European countries, it was not until the early 1980s that the drive toward the West intensified, in tandem with more pervasive shifts in Hungarian political and economic policy.

I should like now to direct your attention more closely to the filmmaker whose work constitutes the primary focus of my remarks here today. In the forefront of Hungarian film directors whose work now reaches the West is Márta Mészáros. Trained as a documentarist at the Moscow Institute of Cinematography in the early 1950s, her features in the early 1970s established the concerns for which she is now recognized: representation of the struggle of working women and men attempting to create a new society against the background of modern political and socio-economic life in post-1956 Hungary. Those films foregrounded women characters, raising issues of power in the framework of class and gender relations. *Riddance* (1973), *Adoption* (1975), *Nine Months* (1976), and *The Two of Them* (1977) represent conflicts between lovers and workers, family and state, young and old. Their making coincided with the director's separation from her former husband, Miklós Jancsó, and their critical esteem emanated rather more from abroad than from within Hungary, for these were not topics favored by Hungarian audiences. In the February 1989 issue of the Hungarian independent journal *Hitel* (Credit), in an interview entitled "A Warrior's Repose", Mészáros states:

> I'm an East European director, and my whole life-unfortunately—
> has been filled with politics; it is a tradition that, good or bad, you
> must deal with politics, especially for my generation, educated
> under Stalinism...All my earlier films were political, though not
> overtly so, addressing political themes from a psychological perspec-
> tive. The general public despised *The Two of Them, Nine Months,* and
> *The Heiresses* (1980) because these films described people who were
> different from them. They called attention to democratic problems
> such as women's right to independence, to live their own lives.
> These are especially important themes today in Hungary, for I know
> no other country that is so conservative about these issues. (Transla-
> tion László Kürti)

The incomprehension and, for that matter, hostility of their reception discouraged the director, who had been working for over
a decade without recognition as a serious filmmaker, isolated as a
woman in opposition to the predominantly male filmmaking establishment. Realizing the limitations of that situation, and having
completed that chapter in her work, Mészáros left Hungary in
search of a wider audience with its attendant challenges on an
international scale.

Mészáros next completed three co-produced films in as many
years: *On the Move,* in 1979, a Polish-Hungarian venture; *The Heiresses,* with Paris-Gaumont, starring Isabelle Huppert, and *Anna* in
1981, also made with French cooperation. In spite—or perhaps because of—their locations abroad, in these films, too, the director
continued to re-work, albeit in more complicated fashion, her previous interests in historical, gender-specific subjects. I questioned
Márta Mészáros about the conditions of their making and reception
during a series of interviews I conducted with her in Budapest last
summer. While *The Heiresses* was highly regarded in France for its
audacious and even courageous treatment of infertility, class, and
female friendship, Hungarian reviews of this period of her work

were overwhelmingly negative. She remarked that she might well have continued to make movies abroad that, however successful, departed from the heart and soul of the vision that had inspired her in the first instance to become a filmmaker.

According to Mészáros, the Polish actor Jan Nowicki, star of nearly all her feature films, warned her then of the dangers of irreparable alienation from one's roots as an artist. His insistence brought into sharp focus the dilemma in which both of them found themselves. For Nowicki too knows well the complexities of dual identity as a Polish stage actor, living in Hungary, returning often to perform in his homeland. On the brink of a precarious status as international celebrity, attracted by the glamorous prospects of continued work in the West, Mészáros had not yet accomplished what mattered most to her as a person and artist. She was to confront, in that anguishing contradiction, the quintessential conflict facing many East Europeans caught between the desire to return to their national origins or leave them behind, perhaps forever.

It was at that point, Mészáros remembers, against the background of the emergence of Solidarity in 1980 and its suppression the following year, that her companion Nowicki urged her to make a decision. As he saw it, the terms of her choice were to "become a third-rate director making popular films in the West", or to return home to embark upon her long-cherished project, the autobiographical sequence she had been contemplating for nearly two decades.

Returning to Hungary, a country already on the road to liberalization and democratization in the early 1980s, she was able at last to realize that long-suppressed dream, the first two segments of her *Diary* trilogy. Its antecedents were already discernible in early documentaries: the 1967 portrait of the sculptor *Miklós Borsos*, for example, is an homage to an independent artist, while the 1970 *Don't Cry, Pretty Girls* announces her interest in rock music and disenchanted youth. Such topics were taken up only considerably later by other filmmakers such as Gábor Bódy, Péter Gothár, János

Xantus, and now Miklós Jancsó with his new feature on the popular Hungarian rock group *Omega*.

In contrast to those earlier films, Mészáros' autobiographical projects *Diary For My Children* (1984) and *Diary For My Loves* (1986) won prizes at Cannes, Munich, and Budapest. They chronicle the tumultuous period of Hungarian and East European history between 1949 and 1956, a period that had been, until then, *terra incognita* in Hungarian cinema. More important still, these films narrate the director's own life story from the perspective of her adolescent alter-ego, Juli, using an innovative combination of semi-fictionalized and documentary material. By validating the importance of reconciliation with what has been repressed or denied—be it family, political affiliation, or inequalities inadmissible under Stalinism—these films affirm the right of both individual and nation to claim their experience, no matter how fraught with guilt, betrayal, or fear. Mészáros emphasizes the protagonist's quest for her lost father who disappeared in the Stalinist purges, her subsequent repatriation to Hungary as an orphan, and eventual return to the Soviet Union as a film student. The third segment of the planned trilogy, *Diary For My Mother and Father*, was to have been completed this spring, but that film, it seems, remains to be undertaken, ostensibly for purely financial rather than ideological reasons. It is to deal exclusively and intensively with the uprising of 1956 and its consequences, an event of supreme importance to Hungarians, as evidenced by the nearly obsessional proliferation of recent films and literary works on the subject.

The international recognition bestowed upon Mészáros particularly for *Diary For My Children* established her credibility as a filmmaker in both East and West. Her latest release, *Piroska es a farkas* (*Little Red Riding Hood and the Wolf*) a Canadian co-production, bears little resemblance to the *Diary* films except for the presence of Jan Nowicki: "I felt entitled to a rest [from politics] by making a movie...about childhood, its sadness, beauty, and pleasures..." It is, according to the director, a folk-tale she knew could not have been made without a foreign producer, a fantasy of childhood, love, and the relations between humans and animals. It is, she admits, also a political film in that it addresses the oppositions between possession and independence. To skeptics, she insists, however, that the Soviet Union is not personified by the Wolf, nor Hungary by Little Red Riding Hood!

The rapidity of political change in Hungary today is such that the events of the Stalinist and Kádárist eras are now sufficiently distant to enable those who lived through them—as well as successive generations—to engage in their own artistic efforts of understanding and reconciliation. With the 1987 transformation of its studio system into independent units, Hungarian cinema production no longer operates under a centralized institution, a potential encouragement to intensified international co-production. Despite severe financial strictures, the 1989 annual Hungarian Film Week boasted some thirty-five new releases, well above the figure for the past two years, among them András Jeles' *Dream Brigade*, banned as recently as the previous summer. A preponderance of theatrically-released documentaries—a long and prized tradition of Hungarian cinema— on such previously censored subjects as drugs, Hungarians in neighboring successor states, prostitution, the status of gypsies, and Stalin-era internment camps in Hungary demonstrates Hungarian filmmakers' efforts to rethink the past, emboldened by a new, more fully international spirit. The formation last year of MODESZ, an Independent Film Artists Union, attests further to the tenacity of such efforts.

East European artists, forced too often into dislocation and repatriation, know all too well the dangers both of obliterating the past and refusing to relinquish it. Caught between languages and the profound consequences of living a multi-cultural identity, Hungarian filmmakers are inscribed within conflicting discourses; they live with a double vision, one that imparts to Hungarian cinema—as well as literature and poetry—its particular pain and glory. For if indeed there are financial and political benefits, surely, too, there are also potential costs beyond those of artistic freedom: uncertainties of artistic livelihood and future, alienation from heritage, culture, and peers.

Although some might argue that her case is unique, I want to conclude by suggesting that the odyssey of Márta Mészáros is nevertheless richly illustrative of the dynamics of ambivalence inherent in the condition of film artists' traversal of East/West frontiers today. A parallel may be found in Péter Gothár, whose 1984 *Time Stands Still* catapulted him to worldwide markets, earning prizes in Japan and the USA. After a muted reception for his 1987 multi-national venture *Just Like America* (produced with cooperation from Hungary, Japan, Israel and the US), Gothár too returned to Hungary to resume the rigorous film and theater production for which he was first appreciated.

As we examine these delicate interconnections in the terrain between East and West, we must recognize that the arts of small East European nations cannot afford to remain marginalized or avoid participation in the current international arena if they are to maintain their national identity. In order for a truly vital national cinema to sustain itself in Hungary, Hungarian filmmakers seem prepared to enact a scenario staged within this intermediate zone; if these examples indicate a pattern, we can, I think, expect to see an increase in such shifts in the future.

In the domain of this third term, neither entirely East nor West, a more complex framework is required, I think, to understand the dialectics of this oscillation. The lure of the West—especially for film artists from those countries known as "the other Europe"— might well be the most effective and creative means of coming more profoundly to terms ultimately with oneself and one's nation. Working in the West is not necessarily tantamount to permanent change in the artist's endeavor, nor to loss of the soul. Departure may also lead to return, and to a deepening, rather than neutralization, of artistic and political vision.

From Eisenstein to Prime Time:

The Film and Television Design Career of Nikolai Soloviov

John E. Twomey
Ryerson Polytechnical Institute

There were three major periods in the life of the late Nikolai Soloviov. The first period, spanning the years 1910 to 1941, included his birth, education, and his years with Eisenstein when he designed, with Isaac Schpinel, the classic film, *Alexander Nevsky*, and began work on *Ivan the Terrible*. The second period, 1941-1952, included his Red Army service, his capture, and forced labour years under the Nazis, his post-war struggle to remain in the West, and his early years in Canada as a displaced person and contracted farm worker in Quebec. The final period of his life, 1952-1976, he spent as the senior art director/scenic designer for CBC television.

For nearly a quarter century, Nikolai Soloviov put his creative genius to work as a pioneer in a new technology and new art form decades before there began to be developed in Canada a theatre industry and a feature film industry.

In her 1987 book *Turn Up the Contrast*, Mary Jane Miller sets out television drama's critical cultural role:

> For most people now under forty, television provided the first formative, direct, and continuous experience of drama. Whether or not this was the case in any particular instance, Canadian television

> drama still played a crucial role for all of us as a window through
> which we saw glimpses of ourselves, acted for and by ourselves.
> Next door on the dial to Milton Berle or *Maverick* were plays writ-
> ten, produced, acted, directed, and watched by Canadians;
> hundreds of plays, performed for millions over the years (193).

I began my "detective" work on the life and work of Soloviov a dozen years ago when at the time of his death, his widow, Joan (a long time friend and colleague both at the CBC and at Ryerson) entrusted me with the body of his creative work. For over a year, working with an assistant, I was able to bring some order to a chaotic collection of sketches, renderings, paintings, floor plans, slides, and photographs, totalling over one thousand items. Among them were scenic drawings from Soloviov's pre-war work, brought out of the Soviet Union by his wife. With the help of a grant from the Ontario Arts Council, some of the items were mounted and displayed in the Soloviov Film and Television Design Exhibition.

Nikolai Soloviov was born in St. Petersburg in 1910. He was seven at the time of the Revolution, when his father, an officer in the Czar's Guard, was killed. He was taken by his mother to live with relatives in Moscow. As a student at the Moscow Institute of Fine Arts, his plan was to become an illustrator. He was asked to help design set for a play while at the Institute, and he showed such aptitude that he made theatrical design his career. After graduating in 1934, his professional life alternated between designing Moscow stage productions and creating set designs for motion pictures.

In 1938, he and Isaac Schpinel, guided by Sergei Eisenstein's drawings, co-designed the sets for *Alexander Nevsky*. Soloviov's responsibilities included the Cathedral and town of Novgorod, and the Tents of the Invading Teutonic Knights.

Later, as Eisenstein began work on *Ivan the Terrible* in January, 1941, he again called upon the team of Soloviov and Schpinel to do the design work.

Eisenstein had completed his first treatment of the projected film in May, 1941. On June 22 Hitler's armies invaded the Soviet Union. In the dark and devastating summer of 1941, when whole army

One of Soloviov's sets for *Alexander Nevsky*

corps were surrounded and captured by German armoured divisions, Soloviov was called into the Red Army and was sent to the front with the rank of captain. It was not long before he was a prisoner of war under the Nazi system that showed no mercy to Jews, officers or political commissars found among the captured.

The means by which Soloviov survived his four years as a prisoner, and the years immediately after the war when most prisoners were repatriated to the Soviet Union by the Allies, was never revealed in any detail by him.

We do know he lived in post-war Germany, earning a living as a photographer and sometime scenic designer for German films. In an effort to distance himself from the efforts and intrigues bent on locating all former Red Army soldiers and returning them to Russia, Soloviov came to Canada in 1949 as a Displaced Person, contracted to work on a farm in Quebec. He was never happy with his life as a farm worker, and was able to move to Toronto where he worked as a labourer. He was a roofer in 1952 when Ivan Romanoff, a chorus and orchestra leader on CBC radio, told him of the advent of television in Canada. Armed with a copy of Eisenstein's *The Film Sense* and a book with scenes from *Alexander Nevsky*, Soloviov persuaded Stuart Griffith, CBC's first Television Program Director, that he had the credentials to be a television scenic designer.

From the day he started, Nikolai Soloviov was the pre-eminent designer among the pioneers of CBC television drama. His first assignment was *Justice*, the second play ever produced on CBC Television. He designed as many as four ninety-minute plays a month during television's first year, supervising all stages of set design from floor plans to construction, through assembly.

Soloviov designed sets for CBC's first Shakespearean drama (*Othello*, starring Lorne Greene in 1953); its first TV opera (*Eugene Onegin*, 1958); and the first TV drama in colour (*Lady Windermere's Fan*, 1967). In 1962, he designed the colour program celebrating the 80th birthday of Igor Stravinsky.

CBC production of *The Importance of Being Ernest* 1956

CBC production of *Eugene Onegin* 1958

During his near quarter century designing for the CBC, Nikolai Soloviov worked with all the major producer/directors, actors and actresses, composers and conductors, and costume designers, as part of the production teams that built the reputation of excellence for CBC television drama.

Many of Soloviov's contemporaries considered him a traditional and "heavy" designer of the European school. Yet any comprehensive review of his work would refute this view. The body of his work shows versatility and flair. While it was true he was regularly given plays by Chekhov, Ibsen, Shaw and Wilde to design, his open area, representational design of Herman Gressieker's psychological drama about Henry VIII and his wives illustrates his ability to incorporate subtlety and symbolic forms in his work.

In addition it is interesting to recall that it was Soloviov who in 1956 designed the sets for Arthur Hailey's *Flight Into Danger*. This first play of Hailey's was the progenitor of his later book and film

Airport, and the play that spawned the whole genre of modern disaster films. The success of *Flight Into Danger* in Canada was followed by its production by both NBC and BBC. According to Mary Jane Miller, Hailey's first drama was "the first widely discussed popular television play: a real breakthrough".

CBC production of *Miss Julie* 1966

His years with Eisenstein did not freeze him in a heavy pre-war style of realism. It did however equip him with some of the techniques used by Eisenstein, such as drawing what a scene is to look like with actors in it. Soloviov's script renderings almost always include actors. He takes the view of the director's shot selection. Because television often brought three cameras to bear on any scene, Soloviov's floor plans included drawings of what each camera would "see" from its particular perspective in the set.

The Soloviov Film and Television Collection provides scholars with a unique opportunity to study systematically the development of design in Canadian television drama and Soloviov's contribution to it. A truly comprehensive understanding of his life and work is now possible but remains beyond the scope of this brief paper.

WORK CITED

Miller, M.J. *Turn Up the Contrast*. Vancouver: UBC Press, CBC Enterprises, 1987.

Discussion and Responses

Session Two

Graham Petrie as discussant:

Catherine Portuges' and John Twomey's presentations remind us that this phenomenon which we are discussing is not just one of the last twenty years, with an overtly political motivation behind the removal of people from their homelands to the West, but this kind of migration has been going on since before the first World War.

George Lellis's presentation on Forman picks up on what was said by Gerald Peary after Session One: that Forman, of all Eastern Europeans who have moved to Hollywood, has taken to it like a fish to water; he has an affinity to the mass market audience which Hollywood requires. There is also a paradox here: his Hollywood career seems to be increasingly disappointing. The splendours of his Czech films, and *Taking Off*, which is still his best American film, and has a lot of the Czech spirit still in it, have vanished. *Taking Off* did not have the big impact he expected and he has retreated to a kind of elitist material with a popular gloss over it, so that audiences can receive the kind of entertainment they're used to and at the same time think they are receiving some sort of serious analysis and information as well. He has captured that market quite well. Works like *Hair*, *Ragtime*, and *One Flew Over the Cuckoo's Nest* are books which have a patina of seriousness over them, but which never really follow through with the implications of the subject matter.

As for the Hungarian scene: three or four years ago I spoke at length with Hungarian directors, at a time when the idea of co-production was a big one. It was a time when film making was shrinking; in a situation in which there were many qualified filmmakers but only a few had the opportunity to work. The solution seemed to be to turn to co-production with foreign capital. This itself caused a crisis. A lot of people felt that one of the glories of

Hungarian cinema in the sixties and seventies was that it reflected a strongly national characteristic which expressed a purely Hungarian reality. With co-production there is an attempt to find a mythical international audience which falls between two stools; losing the Hungarian integrity, but without the flair and the even vulgarity, if you like, needed to capture an American audience. This was causing quite a crisis; some wanting and others not wanting co-production.

Some wanted never to make co-productions, feeling it was the role of Hungarian filmmakers to make films which analyze Hungarian society. Others felt they had to take the chance and that they could not afford to make a film only every ten years. Others were quite hostile to the idea that Hungarian films should remain purely Hungarian: Péter Gothár told me: "It is all right for foreign critics like yourself to come along and tell us how to run our industry; if I can make my films I'm going to make them. No one should tell me I am not being faithful to my Hungarian audience in doing so." This crisis is East European. István Szabó has managed to straddle it, although some feel that he has lost some of the authenticity of his earlier work.

Bart Testa, regarding Forman and genre:

There was a remark this morning regarding a list of Academy Award films which are not genre movies. I would propose that there is a genre at play here, the "prestige production": the pre-sold, well-budgeted, so-called unique production within the Hollywood film industry, and this introduces us to one of the problems just heard: the problem of popularization. In his paper on *Amadeus,* George Lellis talked about "interior strategies" in the film. Perhaps this issue could be broadened to include a history of East Europeans working in this genre since the 1920s and to relate this to the position in which we find Forman in the 1980s.

George Lellis:

There is a tendency for East Europeans to make these movies. I'm not sure that issues like sexuality and masculinity and their relation to culture are not central issues of the composer/biography genre.

Bart Testa:

The composer/biography is a sub-genre of the prestige production.

Unlike musicals and westerns, these were never conceived to be a regular production; it was always a puffed up pre-sold production with cultural credentials and was viewed by the Hollywood studios, even including the Buddy Holly film, as a prestige production.

The game at play is one of popularization; the game of using European directors for the prestige production and placing the burden of responsibility for popularization on their shoulders. They are brought in as art-film directors to make a prestige film which then would also be a popular film. Graham has written extensively about this phenomenon in the 1920s.

George Lellis:

I agree with your remarks but have problems agreeing that there is in fact such a genre as the "prestige picture": there is a lack of a common iconography.

Graham Petrie, in reference to the "prestige production" and the "prestige director":

In the 1920s the studios made a concerted effort to go out and get the prestige directors: like Lubitsch, Murnau and Sjöström. Most of the people who arrive in Hollywood nowadays end up there by accident. Few are sought for to come over; they come over for other reasons; most have had to struggle to establish themselves. Of those who have arrived in the last twenty years, Forman and Polanski have made it biggest, establishing themselves both commercially and critically in North America. Forman has had the shrewdness to get hold of well regarded literary material. He has made just the right kind of films from them, they have prestige, a big budget, are talked about in advance, and consequently get all the Oscars going each year they come out. I don't know that any other directors have had that chance. Even Polanski's *Rosemary's Baby* was not a prestige production; its success was a surprise. He then went on to make quirky films like *The Fearless Vampire Killers*. He didn't slot himself into a predictable "type" of film as Forman did.

Natasa Durovicova:

In American cinema there is an over-emphasis on the romantic. Most East European directors are reluctant to organize their narrative material around a central romance. Perhaps *Amadeus* is a variant where, on the one hand, you have a kind of romantic relationship, a kind of thwarted love relationship between the two men. This provides the narrative's infrastructural romance, yet it is not fully cast in the mainstream of Hollywood prestige productions. A narrative thrust is needed but without the obvious Hollywood sentimentality. Perhaps this is one way for the prestige production to accommodate serious topics and yet remain in the commercial domain.

George Lellis:

I agree with you. One of the issues in my expanded paper is the de-sexualizing of Shaffer's play. The play is obviously heterosexual; Salieri sets out to seduce Constanza. This does not occur in the film. Salieri has a mistress in the play. Salieri offers his chastity to God in return for success. It implies that he is taking a vow. The sexuality in the film becomes repressed.

Alex Batchan:

The film *Amadeus* is a success in Moscow. There is one redeeming aspect: the responsibilities of a genius. There is a minority view in Russian culture that the genius does not owe anybody anything. I would quote the Pushkin-Sinyavsky argument; Pushkin expressed this view in his small tragedy *Mozart and Salieri* (which I think Shaffer knew about when he wrote his play) and Sinyavsky in his *Walks with Pushkin*, written in the labour camp and published in London in 1975, proclaimed that Pushkin was lighthearted and chasing the ladies. This was taken as an insult by Russians both in this country and the Soviet Union. I wonder: was there any mention that Shaffer and Forman read either of these works?

Also, regarding the Hungarian cinema issue: there are other films set in the Stalinist period, such as *The Witness* by Péter Bacsó and *Angi Vera* by Pál Gábor. When I saw *Diary for My Loved Ones* by Márta Mészáros I felt that Hungarian cinema is running out of steam - not because of co-production or some economical problems. They are covering these topics such as the events of '56 and Stalinism far too much, it is time for them to get out of that. It is not their fault; there are certain subjects which the government allows them to cover; now they are allowed to criticize Stalin but not Lenin. Still it is the responsibility of the artist to find ways to cover these things, perhaps by using Aesopian language. They can avoid doing only things which are permitted. This is a danger.

About Soloviov, I don't remember this name, I remember Schpinel, so perhaps you remember if the Soviets mention him, he is a very interesting figure. There is someone else who became famous in North America via Canada, Boris Kaufmann, Vertov's younger brother who was a cameraman for *Twelve Angry Men* and *The Pawnbroker*. I think he started in Canada in 1940 in different circumstances. And now it's a very good time because the Soviets are trying to rehabilitate all these people who emigrated and who are now here. Is he mentioned in the credits?

John Twomey:

Yes he is mentioned by Schpinel in the credits. He is in Eisenstein's book but it is co-designed by Schpinel and Soloviev.

Alexander Batchan:

But do they explain what happened to the man?

John Twomey:

Eisenstein doesn't because his book was written in 1940-1941. There is much of Soloviov's life that I don't know, neither does his wife.

George Lellis:

I believe Shaffer was aware of Pushkin's work, but I have no idea to what degree he influenced Shaffer or Forman.

Catherine Portuges:

Where 1956 and Stalinism are concerned, some Hungarian filmmakers feel that they have not been able to deal with this matter until recently and that they are not through with it. There are documentaries which attempt to deal with current social problems.

Graham Petrie:

Another topic raised amongst Hungarian filmmakers was an irritation with this obsession with the 1950s, saying it was time to get away from Aesopian films set in 1850 that were meant to relate to the 1970s, and to get down to contemporary problems. Two years ago when I was there this was being done through documentaries. Catherine mentioned rock music, drugs, prostitution, and admitting for the first time that there were forced labour camps in Hungary in the early 1950s and taking the testimony of survivors. So, as Cattherine suggested, the 1950s are not totally exhausted and Mézáros plans to do a film on 1956 and Géza Beremenyi who was a scriptwriter of *Time Stands Still*, has just directed a film on the events leading up to 1956. There is, however, a widespread opinion that this has gone as far as it can go.

Barry Grant:

Forman's films have one thing in common, they are based on literary properties. Whether they are suspect I don't know. I think *One Flew Over the Cuckoo's Nest* is a fine novel and it stands apart from the other three. They are all obviously about America; if *Amadeus* isn't, then it is an anomaly. George Lellis did not feel that Mozart and Salieri were "about anything". I wonder if you could consider that their relationship had to do with the basic dilemma of democracy which applies to America: the force of levelling the genius in relation to the common man; this is something which has always been an issue in American culture. It is a hot issue with Harold Bloom.

Skolimowski's *The Lightship* and Conrad

Peter G. Christensen
Marquette University

In an interview with Richard Combs of *Monthly Film Bulletin* shortly after the release of his latest feature film *The Lightship* (1985), Jerzy Skolimowski states:

> Somebody brought my attention to Siegfried Lenz's book [*Das Feuerschiff*, 1960], and I thought there was great potential there for a film. There are similarities to Joseph Conrad's *Victory*, which is something I've always wanted to do. Maybe the geographical situation of Poland makes people specialists in those kinds of issues. *Victory* has been a project of mine for fifteen, twenty years now, so in a way I could make use of the Conradian philosophy which I'd been accumulating on *The Lightship*. Robert Duvall is almost like Mr. Jones in *Victory*, although Lenz had already described that character pretty well. (133)

Further along in the interview Skolimowski adds a few more references to Conrad. He says that there were seven writers of the film, including himself and Conrad, and that what appealed to him about Lenz's novel was the "Conradian setting where the moral issues were strongly established." Finally, he closes by declaring that he has written a screenplay of *The Secret Agent* and that he hopes he will be able to film it. [1]

Despite these several mentions of Conrad, it never becomes clear what Skolimowski has in mind by the "Conradian philosophy." Considering that there are many different interpretations of Conrad's themes and ideas, we have little to go on here in trying to

interpret the film. Furthermore, there are so many differences between *The Lightship* and *Victory*, including the complete absence of
a heterosexual love story in the film, that the director's stress on
these similarities needs clarification that he does not provide. Nevertheless, an exploration of Skolimowski's debt to Conrad in the
making of this film is in order.

There are no critical overviews of Skolimowski's work to help us
gain our bearings. His career has moved through distinct phases
that are initially hard to link together. First he published several
books of poetry in Polish in the 1950s.[2] Then he co-wrote screenplays for such films as Polanski's *Knife in the Water* and Wajda's
Innocent Sorcerers. In the early 1960s he began to make short films
and then graduated to features such as *Ryopsis*, *Walk Over*, and
Barrier. In the mid-1960s he became an international director, working in many different nations, such as Belgium for *Le Départ*. His
career went into a slump with two adaptations, *The Adventures of
Gerard* and *King, Queen, Knave*. However, beginning in 1978 in
Great Britain he reasserted himself with three complex films, *The
Shout*, *Moonlighting*, and *Success Is the Best Revenge*. *The Lightship*,
his first film in the United States, appears much simpler than the
films of the British period. However, on closer analysis, it seems to
have almost as much ambiguity as the films that immediately
preceded it. Like *The Shout*, *The Lightship* deals with a violent
intrusion. With *Moonlighting* it shares the theme of a man trying to
keep his subordinates in line. It is similar to *Success Is the Best
Revenge* in its treatment of father-son conflicts. Thus Skolimowski's
first American feature can also be considered a summary of his
British period films.[3]

Although Skolimowski and Conrad were both Poles displaced
in England, the fact that they were exiles is not the main similarity
between them. Instead, Skolimowski's debt to Conrad can be felt
in four ways in *The Lightship*. First of all, there is the depiction of a
morally difficult situation, which is characteristic of much of Conrad's fiction, including sea fiction such as "The Secret Sharer" and
The Shadow Line. Skolimowski takes the material from Lenz's novel

and renders it more complex by making the Captain less admirable. Second, a Conradian motif of suppressed homosexuality is added to the characterization. Third, as in *Lord Jim* the dangers of identifying with evil (e.g. Gentleman Brown's tempting of Jim), are expressed. Fourth, like *Victory*, *The Lightship* presents the inadvisability of retreating from the world and falling into inactivity.

Perhaps the most obvious influence of Conrad on the film is the most general one. In line with Conrad's exploration of moral ambiguity, Skolimowski elaborates on the complexities of the novella in three ways related to the characterization of the Captain.

First, by closing the film with the voice-over of the son Alex reconciled with his dying father, Skolimowski gives us no final word as to how we should judge the Captain's questionable behavior throughout the shipboard crisis. On the one hand, we may feel that Miller is a man who has so habitually withdrawn from life that he is too paralyzed to oppose the three criminals. His refusal to resort to arms proves foolish, as his lack of leadership endangers the lives of others under him. He places too high a value on devotion to the ship. Ultimately, Alex proves more resourceful, for he kills the dangerously unbalanced Eddie. On the other hand, it seems possible to give an almost diametrically opposite significance to the events. Miller's watch-and-wait tactic recognizes that he cannot stop violence with more violence. Although he dies, he maintains his principles and reestablishes contact with his estranged son. The latter reading is closer to Lenz's novel, but the former one, stressing the inadequacy of the Captain, seems to me a better reading of the film and one closer in spirit to Conrad's *Victory*.

Second, not only is the wisdom of Miller's actions brought into question, but the relationship of the father and son as well. Their reconciliation is possible only because Alex kills Eddie, who has previously spared his life. Miller probably would not have condoned such a murder. More significant than the brief reconciliation could be the fact that the death of the father frees the son to be himself.

Third, by giving the audience little sense of the interior life of the

Captain, who does not reveal himself in voice-over narration like Alex or in weighty conversation like Calvin Caspary, Skolimowski also keeps us from easily judging the existential slant of Caspary's ideas. As the person who can assume another's identity (his brother's) and who acknowledges no ties to the past or any crimes in it, Caspary represents a sinister brand of existentialist, the great criminal. However, Miller's reclusiveness after the inquiry into his actions during World War II and his symbolic connection to the daily entries in the ship's logbook also suggest that an inability to shake off one's past can limit life's possibilities dramatically.

Skolimowski says that he had no desire to make a direct transposition of Lenz's novella from German characters in the Baltic to American characters off the coast of Virginia. As a result, he does not hesitate to treat his Captain less sympathetically than Lenz's. The Captain in the novella is more intelligent and alert, strong-principled, conscientious, shrewd, and free of the weight of the past than the Captain in the film.

In the novella, when Caspary tells the Captain that the ship's refusal to move is not an indication of duty and virtue but of imprisonment, Captain Freytag gives a more graphic and philosophical defense of his actions than does Miller, his counterpart in the film.

> "Prisoners have a power of their own," said Freytag. "The masters are far more dependent upon their prisoners than the prisoners on the masters. If we didn't exist you would have a well-filled ships' cemetery here, and the spars of sunken ships would stick out all over the bay like nails from a fakir's bed. The whole bay would be full of wrecks, and out there, where the minefields used to be, they would lie side by side or even one on top of another. The others can only sail about because we lie at anchor and they can rely on our signals. Where a lightship lies, there is something wrong. They know that, and they are on the alert as soon as they see us." (27-28)

Freytag's use of Hegel's master-slave dialectic, along with the vivid images of disaster, gives the reader the impression that he is more forthright and articulate than the Captain in the film.

Early in the film, before he picks up the three unknown passengers, Miller hears radio news that three criminals have escaped. Thus we wonder why he wasn't more alert when he sent a boat out to help strangers. He waits passively for events to happen and does not take the initiative.

Freytag seems to be a person of greater resolve. He tells his son Fred:

> "You know nothing," said Freytag. "So long as you imagine that the only course open to an unarmed man is to argue with gun muzzles. I don't give a damn for what you know. I'll tell you something, lad. I have never been a hero and I don't want to become a martyr; both of those types have always seemed very suspect to me: they died too easily and even in death they were still certain of their cause—too certain, I think, and that is no solution. I have known men who died in order to settle something. They settled nothing, they left everything behind. Their death helped them but nobody else. A man with no weapons and no power still has more chance than a dead man, and I often think that behind this desire to offer oneself at any price to the muzzle of a gun lies the worse egotism." (66)

Freytag looks at the unconscious motives that surface when one tries to become a hero. He addresses a type of cowardice in facing the problems of daily, non-heroic life. In the film this idea is not expressed, and Miller's actions seem less self-assured.

Freytag in the novel is presented as writing down the events in the ship's log as accurately as possible in order that his controversial behavior may be understood later. Caspary comes in and tears out this entry. Although in both novel and film, the logbook prompts a discussion by Caspary of the will to forget, only in the novel do we actually see the Captain at work at his official function of recording events. Thus Alex's voice-over statement that he has no idea why his father is acting the way he is or what game is going on between him and Caspary is justified because Miller never seems to represent a carefully considered position toward danger.

The presentation of the Captain's rather than the son's interior thoughts in the novella makes us more sympathetic to Freytag than to Miller, not only because we tend to sympathize with characters whom we understand, even when they are weak, but also because these passages reinforce the idea of the Captain as a man with a reasonable strategy. Freytag recognizes the seriousness of the crew's situation late in the novel:

> *So he caught on*, thought Freytag, *he realized what I meant to do, because Soltow can't have told him, and Soltow is the only one who knew. He saw through everything: that we only wanted to push them out a mile into the bay, where they would have been a sitting target for the police.* (98)

It is never as clear in the film that Miller's delaying tactics will have the same effect of necessarily getting the criminals into a position from which escape will be impossible.

Last, and most significantly, the Captain gives a different account of the experiences in World War II that have haunted his life. In the film, the U. S. military ship which Miller's ship was guarding was attacked by a submarine. Men had to jump into the burning flames, and he could hear them screaming. However, he took his ship after the enemy submarine and sank it. There was an inquiry, and he was cleared of charges. Nevertheless, he still feels responsible for the deaths of the men. Alex responds somewhat sympathetically to this story, which he has never heard before.

In the novella Freytag's account is provoked by a greater antagonistic outburst on the part of his son, Fred. The teenager accuses his father of having left a comrade named Natzmer to his death because he was afraid of danger to himself (58). Fred believes that the whole crew "wanted to go ashore and fetch Natzmer" (60), but Freytag prevented them because he was a coward.

Freytag explains that he, Natzmer, and another seaman named Lubisch (64) were taken prisoners by the Greeks. After some time, Freytag and Lubisch were led to the shore and allowed to swim toward their ship. Lubisch tried to turn back for Natzmer, but Freytag prevented him because it was a foolhardy idea. On shipboard, they had new orders to sail to Rotterdam, and Freytag obeyed them. From the Captain's account, it seems that he had drawn the only reasonable conclusion under the circumstances. He would only have been risking the lives of his men to return and confront the heavily armed enemy. However, the immature Fred is too blinded by anger to understand.

In short, Freytag's story shows him to be a man of perspicacity and principle. Unlike Miller, he was not really facing a profound moral dilemma. Miller chooses to do what is his military duty, and in so doing, arrives too late to rescue his comrades. Thus it is not surprising that he should still feel responsible, whereas Freyag does not. The viewer fears that Miller may make the same mistake again and put his duty to his ship over figuring out how to protect the lives of his crew. This one incident best exemplifies Skolimowski's turning the Captain into a less admirable figure.

Skolimowski also complicates the film by including homosexual attraction to characterize temptation in the film. The relationship between the Captain and Caspary is simpler in the novella. Freytag's evaluation is that Caspary is a madman, which is revealed in his interior thoughts:

> He's crazy, thought Freytag, he is one of those who have been dropped on their head. He's just one of those fellows for whom life isn't enough, because they don't manage to make a success of one single thing. (96)

In contrast, in the film, homosexual attraction plays a part in the interactions between the Captain and Caspary and between Alex and Eddie. Both the crew on the lightship and the three intruders are men without women in their society. However, no tangible warm feelings circulate among the grown men on board, whereas Caspary is very chummy with his two dangerous assistants. We even see Caspary dancing playfully with Eddie. When Caspary first meets Alex, he asks him what things he does with his girlfriend in a tone combining curiosity with complete indifference.

In the film Caspary is less a madman than a dandy whose homosexual appeal is made most apparent in the bathtub scene. This is the occasion when he tells the Captain that the ship is chained down. He asks Miller if he has ever thought of wrecking the ships dependent upon him. After all, he does have freedom of choice. Caspary looks at a framed photograph of former captains of the lightship, and he puts on the Captain's hat. Drinking from a flask, he toasts the captains "happy in their chains." The invitation to evil made by the naked and playful Caspary, rakishly sporting the Captain's hat, has an obvious erotic touch.

Eddie Waxler appears to be physically attracted to Alex. After he hears his father's story, Alex goes out on deck during a storm. The heavy-set Stump is drunk and nostalgic. Remembering his early years as a prizefighter, he asks Alex to punch him in the stomach. "Don't be a pansy," he taunts cheerfully. Alex hits Stump so that the middle-aged man can have the opportunity of saying that his stomach is still like steel. Then Eddie and Eugene come on the scene. They are not amused, and Eugene malevolently punches Stump in the crotch and calls him and Alex "pussies." Eugene kicks Stump, and it is at this point that Eddie tells Alex that he is as pretty as a girl and kisses him. The combination of the blow in the genitals with the kiss suggests that the erotic attraction between men has its castrating and degrading side. This scene is completely absent from the novel, as is the later scene when the severely seasick Eddie confronts the armed Alex, who has the opportunity to kill him. Instead, Eddie disarms Alex and hits him. The humiliated Alex tells us in voice-over that he is not as different from his "old man" as he would like to believe.

It could be that the film has an offensive, homophobic overtone with the villains presented as homosexuals trying to lure the Captain and his son not into sexual activity but into moral bankruptcy. The other possibility is that Skolimowski has tried to use same-sex attraction to underline the danger of identifying with other men when suspending value judgments. Even so, the film has a regrettable fear of same-sex attraction that also characterizes Conrad's *Lord Jim*.

The strengthening of this theme of homosexual attraction could be either a conscious or unconscious harking back to Conrad. An excellent article by Robert R. Hodges in the Summer 1979 issue of the *Journal of Homosexuality* examines significant homosexual themes in the life and work of Conrad. He locates the sea fiction "The Secret Sharer" and *The Shadow Line* as the works in which Conrad expresses homosexual attraction in the most sympathetic way he was to allow himself. In contrast are *Chance*, with its unkind portrait of a lesbian, and *Victory* with its caricaturized woman-hating homosexual Mr. Jones. Between these two poles falls *Lord Jim*, in which, Hodges notes, the erotic attraction of Jim on Marlow and other older men is hinted at but never openly labelled. He concludes that "Marlow, as he struggles not to sympathize too much with Jim, suggests a man battling against a forbidden amorous attraction" (384).

Hodges stops just short of taking his conclusions one step farther by relating Marlow's distancing of himself from the physically attractive Jim to other themes in the novel. As Robert Ducharme has suggested in a recent paper on *Lord Jim*, homosexual attraction is implicitly cast in a bad light because the novel, backing up Marlow, contends that we must not allow ourselves to identify with those who have done something morally wrong, such as Jim, who has deserted the *Patna*. The novel ends up tarring three completely unconnected ideas with the same brush: identification with evil, a romantic view of life (as represented by Jim's daydreaming and inability to know himself), and homosexuality. As Marlow tries to maintain that decent people would not have done what Jim has done, the romantic view of life represented by Jim and same-sex attractions are also criticized. In *The Lightship* we have a similar situation, although here Caspary's existentialism (with both a Nietzschean strain of forgetting the past and a Gidean touch of the *acte gratuit*) takes the place of romanticism.

In *The Lightship* much of the ambiguity comes from the theme of identification and its relationship with judgment, which is also an important issue in *Lord Jim*. A central question arises: when should a person identify with another (particularly one man with another man) out of a common fallen humanity, and when does identification get in the way of making value judgments, and thus represent a temptation to evil? The film suggests that although good people may be erring and weak, they must not be tricked into identifying with the forces of evil in the world.

Unlike Jim, who is unable to resist being tempted by Gentleman Brown, the Captain resists being tempted by Caspary. Gentleman Brown is described by Marlow as having "a satanic gift of finding out the best and weakest spot in his victims" (Chap. 42, 235). In order to escape from Patusan he suggests to Jim that they have much in common. Although he does not know the secret of Jim's past, he indirectly preys upon Jim's memory of the *Patna* disaster when he abandoned ship with hundreds of pilgrims aboard. Brown makes it sound as if he, the criminal, and Jim, who has tried to lead a new, responsible life, are doubles. Thus he is able to get Jim to agree to let him and his men leave Patusan in safety. Marlow later interviewed Brown, and he writes:

> It was as if a demon had been whispering advice in his ear. 'I made him wince,' boasted Brown to me. He very soon left off coming the righteous over me. He just stood there with nothing to say, and looking as black as thunder—not at me—on the ground.' He asked Jim whether he had nothing fishy in his life to remember that he was so damnably hard upon a man trying to get out of a deadly hold by the first means that came to hand—and so on, and so on. And there ran through the rough talk a vein of subtle reference to their common blood, and assumption of common experience; a sickening suggestion of common guilt, of secret knowledge that was like a bond of their minds and of their hearts. (Chap. 42, 235)

The situation ends disastrously for Jim, since Brown does not go away peacefully. He attacks Jim's village, and Dain Waris, the son of the chief is killed. Since Jim has given his own life as a pledge, he forfeits his life to Dain Waris's father.

Murray Krieger summarizes the encounter of Jim and Brown nicely when we writes:

> So Brown comes to be the case for common guilt a fortiori, as a gratuitous murderer the worst possible of his kind. But, ironically, Jim must disdain moral hierarchy and see likeness rather than difference. As Brierly saw himself as Jim—and not utterly without reason—Jim goes the full length and beyond all reason and sees

himself in Brown. Mere ethical judgment becomes impossible when the judge sees himself as the accused, finds the same dirt on his hands. When Jewel asks Jim if these men are very evil, Jim answers significantly, "Men act badly sometimes without being much worse than others." (446)

Tony Tanner describes another side of the case when he writes that Brown is successful "because he has an uncanny instinct for attacking just those faults of self-deception and inaction and shame which mar Jim's armour of idealism" (454).

Fortunately, although Caspary tries the same approach on the Captain, he is unsuccessful. We can see that this Conradian temptation-through-identification motif is already in Lenz's novella, and it surfaces on at least three occasions. Shortly after the criminals come aboard, we read, "'We have understood one another, Captain,' said Dr. Caspary. 'There is probably no one on board with whom I can achieve such understanding as with you'" (46). Caspary cuts the small boat loose and takes advantage of his extra time with the Captain to reveal more of his story:

> . . . I have never before met a man in whom I have confided like this, Captain. What can that be due to? To the completeness with which we understand one another? To your and our situation? Or do I want to tell you all about myself because we each hold the other in the palm of our hand? Every man resembles his adversary, he has no more intimate relationship to anyone." (98)

These two statements are only warm-ups for the final expression of the theme when Caspary offers the Captain money and asks him to put him on the coast at a point where he will be safe.

> I have met in you a man who is closest to myself. Our closeness does not spring from what we have in common, but from the completeness with which in every respect we contradict each other. You would be dismayed if you know how well I understand you and how close we are as we face each other. Your life, Captain, would have been the only one I could have led if I had not decided upon my life, or upon my three lives. (111)

Not only does Caspary declare that they are alter egos for each other, he also stresses that men without exception are sinful. Every person has in his past life something which "according to the law of the land would cost him two years in jail—without an excessively harsh sentence" (112). Freytag pays no attention to this line of reasoning, and he reminds Caspary of the dead body of Zumpe down below. In the film this dialogue is shortened, and Caspary tells the Captain, "Every man resembles his enemy. We are as intimate as lovers."

The Gentleman Brown—Jim duo is repeated with less success, as Mr. Jones-Axel Heyst in *Victory*, according to Alfred G. Guerard, in his influential book on Conrad:

> . . . Mr. Jones . . . seeks to paralyze Heyst by insisting that they have much in common. Yet this scene, using again one of Conrad's most striking psychological intuitions, seems untrue or at least unimportant. The essence of Gentleman Brown's power lay in his shrewd appeal to a common guilt. The only genuine identification in *Victory* would connect Heyst's diffidence with Mr. Jones "horror of feminine presence." (275)

Although it is possible to point out minor similarities between Axel Heyst and Mr. Jones, I agree with Guerard that the characterization of the novel is weak, and that the temptation that Heyst faces is of far less interest than Jim's.

As Frederick Karl (23) notes, *Victory* is the most controversial Conrad novel in terms of its artistic merit. Some critics, including Karl, see it as one of Conrad's best novels, whereas others such as Guerard consider it as an unconvincing work marking the beginning of the end of Conrad's creativity. In addition, we should note that there is no consensus about its overall statement about life. One group of critics (Daleski 39, Martin 211, Schwarz 63, Ressler 154), following in line with Conrad's stated intention in the preface, finds the novel a warning about the dangers of isolating oneself from humanity. Another group (Purdy 122, Rieselbach 133, Watts 75) describes *Victory* as either nihilistic or, at best, deeply despairing.

Given the debate about the novel, is it possible to say from *The Lightship* how Skolimowski read *Victory*? What was the "Conradian philosophy" that he found in this work? There is one obvious plot similarity between the two works. In *Victory*, three grotesque criminals endanger the lives of basically decent people. The woman-hating dandy Mr. Jones, his secretary Ricardo (for whom he feels a strong attraction), and the beast-like Pedro arrive by boat on Samburan, the secluded Indonesian island settlement of Heyst, his lover Lena, and the Chinese servant Wong. They have been urged there by Schomberg, a hotel keeper who despises Heyst and covets Lena. He has told the criminals that Heyst has stored up secret wealth on the island, and they are there to seize it. Heyst fails to understand or love Lena adequately, and she, in trying to preserve them from the criminals, gives up her life. Mr. Jones shoots Lena and Ricardo. Heyst kills himself, and apparently Jones also chooses suicide. Finally, Wang shoots Pedro. He is the only survivor of the criminals' attempt to take a non-existent treasure. Heyst was not able to help him. He saved himself.

In the novel's preface Conrad takes Heyst to task for his detached attitude toward life:

> It is very obvious that on the arrival of the gentlemanly Mr. Jones, the single-minded Ricardo and the faithful Pedro, Heyst, the man of universal detachment, loses his mental self-possession, that fine attitude before the universally irremediable which wears the name of stoicism. It is all a matter of proportion. There should have been a remedy for that sort of thing, And yet there is no remedy. Behind this minute instance of life's hazards Heyst sees the power of blind destiny. Besides, Heyst in his fine detachment had lost the habit of asserting himself. . . . Thinking is the great enemy of perfection. The habit of profound reflection, I am compelled to say, is the most pernicious of all the habits formed by the civilized man. (x-xi)

Conrad wishes to tell us that chronic inactivity has led to the debilitation of Heyst's will, and he is unable to stand up to the three dangerous intruders.

If we try to see *The Lightship* as a film transposing this theme to the U.S. during the 1950s, then we must accept two propositions. First, Miller's attempts to do his duty, preserve his men, and cope with the criminals must be seen as insufficient. Second, Miller's inadequacy must stem from his retreat from life and his choice of contemplation over action. These two statements can not be maintained unequivocally. There is enough ambiguity to the film to claim that Miller's watch-and-wait tactic is as legitimate a choice as the surprise attack proposed by the crewmates, which, after all, does fall through and lead to a death. Furthermore, the lack of access to the Captain's mind does not make clear the extent to which the submarine incident in World War II is influencing his current actions. However, it is possible to see the Captain's years of isolation on his boat as a type of detachment from the world which hinders him from acting effectively in a crisis.

If we look at some of the alternative readings of *Victory*, we do not come up with other theses more applicable to the film. Dwight H. Purdy writes that Conrad shows that "human love is impossible . . . or ineffectual. . . and that human evil is ineffectual. . . or ridiculous. . . in a world that prizes coal above diamonds" (122). For Helen Frank Rieselbach, Conrad's message is that "to trust in life is to invite betrayal" and that "the spirit of Heyst's father's nihilism" prevails (133). Cedric Watts seconds this notion, stating that the novel justifies Heyst's father's maxim, "Look on—make no sound" (75). Such pessimism should not be read onto Skolimowski's film. *The Lightship* ends with the defeat of evil. Caspary is captured, and Eddie and Eugene are dead. Although the Captain and Stump have been killed, Alex survives with a new fondness for his father.

Skolimowski, in his interview with Richard Combs, overemphasizes the importance of *Victory* to *The Lightship*, although he is accurate in speaking of Conrad's work in general as crucial to his making of the film. He suggests that there may be other significant literary influences on *The Lightship*. For example, he states that he wanted to make "Caspary's two hoods" like characters out of *Key Largo*. He does not say if he means Maxwell Anderson's 1939 stage play or John Huston's very different 1948 film "based on" it. In either case we are turned to another drama about decent people confronted by a group of criminals. Nevertheless, *Key Largo* does not provide the two motifs which are most interesting about *The Lightship*, the representation of temptation in connection with both the common fallen state of humankind and male homosexual attraction. Although Skolimowski does not announce these themes as his major ties with Conrad, they are the two crucial ones.

NOTES

1. *Victory* was filmed in the U.S. in 1919 with Lon Chaney as Ricardo. There was also a 1960 NBC television production directed by Daniel Petrie with Art Carney, Eric Portman, Oscar Homolka, Richard Harris, and Ruth White.

2. For two brief overviews of Skolimowski's career, see Paul Coates' *The Story of the Lost Reflection: The Alienation of the Image in Western and Polish Cinema* (144-47) and Mira Liehm and Antonin J. Liehm's *The Most important Art: East European Film after 1945* (passim). A filmography of Skolimowski's work up to 1982 can be found in *Revue du Cinéma*, July-August 1984, p. 64.

3. Little of Skolimowski's extensive work as a screenwriter has been published. His collaborative work on *Knife in the Water* is still available. Out of print is a German edition *(Der Start)* of his French-language film *Le Départ*. The Library of Congress gives entries for two of his books of poetry, but there are apparently others.

BIBLIOGRAPHY

Coates, Paul. *The Story of the Lost Reflection: The Alienation of the Image in Western and Polish Cinema*. London: Verso, 1985.

Combs, Richard. "Under Western Eyes: Skolimowski's Conradian Progress." *Monthly Film Bulletin* 628 (May 1986): 133-34.

Conrad, Joseph. *Lord Jim*. Ed. Thomas C. Moser. New York: Norton, 1968.

—. *Victory*. Garden City: Doubleday, Page, 1924.

Daleski, H. M. *Joseph Conrad: The Way of Dispossession*. New York: Holmes & Meier, 1977.

Ducharme, Robert. "Forms of Resistance: Some Questions about Lord Jim." Paper presented at the NEH Summer Seminar on the British Novel in the Early Twentieth Century, Ithaca, 28 July 1988.

"Filmographie de Jerzy Skolimowski." *Revue du Cinéma* 396 (July-Aug. 1984): 64.

Guerard, Albert J. *Conrad the Novelist*. Cambridge: Harvard U P, 1958.

Hodges, Robert. "Deep Fellowship: Homosexuality and Male Bonding in the Life and Fiction of Joseph Conrad." *Journal of Homosexuality* 4.4 (Summer 1979): 379-93.

Karl, Frederick R. "*Victory*: Its Origin and Development." *Conradiana* 15.1 (1983): 23-52.

Krieger, Murray. "The Varieties of Extremity: *Lord Jim*." Joseph Conrad. *Lord Jim*. Ed. Thomas C. Moser. New York: Norton, 1968: 437-62.

Lenz, Siegfried. *The Lightship*. Trans. Michael Bullock. New York: Hill and Wang, 1962.

Liehm, Mira, and Antonin J. Liehm. *The Most Important Art*: East European Film after 1945. Berkeley: U of California P, 1977.

Martin, Joseph. "Conrad and the Aesthetic Movement." *Conradiana* 17.3 (1985): 199-213.

Purdy, Dwight H. *Joseph Conrad's Bible*. Norman: U of Oklahoma P, 1984.

Ressler, Steve. *Joseph Conrad: Consciousness and Integrity*. New York: New York U P, 1988.

Rieselbach, Helen Funk. *Conrad's Rebels: The Psychology of Revolution in the Novels from "Nostromo" to "Victory."* Ann Arbor: U M I, 1985.

Schwarz, Daniel R. *Conrad's Later Fiction*. London: Macmillan, 1982.

Skolimowski, Jerzy. *Gdzies blisko siebie*. Katowice: Slask, 1958.

—. *Siekiera i niebo*. Warsaw: Czytelnik, 1959.

—. *Der Start: Protokoll*. Frankfurt am Main: Verlag Filmkritik, 1968.

—, Jakub Goldberg, and Roman Polanski. *Knife in the Water*. Trans. Boleslaw Sulik. *Three Films by Roman Polanski*. London: Lorimar, 1975.

Tanner, Tony. "Butterflies and Beetles—Conrad's Two Truths." Joseph Conrad. *Lord Jim*. Ed. Thomas C. Moser. New York: Norton, 1968: 444-62.

Watts, Cedric. "Reflections on *Victory*." *Conradiana* 15.1 (1983): 73-79.

Exile and Identity

Kieslowski and his Contemporaries

Paul Coates
McGill University

How the West was Won is the title of the East European producer's unrealized dream film: a horn of plenty discharging hard currency into the coffers of its debt-ridden country of origin. At a time when hopeful speculation is resurrecting the spectre of Central Europe, however, it may be worthwhile asking just where the West is. As a purely Utopian image in the East European consciousness, it may be located across the Atlantic; as a place of relative material wellbeing one may visit and work in, it may—for the Polish actor or actress—go by the provisional name of Hungary. (Or—if one is Wajda or Zanussi—West Germany or France.) Does the West exist wherever a Westerner is present? Such questions are prompted by the problematic nature of borders, which are far more prone to shift at the behest of the world market than their apparent post-Yalta fixity would lead one to suspect. As the world economy becomes increasingly tight-knit, it is ever harder to determine just where the East and West lie. The growing frequency of co-productions—of equal interest to Western companies seeking to trim budgets by using non-unionized labour, and to Eastern countries needing hard currency to service their debts—blurs the borders. As borders become increasingly mobile, however, it may be salutary to remember that there may well be something that resists the law of exchange. One might be tempted to term that thing identity, were it not that in one of its senses the word itself embodies the notion of exchange. The ambiguous designator of both individual selfhood and its loss, the word "identity" may in fact be a lynchpin in the workings of ideology—a key term in a Marxist version of the Freudian lexicon of primal words—as it seduces one into the system by implying that one can both conform and remain oneself, become identical and retain identity. As an increasingly identical economic totality subsumes into itself all individual identities, it may be preferable to speak of the individual as non-identity vis-à-vis the false whole. It will be the thesis of this paper that such a position of non-identity is occupied virtually uniquely in Poland by the work of Krzysztof Kieslowski.

I. Kieslowski and his Contemporaries

A certain stereotype exists concerning Polish directors: the daring ones either leave for the West, or visit it periodically to escape the native chill. The stereotype derives from the careers of Polanski, Skolimowski and Borowczyk, frozen out of Polish cinema by the stultifying cultural policy of the early sixties; from those of Wajda and Zanussi, with their intermittent excursions to the West; and from that of more recent figures, such as Agnieszka Holland, whose *To Kill a Priest*—a fictionalization of the murder of Father Jerzy Popieluszko—could hardly have been filmed in Poland itself. (Though one should note here that the film's silence concerning the State televising of portions of the murderers' trial pretends that official reference to such events is impossible in Poland thereby simplifying the country's contradiction-laden reality.) It is assumed that sooner or later the director of integrity will be compelled to go into exile, re-enacting the primal drama of a Mickiewicz or a Milosz—or, at the very least, to do some work abroad. And should one come home, it will only be to do a co-production. The problematic nature of these options can be gauged through brief consideration of two films: Zanussi's *Year of the Quiet Sun* (*Rok spokojnego slonca)* (1984) and Agnieszka Holland's recent *To Kill a Priest* (1988).

The Year of the Quiet Sun, Zanussi's first Polish-language film in several years, was a co-production in form (the co-sponsors were companies in Berlin and New York) and in content also: like Wajda's near-contemporaneous *A Love in Germany*, it reflects on wartime relations between Poles and non-Poles, forty years after the end of World War Two. It is a strangely willed and yet half-hearted film. The mixture of Scott Wilson's nervously lachrymose intensity in the role of Norman, the American ex-POW, and the mannered, head-tossing spinsterly stoicism of Maja Komorowska's Emilia, is a tragedy of errors, with the man too self-doubting to press his claims and the woman too intent on remaining pure in the sight of her own conscience to wish to be saved, but the details of their relationship never quite ring true. There is a clear, almost banal reason for this: Zanussi never really solves the problem of how the two communicate across the language barrier. He is too sophisticated to invoke love's telepathy or animal magic, but their complete linguistic incompatibility and the evident uselessness of their interpreters render it hard to guess how they built up a rapport. The film tends to be both flat and cryptic, particularly in Norman's memories of his humiliation as a POW. Even the fine closing vision, showing an ideal encounter in which the two dance in an American desert dreamland, is uncanny in tone, and somehow self-frustrating. The dance motion seems too fast, with an air of nightmare, and it is eerie that the camera should concentrate so on the dust at their feet and then lose them in the distance of the longshot. The sequence is placed further offkey by the fact that *Stagecoach*, whose Monument Valley setting it employs, had earlier been mentioned as the favourite film of Emilia's *mother*. (There may be an implication here that Emilia's identification with her mother is so deep that it even pervades her dreams.) The film's tragedy irritates, because it feels forced: Emilia is unable to escape to the West because she has insufficient funds to smuggle both herself and her mother out— knowledge of which causes the mother to induce her own death to allow Emilia to leave with the love of her life. Could not Emilia have explained the necessity to Norman, before her mother offered her the present of death she then refuses to accept? When Zanussi allows her to tell Norman that there can be happiness even in suffering he hints at a masochism whose aetiology he refuses to probe further. And when Zapasiewicz, as a brutal black marketeer turned Party member, warns Emilia that she won't be able to leave without official permission, his petty viciousness is cloaked in the inappropriate ominousness of Fate in a Hardy novel: *diabolus ex machina*. The film's vision of the nobility of sacrifice is clouded by one's doubts regarding its necessity. One is almost tempted to conclude that repeated work in foreign languages had dulled Zanussi's sense (threatened in any case by his preoccupation with near-autistic protagonists) of the mechanics of human interaction.

To Kill a Priest opens with an image whose resonance raises one's expectations of the film to follow. A mundane activity becomes a powerful metaphor: using a coin, a hand scrapes a hole in the frost on the inside window of a bus; the young scout holding it— already an insider in Polish society—peers out at the scene that has been revealed, a group of people marching with Solidarity banners. Holland's image rejects the metaphor that would speak of a 'thaw' in the frost of People's Poland; the freeze continues, though it can be punctured at points by scraping back the ice. A thaw would embrace society as a whole, but the disparity between the uniformed scouts inside and the motley of Solidarity outside indicates that the hope for change is far from universal. The theme of partial visibility intriguingly—and probably inadvertently, for the two directors were working independently of one another—echoes the central device of Kieslowski's *Short Film About Killing* (Krotki film o zabijaniu) (1988). Unfortunately, little in the subsequent film matches the promise of this opening moment. There is probably only one other moment of similar suggestivity, when Stefan—the Interior Ministry spy assigned to the turbulent priest, whose seeming impunity galls him—slows down a videotape of the priest addressing the faithful. He can only control the man's reflection in an image, not his reality; and as the priest's voice slows down into a prehistoric, subverbal roar, its sound evokes the would-be controller's nightmarish sense that he is failing to make any progress, as well as suggesting that the two men will meet on an atavistic plane of sheer suffering.

Holland's film is, of course, an international production based on the murder by Polish State officials of the awkward pro-Solidarity priest, Father Jerzy Popieluszko. The original event, which took place late in 1984, precipitated a lightning investigation and the unprecedented spectacle in the Eastern bloc (and perhaps anywhere) of the televised trial of the three guilty secret policemen. Like Kieslowski in *A Short Film About Killing*, Holland omits their trial; though where Kieslowski does so on aesthetic grounds, omitting the inessential, Holland's grounds seem to be more ideological: it would complicate her simplified image of how the Polish state works. It is in fact only to the extent to which it removes itself from the story of Popieluszko himself (here called Father Alek) that the film is interesting. Frustratingly, it prompts one to speculate on the work that might have been had Holland made more of the licence created by fictionalization, rather than engaging in a two-dimensional hagiography spiced up with banal hints of "human interest" (a girl floats around Alek, who manfully resists seduction). The treatment is not the TV movie it could so easily have become, though there are moments that come dangerously close, such as the clumsily-staged sequence showing the imposition of martial law, where the dialogue is wooden and improbable. The film is tantalizing in its failure to realise its possibilities, such as the potential for irony built into the parallel plots: the encounters between Stefan and Alek and their respective political superiors could have been pointedly contrasted presentations of each as a martyr to his cause, with Stefan the more consistent communist, and Alek the better Christian, than his superior. Most of the squandered possibilities concern Stefan: the playing of Ed Harris suggests that he could have been the centre of an hallucinatory, *Conformist*-like evocation of the political heart of darkness. Holland's inability to shift the film's centre of gravity to Stefan is an artistic miscalculation. One applauds the film's courage even as one recognizes that having one's heart in the right place is no guarantee of a masterpiece. And even the film's most interesting aspect—the image of Stefan as a self-hating inquisitor, a figure from Bertolucci or Scorsese—is vitiated by its function as revenge fantasy: no one loves Communists, who are all either paranoid or insane, Holland argues. (Stefan's wife hysterically demands of him why "they", the Solidarity activists who supposedly threaten his life, cannot simply be locked up.) The film reaches a nadir of tendentiousness in the names it gives to the dogs Stefan and Alek keep: "Pope" in the former case, and "Spy" in the latter. What is more, Holland's hagiography is tainted by an ambiguity that brings it to the verge of two-facedness: Alek has no answer to the soldier facing execution for training his guns on his superiors, and who is critical of the utility of the non-violence the priest preaches and practices; the criticism is reiterated at the end by Alek's chauffeur, who says that although Alek could forgive, "we" cannot. If Alek's non-violence is not to be emulated, the film is simply pretending that he is its hero—perhaps half-reluctantly hitching a ride on a religious bandwagon that may at present be the strongest alternative to the Polish state, but whose final destination is very different from Holland's.

The preceding examples (which could be augmented with many others) begin to help one understand why Kieslowski's work has a cohesiveness lacking even in the oeuvres of a Wajda or a Zanussi. If every artwork is, in Adorno's words, an "urteiloses Urteil", then those of Kieslowski pass judgement on those of his contemporaries; a judgement, one hastens to add, which the director himself would never extend to the *persons* of Wajda or Zanussi. With admirable acumen and tenacity, Kieslowski has grasped and exploited the change in the rules governing cultural production in Poland: one may still need to use one's wits to slip radical work past the censor—as was the case with *A Short Film About Killing*, smuggled through behind the protective shield of a clutch of films based on the Decalogue—but the current desperation of the authorities for any sign of participation in the public sphere has blunted the censor's scissors. In this changed climate, however, it is no longer sufficient to make the allusive critical gestures that served a purpose in the past; in order to avoid co-optation, one's gesture must be as dark and radical as that of *A Short Film About Killing*.

II. *Blind Chance* (Przypadek): Kieslowski, Bertolucci and the Dead Father

The preceding remarks may seem to be underpinned by a form of nativism: the implicit thesis may seem to be that only the Polish director who resists the blandishments of the West can be truly significant. Framed in these terms, the thesis recalls compromised nationalist traditions of rejection of "the cosmopolitan". It would be a disservice to Kieslowski, however, to allow my remarks to be taken thus: the director of *No End* is in fact one of the most cosmopolitan and intellectually sophisticated directors at work anywhere in the world. Where Wajda has succumbed to academic frenzy, and the early Zanussi's passion for the crystalline has become somewhat theoretical and bloodless, Kieslowski offers fiercely conceived structures that embody the haunting possibility of a recovery of the lost intellectual legacy of the late sixties. Profound immersion in the particular has enabled him to distill the image of the universal; the most Polish of directors is thus the most Western. Certain of Kieslowski's works reinvent the passionate, unstable mixture of politics and auto-analysis that characterized the early Bertolucci. In particular, *Blind Chance* (Przypadek) (1982) fuses preoccupations usually polarized between "East" and "West".

Blind Chance marries a "Western" preoccupation with the effects of the death of the father—with the sense of arbitrariness that afflicts choice in a world emptied of paternal prototypes—to an "Eastern" reluctance to renounce humanism by invoking such psychoanalytic scenarios as the Oedipal one. Arbitrariness dictates the very form of the film, which gives three different versions of a crucial period in the life of one young man, Wit Dlugosz. Each version begins like a dream, with the young man running to catch the Lodz-Warsaw train. In the first version he succeeds, and becomes a Party activist with a bad conscience; in the second, he fails and becomes a dissident; and in the third his failure causes him to stay at home, marry, become a trainee doctor, and die in an aircraft explosion (the failure to reach Warsaw is interpreted as the equivalent of remaining in the antechamber of political awareness). In each case the decision to leave for Warsaw follows the death of the father, whose earlier wish that his son become a doctor loses its binding force. "Nic nie musisz" ("you don't have to do anything"), the dying father tells his son through a telephone that seems also to relay a voice from the interior. The bereaved son requests a leave of absence from the medical academy's dean, and seeks an alternative to the paternally-prescribed path. The father's death thus frees both son and film from necessity—this particular linkage of form and theme being one of the features that recalls the early work of Bertolucci, particularly *The Conformist*, whose simultaneously exuberant and deranged formal play is soul-murder of Godard, Bertolucci's cinematic father. Stylistically the first section is the most arresting, beginning with images presented as rapidly and laconically as at the start of *Pierrot le Fou*, and then modulating into a Tarkovskian adherence to the line of "real time": no time is edited out of any of the sequences in this section. The second version is edited more conventionally, highlighting the "key" moments in a scene—those that advance the dramatic conception—and omitting all else. The final version is edited most conventionally of all, virtually in the no-nonsense manner of a TV movie, with point-of-view shots, shot/reverse-shot, and so on. Asked whether or not any one of the three versions should be privileged as "the true one", Kieslowski has stated—with sibylline cunning—that it should be the last one, because it is the most conventional. It is clear, however, that the conventional is of no great interest to Kieslowski: this section is brief and brisk, and its protagonist is blown up in the end. The almost disdainful destruction of the protagonist suggests that Kieslowski feels that Filip Mosz, the hero of *Camera Buff* (Amator) (1979), was wrong to choose peace and mediocrity rather than follow the pull of filmmaking to Warsaw. One suspects that in fact Kieslowski prefers the first version, given his stated admiration for Tarkovsky's long takes and the amount of thought that has gone into this section. If the final section *is* to be privileged, it is rather for a reason Kieslowski did not mention when I discussed the film with him: because it allows one to place the film's first image, which shows a man screaming "Nie". We recognize him as Wit on the plane, following the first small explosion in the fuselage, and anticipating the fatal second one. The final section is privileged in that it confronts its protagonist with death.

In each section figures who played major roles earlier on are recast in minor functions. The Communist old believer, an influential substitute father in section one, becomes a passer-by later on; the priest of section two is glimpsed incidentally at the airport in section three, about to lead the group excursion to France from which the authorities had debarred Wit in that earlier "life". In all three sections, however, Wit is "the same" person. He is always preoccupied with the degree of coincidence in people's lives (it is as if he suspected that the life he is leading is merely an accidental variant of an alternative ranged alongside it): he drops to his knees and clutches his forehead in moments of crisis (in version A—after the secret police car has sped away with his girlfriend; in B—when a fellow-conspirator demands the return of the key to the secret printing shop the militia have discovered; and in C—when his girlfriend announces her pregnancy). The film is profoundly subversive of ideas of destiny; fate belongs in the mythical world of the fathers, whose ending precipitates one into the new world of fortuity. In the process it subverts the black-and-white notions of character that are so prevalent in a Polish ideology which deems one either one of "us" (a martyr) or one of "them" (a traitor). In each of his first two lives Wit is the victim of these stereotypes: in the first his girlfriend ostracizes him after her release from custody, assuming that he used his pull as a Party member to secure her freedom; and in the second a colleague assumes that his non-arrest when his conspiratorial cell was breached indicates complicity with the authorities. One can just as easily land on one side of the party line as on the other. The film's subversiveness extends into a doubt of memory, in the manner of Resnais: the first section shows us a boy bidding Wit farewell before going up a hill to a VW; in the second section we learn the boy's name, Daniel (he is the brother of a girl with whom Wit has an affair), and discover that the goodbye preceded Daniel's departure for Denmark. And yet he says there was no automobile on the scene. His words confirm the fact that the farewell with the car was part of a different life, but they disturb one by extending the principle of arbitrariness into the distant past. As they suggest that memory is creative, they question the cinematic dictum that seeing is believing.

The first time we see Witold he is a child, reflected in a mirror, doing homework; his father says he makes a certain figure as his dead mother did. The presentation of the protagonist as a mirror image is typical of the openings of Kieslowski's recent works: it is thus that Antek first appears, reflected in a bookcase, in *No End*, whilst in *A Short Film About Killing* Jacek is first seen mirrored in the glass covering the *Wetherby* poster in the new section of the Old Town. The films thus begin by reminding us that what we are seeing is not reality but an image; that the true life is perpetually displaced. The life we live is governed by coincidence (one translation of the title "Przypadek")—rather as coincidence carries the taxi-driver (as he bypasses two sets of potential passengers) to his encounter with Jacek. There is no Platonic form of the true life; neither—equally importantly—is there any such archetypical form of the false life as Bertolucci offers in *The Conformist*, with its pat explanatory primal scene. All Kieslowski's work appears to be about the effects of the loss of the prototype; and the theme may be fuelled by autobiographical forces, since Kieslowski lost his father when still young. The loss of compelling reasons why one should do one thing rather than another may also be an argument against leaving the country, that is—against a potentially *irrevocable* choice (the desire to return after having crossed a border is found in double form at the beginning of *No End*, in Tomek's return to Poland and in Antek's return as a ghost; one may even see it in the title). By staying in Poland one haunts the grave of a father one lost rather than killed. The Pole does not define himself through Oedipal parricide, for the father is not perceived as the locus of power: power lies elsewhere, with the true rulers who pretend merely to be brothers, ever-ready to provide "fraternal aid". One does not kill the father, for his murder has been carried out by the alien powers. (And in *Blind Chance* even the mother has been killed in a sense by Poland's alien order: she dies giving birth to Wit during the Poznan protests of 1956, and a recurrent memory flash shows a man being dragged across a floor, leaving a trail of blood—as if this bloody dragging forth is Witold's birth.) This is surely the key difference between a Kieslowski and a Bertolucci (in other words, between the East European and the West European director); it is a difference that severely threatens the likelihood of any East European producing his or her most valuable work in the West. For the Pole the father is castrated, powerless, the dead father of *Blind Chance* or *Man of Iron*; and so when Wajda casts the same actor as both father and son, it is to underline their fundamental spiritual identity, not—as in Bertolucci's *Spider's Stratagem*—as a metaphor for Oedipal or mimetic rivalry between them. (*The Spider's Stratagem*, incidentally, demonstrates that despite Girard's polemical opposition to Freud, mimetic desire is quite compatible with Oedipal desire, and may even be one of its forms.) Hence the dynamics of East European cinema are not—like those of the West—linked to the Oedipal triangle. The East European director who comes to the West may deal with father-son relations, but it will be on the understanding that the father is more helpless than tyrannical (see, for instance, Szabó's *Father* or Skolimowski's *The Lightship* and *Success is the Best Revenge*). And it is this sense that power lies elsewhere that renders East European cinema so bewitchingly accurate a mirror of our era—the era so often described as postmodern—since the crumbling of nationality before the pressure of the empire of the world economy defines power as something that continually relocates itself on the far side of continually displaced borders. The knowledge that the cause of the effects we feel is perennially absent pervades Kieslowski's work (one never learns why Jacek kills the taxi-driver). Its base in Poland gives it a deeper consciousness of exile than is available to the exile who thinks there is a homeland.

ENDNOTE

1. I would like to thank Krzysztof Kieslowski for making time for me in the midst of a hectic Canadian schedule and granting me an interview on Wednesday January 25th, 1989.

Auditioning for America

Method, Madness and Banality in *Anna*

Natasa Durovicova
UCLA

About a year and a half ago a film made by a Polish director and a Polish screenwriter, featuring prominently a young actress with an unmistakably Czech name and accent, received a mixed critical reception in the country of its origin, the USA. Praise, awards, even that keystone element in the curve of commercial success, the Oscar nomination, came to the unknown middle-aged American actress in the role of a faded Czech film star. By contrast, the critics' negative responses kept returning to a peculiar claim— that the film's representation of "Eastern Europe" was *banal*. Far be it from me to assume automatically that American film journalism is never wrong, or, for that matter, that a Polish or Czechoslovakian filmmaker has never been known to turn out a cliché; still, the charge of banality in representing the world of one's own origin, coming as it does from those unlikely to be deeply familiar with that world, might be worth pursuing insofar as it ultimately testifies more to the conditions of reception than to the intrinsic value of the object of criticism itself. What exactly is, then, the nature of "East Europeanness" in Jurek Bogajewicz's and Agnieszka Holland's *Anna* (1987) that it should have so readily confirmed the expert opinions of the New York and Los Angeles critics? And conversely, to what extent does this accusation suggest the gap between authorial intention and generic expectations that is conventionally assumed to mark the difference between *all* European cinema (not just that from the "East") and Hollywood — a question that is also one of the topics for this conference.

To begin with, it has to be noted that the film hardly comes to us "straight". An outline should allow us to recognize the highly layered and allusive character of *Anna's* plot. From the first shot surveying the Manhattan skyline, the ringing of a phone draws us into a modest apartment. When the phone finally gets pulled toward a dishevelled bed, it is answered by an equally dishevelled middle-aged blonde with a heavy Czech accent: the off-off Broadway actress Anna Radková (Sally Kirkland) is reminded by her furious agent that one of her rare auditions is about to begin in fifteen minutes. Arriving in a chic black outfit highlighting her spectacular legs, the energetic and only a little ravaged Anna looks an unlikely candidate for the slot of an "older woman" in what seems like the work of a lesser Polish absurdist. The lunatic audition over, she is accosted outside by a bundled up figure, introducing herself in fluent Czech as a fervent admirer from their former homeland, just arrived in New York and ready to wash dishes simply to be near her idol. When the young girl faints from hunger on her suitcase full of old clippings and snapshots documenting the actress's brilliant career, Anna takes her home. When her agent lets her know she is on for the play, she announces to Daniel, her "lover, a little" (Robert Fields) that she is keeping Krystyna (Paulína Porízková) "for luck".

With Krystyna's appearance and English groomed by Anna and Daniel respectively, the girl flourishes: a photomontage of the two women bridged by a voice-over letter to Krystyna's little sister in Czechoslovakia details the enthusiastic embrace of America where everyone is very nice but "good teeth are very important" (her own being almost comically bad). While the increasingly depressed Anna continues to watch from the wings the repetition of the mad play in which her role turns out to be the understudy for a cast of seven women, Krystyna, with a newly-bonded smile, soon lands a major "Mata-Hari sort of a role" from the world-famous director Baskin (Larry Pines).

In a part-motherly, part-sisterly mood, Anna makes a present of details from her complicated past to her protegée so the latter can "make what she wants of it": from stardom at the crest of the Czech New Wave under the tutelage of its best young director, (subsequently her husband Tonda), through post-invasion persecution that included imprisonment, loss of a small child and expulsion from her homeland, and finally to a rejection in New York by the now fully Americanized Tonda. Repeating to herself the narrative's most emotional turns, Krystyna seems deeply moved. Yet on her first TV show, answering a question about her life, she uses the same words and the same story, carefully rehearsed, to provide herself with a dramatic past proper for an Iron-Curtain star. In a precipitous series of events, the distraught Anna throws out Krystyna, finding that in the process she is also losing Daniel, who wants to move to Los Angeles as Krystyna's "manager", and subsequently watches an old film of hers burn up when it is caught in a jammed projector in a mostly deserted movie theatre. Drunk and crazed, Anna then uses her one evening on the stage to curse loudly the play's audience. Finally, we see her on a beach: she climbs over a dune, steps carefully over a sleeping boy in a blanket, pulls out a gun and, aiming badly, shoots. Her target is Krystyna, who is emerging in a white dress from the ocean for the benefit of a battery of cameras and a film crew. Krystyna is wounded but runs to embrace the older woman. The two weep in each other's arms while, in voice-over, Krystyna calmly reads a letter to her sister in which she describes Anna's behaviour as a minor break-down. She claims her own wound is insignificant and tells of their future plans, which involve Los Angeles, film work and a face-lift for Anna.

From this summary it is fairly evident that the film employs the Dorian Gray or Pygmalion-like plot of the young woman usurping the existence of the aging star which is the narrative core of most "backstage" musicals (e.g. *Singin' in the Rain, A Star is Born*). It is also familiar from melodrama in a wider sense: as a maternal melodrama in *Stella Dallas,* or linked more explicitly with generational shifts between stage or screen performers in *Sunset Boulevard, Fedora* and, most evidently, *All About Eve.* There is no question that the "star is born" trajectory is a quintessentially generic one, migrating from a 19th century dramatic arsenal into Hollywood cinema (or, via a different route, from Strindberg's *Kammerspiel* as taken up in Bergman's *Persona*— frequently alluded to in *Anna*). In this respect, then, criticizing its predictability is roughly like blaming Westerns for their all too conventional use of shootouts. Indeed the reply and quotation of a generic Hollywood formula has been a core device of a number of national cinemas' "New Waves"— most obviously the French and the German (while its relative rarity may perhaps be one of the hallmarks of the Czechoslovakian, Polish, Hungarian and Soviet national cinemas).

While the *frisson* of the standard version of this plot resides in the carefully controlled sadism of subordinating a well-known star performer to a newcomer's relative anonymity, as if the system ritually wished to purge itself of all traces of "transcendence" in favour of a popular aesthetic, *Anna* plays out this trajectory in a different register. Far from shedding the excess glamour accrued during years of top billing, à la Bette Davis in *All About Eve,* or Gloria Swanson in *Sunset Boulevard,* the task of Sally Kirkland, in her first important role on screen, was first to build up the resonance of stardom, then cover it by twenty years of failure, and finally sum up the contradiction in the requisite self-destroying *tour de force.*

It is thus clear why the film's scriptwriter, Agnieszka Holland, whose initial training was with the master of improvisation, Milos Forman, and whose preoccupation with the figure of the actor is shown in her 1979 film *Provincial Actors*), and the director, Jurek Bogajewicz, a product of Jerzy Grotowski's theatre laboratory with its emphasis on ritual forms of performance, would have chosen to work with a Method-trained actress, the hard-core Strassberg disciple Kirkland. Imported from Stanislavskij's Moscow Art Theatre to the USA in the late Twenties (to clear the American theatre from leftovers of the stylized Delsartrean acting technique), the Method emphasizes the technique of "affective memory" in which the actor works by "re-"constructing an imaginary past for his or her character, layering the persona into a constellation of internal choices and contradictions; the final aim is a convergence of affect and role, a bypassing of acting as "pretending" in favour of an "authentic experience" on stage.

This highly prized effect of emotional authenticity, strengthened in *Anna* by the *ex nihilo* appearance of the middle-aged performer, is in turn laminated with another layer of extratextual reality, that of history proper, in particular that of "August 1968". The photographs of the invasion, a crisis point both in Anna's fictional biography and in the historical continuum of Czechoslovakia, appear in Anna's scrapbook collection on a par with "her" early photographs and clippings, both equally valid iconic proofs of a life lived. Much like the documentary footage incorporated into a re-enactment of the same events in *The Unbearable Lightness of Being*, or the documentary footage of the 1956 events in Péter Gothár's *Time Stands Still*, in Andrzej Wajda's two-part trilogy and in much of Dusan Makavejev's work, these usurped images serve to underwrite an effect of presence for the spectator, bracketing the fiction and breaking through to a level of historical immediacy. This effect may be compared, for instance, to the footage of *Queen Kelly* which appears in *Sunset Boulevard*—aligning the latter film within the hermetic unfolding of film history—but should also be recognized as belonging to a different epistemological order in that the truly documentary examples differentiate, litmus paper-like, in their emotional charge between those for whom the pictures are a *déjà vu* and those for whom they merely allude to what it would be *like* to have a *déjà vu*.

It is proper, of course, that this heightened attention to structures of emotional authenticity should appear in a film whose key event is Krystyna's theft of Anna's "depth", that accumulation of experiences and memories that makes a person into a *persona*. This dimension Krystyna lacks completely: indeed the two photo-montage/voice-over sequences of her letters home, a device which would normally allow a viewer a privileged access to the character's subjectivity, serve here mainly to highlight the girl's absolute banality. Neither vicious nor ambitious, Krystyna is literally a blank surface that needs depth to be converted from just another pretty face (a face supplied, appropriately, by the world-famous photomodel Porízková) into the emotional ensemble that would comprise a dramatic performer, especially if that performer is to exude the "Mata-Hari mystique" requisite for media appearances. Anna's guarded privacy sets up a stark contrast with Krystyna's later betrayal of it: having herself refused to "bare her innermost sexual experience" as audition material for an improvised monologue, she later watches Krystyna who, facing a synthetically sympathetic TV talk show hostess, does not hesitate to use the story of Anna's past, her most concealed emotional stratum, to achieve a look of instant profundity and humaneness. The pathos of the East European emigré becomes here the perfect publicity packaging.

As behooves a generic plot, then, the dichotomy could not be more apparent, nor the dice more loaded: on the side of privacy, tragedy, depth, self-knowledge, exquisitely bitter irony—Anna; on the side of self-display, pleasure, trivialization, naiveté, commercialism—Krystyna. Yet not unlike Sergio Leone, who had a habit of casting his Westerns against the grain ("Henry Fonda as the bad guy") to disrupt the genre and to reinforce complicity with his fans, *Anna* too disrupts the conventions and animates the relationship with a select part of its audience through two key choices in casting. The film thus circulates with a supplementary layer of information, at once outside of and a part of the text itself, carefully managed for a fully stratified effect. As is obliquely confirmed by a line of acknowledgement in the film's credits (and discussed at length for instance in a piece in *New York Magazine* 1/4, 1988) *Anna* may be taken as a thinly veiled biography of Elzbieta Czyzewska, the brilliant Warsaw stage and film actress whose complicated involvement in the late 1960s with the Polish authorities as well as the cultural establishment led her to settle in New York, where, despite several attempts, she failed to re-establish a career in the American theatre. Legendary among emigré Polish artists, as well as some American actors (Meryl Streep credits her with her Polish accent in *Sophie's Choice!*), Czyzewska was apparently instrumental in arranging the debut of Joanna Pakula in *Gorky Park* under circumstances not dissimilar to the relationship of the two women in *Anna*. Conversely, Porízková's own biography is similar in outlines, if even more flamboyantly melodramatic, than that which her character is castigated for "stealing" from her mentor. Left in Czechoslovakia as a small child by her parents, who failed in all their subsequent efforts to get her released through legal channels, she was to be kidnapped by her then pregnant mother and two Swedish journalists in a rented plane. The action was interrupted by the Czechoslovak police and the mother jailed for several years, giving birth to her second child in prison, until authorities gave in to massive international pressure and released all three back to Sweden. Unlike Czyzewska's story, a compressed version of these events accompanied the film in its press packet, and was circulated as a part of the film's publicity campaign around the time of its release.

Given how closely fiction, history and biography are made to overlap here, and more importantly, given how fundamentally the plot as well as the marketing cachet of the film is invested in this overlap, two questions beg to be asked: why was Czyzewska in contrast to Porízková, not asked to play the role of "herself" in the film? And the other way round: why was Porízková made to deliver the autobiographical story only to have it immediately overturned as a lie? In both cases, then, the film at once carefully sets up (i.e. authenticates) and disenfranchises (i.e. refutes) the highly overdetermined composite of performer and persona: in its totality *Anna* the film "behaves", as it were, not unlike Krystyna the character, recasting a story to match the generic circumstances and the prettier face, cannibalizing its real protagonist's authenticity for her new media existence. In view of the unquestionably critical distance the spectator is encouraged to take toward this "existential misappropriation" within the plot, how can the process be squared with the displacements and revisions that went into aligning the film with the external generic requirements?

Indeed, the isomorphic fit of the internal and the external "story" seems to me to be, if not a comment on, then at least a clue to, Holland's and Bogajewicz's choices (whether it is the former's or the latter's depends probably on how one evaluates the status of authorial intentionality). Facing the slotted perspective of American mass media, Krystyna adapts: if, as Baskin's agent opines, all East Europeans have bad teeth, preventing them from ascending toward artistic triumphs on American TV, she gets hers fixed; if all East Europeans have to have a life's story in order to capture the heart of kind TV hostesses, she gets one. A media star is, after all *always* a synthetic body. And if "*Anna,* the movie" wishes to achieve this kind of notoriety on the American media scene, it too must follow the outlines laid down in the warp of expectations, be they encoded in generic plots or in cultural prejudices. To put Czyzewska in front of the camera as herself would thus have been "too much": neither sufficiently neutral/blank nor sufficiently aligned with the *code* for a certain kind of "authentic" performance, her presence would have called attention to the fundamentally conventional nature of the character she was asked to play, that of "a woman made by forces of destiny to be a small-scale tragic heroine". Specific names, dates, details would be circulated in press releases, specific questions asked: authenticity as an aura, useful for valorizing a wrecked career by putting quotation marks around it, would have been disturbed when checked against a historical past; the careful dosage of it in genre mythology as a kind of homeopathic medicine, a sample of which immunizes against the whole, would have suddenly risked tasting artificial.

That the American cultural idiom is not entirely unaware of the paradox of its own voraciousness is evident precisely from the generic convention we have been looking at: the exclusive bravura of high art in contrast to the more democratic pap of popular forms of expression, the elitist hauteur of traditional theatre in confrontation with the streamlined dynamism of Broadway—these motifs are recurrent in the backstage formula. This is, in a way, exactly why "Eastern Europe" was such a perfect conceit for this formula's inflection: as a part of the world generally imagined to be unblemished by the contradictions of popular media, exclusively dedicated to high art (a world, in other words where even the little snippet of Anna's first international success, "Enchanted Days", is meant to signify an ineffable mood and tone entirely different from anything aspired to by any comparable American romantic comedy), it is a commercially uncorrupted universe in which even pop stars' triumphs are measured exclusively in terms of their moral fortitude. For Hollywood, this world is thus a perfect "other".

The final, the ultimate irony of *Anna,* and one which, in my view, finally warrants the film's interest (in contrast to those savvy journalists who reject it, thinking themselves beyond the simplified East European world I have just sketched out) is that some of these banalities are indeed true: that Porízková's story sounds like something out of *Reader's Digest* doesn't really make it any less true; that Czyzewska's mythical status could seem all too exaggerated would only ignore the real value nostalgia has for any dyed-in-the-wool emigré; that the sight of the August 1968 photographs among Anna Radková's dusty paraphernalia seems too blatant a way of yanking at the heartstrings of the non-postmodern cultural workers doesn't make the sentiment any less pertinent. Finally, that Bogajewicz and Holland made their way into the American film industry a little bit like Ulysses out of the cave of the Cyclops, bound up under the belly of the sheep of banality, should not prevent us from appreciating the expertise of their passage.

A Polish Filmmaker in the United States

Slawomir Grunberg
Ithaca College

A quite sizeable group of filmmakers from Poland has settled down in the USA during the last 20 years. They are graduates of the Polish Film School for Directors and Cameramen and include Adam Hollender, director of photography for *Midnight Cowboy*; Zbigniew Rybczynski, who received an Oscar for his short film *Tango*; Andrzej Bartkowiak, director of photography for *Prince of the City* and Marian Marzynski, a documentary producer who has successfully exhibited his work on PBS (*Nova* and *Frontline*). These find themselves in the artistic elite, and their names are quite well known in this country. Others are still climbing the ladder looking for their places in this competitive discipline. It is not an easy route. You have to be consistent, have a tough skin and be resistant to rejections. Besides that you have to work hard and have a lot of luck.

Witold Orzechowski, who directed several films in Poland, is preparing a script for his first American feature. Adek Drabinski, who emigrated before he had a chance to experience any major production, also concentrates on writing scripts. Director Lech Majewski has completed his first feature, titled *Spruce Goose Flight*. He had been trying to collect funds for this project for three years until finally Michael Hausman, producer of *Amadeus*, decided to sponsor it. Darek Wolski and Feliks Parnell, both cameramen, are getting ready for their first major feature productions. Another cameraman, Tomasz Magierski, just completed an independent feature project in New York, working there as director of photography.

The Polish Film School still opens many doors in the film industry. The school educates cameramen, production managers, and actors; but its real claim to fame is its directing department, whose graduates, such as Andrzej Wajda, Roman Polanski, Kszysztof Zanussi and Jerzy Skolimowski have received awards at prestigious ceremonies around the world, including Cannes and the Academy Awards. Another reason for this forty year old school's good reputation is professors such as Leon Schiller, Stanislaw Wohl (who was also involved in the founding of the American Film Institute), Jerzy Toeplitz (who later organized a Film School in Sydney, Australia), and finally Jerzy Bosak, a renowned documentary film producer, who is at present head of the Directing Department.

Students who are accepted to the school learn that they will be making their own films in the first year of study and that these films will be produced in 35mm format. They also learn that teachers act more as consultants and executive producers than as instructors who tell them what to do. It is this reputation for hands-on learning that makes for such stiff competition to get into the school. Hundreds apply each year but only about six Polish students and six foreign students are accepted to study directing. Of these, only three or four complete the demanding four year program. The entrance exam for the Polish students is given over a three week period which is broken up into three parts.

As a graduate of this school, you are theoretically guaranteed a job in the Polish film industry. But since the country produces only thirty full length features a year and each graduate wants to direct, rather than do an assistantship or go to the two existing documentary production units, very few can be employed. Those who are extremely talented or have good connections are the lucky ones. The rest join the group of frustrated filmmakers writing scripts which are never produced, or move to another lucrative position in Polish free enterprises (which anticipated Gorbachov's *perestroika* by at least ten years).

Poland brought up its citizens to expect that work is guaranteed by the state, and that a certificate means power. A graduate from the Polish Film School has a document in his hand which opens doors to an otherwise well sealed industry. On the other hand, there are many talented people without such a paper who have no chance to break into the industry.

Under this system, if you want to write scripts, you have to complete your studies in the scriptwriting department. A talented outsider without such a diploma has no chance even to be considered.

Those who find their place in the Polish film industry quickly learn that the Communist government takes seriously what Lenin stated years ago: film, as "the most important art", should convey political messages and infuse citizens with a sense of historical purpose. In the United States, the connection between film and politics has traditionally been more indirect, though it is a testimony to the power of cinema that the fortieth American president first came to the public's attention as a movie actor. From the propagandistic "social realist" films of the Stalin era to such boldly critical statements as *Man of Iron* by Andrzej Wajda, the best and even the worst films reflect the peculiar role a film artist can play in the absence of political democracy. Attaching themselves to the humanistic mission envisioned for the cinema by the regime, film-makers have at times served the state's cause loyally and at other times cleverly raised issues in a critical vein. Those who make films that support the regime's official interpretation of social reality give us a vivid picture of Communism's self-image. More interestingly, those who have succeeded in playing the role of social critic have shown us something of the truth of themselves. Their fight with the censors has sharpened their artistic vision and honed their techniques to a fine point, often escaping censorship through the very subtlety of their presentations, yet managing to put across in unmistakable terms a political or philosophical message that poses a challenge to the regime's version of the "truth".

During the sixteen months of democracy during the Solidarity era, many filmmakers in Poland could look more critically at their role in society. After the crackdown, some of them decided to remain silent, some emigrated to the West, and some took advantage of the political changes and initiated their careers. Only a few of my colleagues from the film school remained in Poland. The majority emigrated. Some, like myself, who were at this time already abroad, decided not to come back after martial law was imposed in Poland and the Solidarity movement was crushed. Some decided to leave the country a few years later.

When I came to the United States in November of 1981, I had planned to stay there for two months. I had just finished a major documentary project in Poland titled: *Anna—Proletarian*. It was a story of a Gdansk Shipyard worker, Anna Walentynowicz, who, disillusioned with the Communist system, started to organize unofficial trade unions. The film showed her story from the time when she was a young Communist activist and follows her through thirty years. Finally, we see her being fired from the shipyard in August, 1980. A demand for her return to work started a Solidarity strike in Gdansk Shipyard. I managed to produce this documentary from Solidarity funds. Walesa signed an agreement with the Polish Film School that created a rare precedent in the Communist system where a film was produced outside official state sponsorship and out of the hands of the censor. During martial law the Polish *Military Daily* classified my documentary as anti-Communist propaganda, after Anna Walentynowicz, a main character of the documentary, and its executive producer had all been arrested. The official copy of the film was locked away and is still not allowed for public screening.

When I decided not to return to Poland, I realized that I was one of many graduates from the Polish Film School living in the U.S. We have created a group of Polish filmmakers in exile. The quote from our brochure says: "The August 1980 revolution that sent democratic shockwaves throughout Polish society gave us the opportunity to act on these desires. We have formed an autonomous, self-directed group of filmmakers to help contribute to this revolution." This group, later as a non-profit organization called the New York Group of Young Polish Filmmakers, gave lectures on Polish Cinema, arranged screenings of Polish films in major academic centres around the country, and even produced one documentary. Two years later, due to the fact that some of its members had dispersed around the country and others decided to come back to Poland, the group was dissolved.

When you come from a country where being a filmmaker means prestige, elite privileges and quite often money, it is difficult to say, "forget it", and start everything from the beginning. One must join hundreds of other immigrants who have to learn, not just another language, but also a completely new culture. It happens very rarely that a filmmaker from Europe succeeds in the United States.

Marian Marzynski was one of the most talented filmmakers in Poland and produced over thirty documentaries and several television shows, regularly drawing the biggest television audience ever. He was at the height of his popularity when he decided to emigrate. The wave of anti-semitic hysteria in Poland of the late sixties helped him to make this decision. Twelve years later his first documentary made it into American public television stations. It took him another three years to follow up his début. He was 45 and his career had barely touched the level he had achieved in Poland. Today Marzynski's documentaries are shown on major television stations and his name is recognized in this very closed field of journalistic documentary. Marzynski is an example of the success of a Polish filmmaker in America, a success which can compare only with the achievements of Roman Polanski in Hollywood. These examples serve also as a myth, which drive many filmmakers to the West. Here they quickly realize that the audience to whom they want to address their work is quite different than the one in Europe and has nothing in common with the one they know from Poland.

When you arrive from a country where the entire culture is governed and financed by the state, you can be shocked that film and television are privately owned.

When you worked in a country where the censorship was in the hands of a small group of people sharing power, and everything you planned to produce had to be politically approved, you can be surprised that subjects are only limited by your imagination.

When you were used to sending your messages between the lines and to conveying political thoughts through metaphors, you may be shocked how straightforward you have to be in order not to lose your viewers.

When you produced in a system in which the state covered all the expenses of the project, you may need to learn the skills of obtaining funds before you can show how good you are at directing actors.

When you used to enjoy working in 35mm film format, you may need to find out that 16mm is also not a bad one.

When you didn't learn in your film or television education what a portapac video system is, you may also need to develop your knowledge in this technology.

When you realize that the words "independent producer" don't exist in the Polish dictionary, you may also need to learn terminology such as grants and deadlines.

It is a major change for filmmakers coming from behind the Iron Curtain. Those who like this challenge stay. Most, after some years, will give up and change their profession. A few will return to the country of their origin. Learning takes years and the competition is tremendous. In the United States students can study film or television courses at over one thousand universities. At Ithaca College, where I now teach, eight hundred students major in Film and Television. This is more than all the graduates of the Polish Film School over its forty years of existence. In order to succeed in this country, you have to compete with a whole world.

I started my United States career on the streets of New York City selling peanuts as a street vendor. Soon I discovered I had another hidden talent and became a teacher. From photography I moved to film aesthetics and to film and video production. I have experienced several different colleges and universities, moving around the country, developing teaching skills and, whenever there was an opportunity, I made a living by teaching. In the meantime, I have produced twenty documentaries and assisted on several others. I was able to obtain some major grants for my video productions and have also been fortunate enough to obtain a few awards for my projects. My work has been shown at several festivals, including some international presentations.

Looking back, I can only thank the wave of political changes in Poland which made me stay in the West. I enjoy this new challenge and, even knowing that there is still a lot to learn, I am glad to remain a permanent student of my new country.

Remarks on the Polish Session

Patrick MacFadden
Carleton University

The deeper we move into the topic of the expatriate filmmaker, the more I feel the topic comes close to dissolving. This is because it is not easy for me to think of these artists as being other than significantly different from one another. For example, Peter Christensen reminds us that Skolimowski had two collections of poetry published before he ventured on his first film. I would have thought this made him *sui generis* not only among expatriate filmmakers but in the entire lexicon of directors. Paul Coates queries the notion of some permanent statehood ascribed to an artist. I find myself asking what, for example, is a Yugoslav? In a conversation last year with Zanussi, he readily agreed that he was not perhaps entirely representative of the embattled artist.

Slawomir Grunberg's formidable list of Lodz graduates working in the United States is a success story; and his description of directors in Poland who cannot find a way to make a film is a familiar enough story in this country—although I should add that in Canada we would be extremely grateful to have thirty feature films every year. And I shall certainly pass on to my own film students his valuable information about the imaginative and commercial possibilities of becoming peanut vendors on the streets of New York.

Recently, in conversation with a visiting correspondent from *Literaturnaya Gazeta*, I was amused by an observation made by the

Soviet journalist: "In our newspapers we are used to reading between the lines; when we try that with your newspapers we find there is nothing between the lines".

In a sense the witticism addresses some of the larger questions raised by Natasa Durovicova's tracing of the perils of *Anna*, questions having to do with the reception of East European films in the West, and the difficulties involved in what she calls "the conversion of cultural models". (When I say East European I am conscious of the unbearable heaviness of Milan Kundera's plea: that we in the West seem to have obliterated what he prefers to call Central Europe.)

In relation to the reception of such films, we have two cultures that distribute films and related material. One is the everyday communications industry, now more or less *Time-Warner*. As Graham Petrie remarked earlier, the laws governing this operation tend to be restrictive. There is another channel of cultural distribution encompassing art house and repertory cinemas, subsidized magazines discussing the products of such cinemas, public radio and television, this latter often called "educational" television, and so on. With the exception of certain parts of the United Kingdom, this duality is peculiar to North America.

So which of the two does the expatriate cinema artist aim for? Are these two systems part of our much vaunted pluralism? Is the smaller one made possible by the surplus generated by the more central one? Or to put the matter another way, where do we in the West expect expatriate filmmakers to position themselves? Do we see them as the last carriers of Modernism? Or should they work "in the industry" as many do? (Konchalovsky takes a classic Hollywood genre of jailbreak and subsequent hunt in *Runaway Train* and uses it as an agora for a Dostoevskeyan meditation on the nature of Man.)

But of course it's not particularly useful to generalize from such examples. We talk easily about "commercial success" but the idea remains elusive. And by that I have in mind the art house-repertory success. If, as Alexander Batchan remarks, *Liquid Sky* was the biggest cult film shown at the Waverly Cinema, was that because the management refused to entertain *The Rocky Horror Picture Show*? Andrew Horton tells us that *Who Framed Roger Rabbit?* is doing well at the box office and among the Oscar selection committee. Is this because it's got an animal in the title? I mention these matters to reiterate a point made by Gerald Peary this morning, having to do with the dangers of thinking of filmmakers who come from Eastern Europe and the Soviet Union in a monolithic way. A conference hosted by a university department concerned with East European and Soviet matters understandably deals with that part of the world. But that should not blind us to the fact that all kinds of filmmakers from all over the world will come to California to make films and then to stay or not. And what is of interest is the kinds of insights or practices they bring, available perhaps only to the outlander's eye: the American Southwest as seen by Wenders or Adlon, for example. But I also have in mind a sequence in *Moonlighting* where Skolimowski has his Polish workmen exposed for the first time to that central icon, the supermarket. Twenty metres of toothpaste, one hundred metres of toilet paper. Heaven! Then his camera tilts up to show the other camera, the one in the ceiling that guards against unofficial property redistribution; the workmen now see the market in a different light, as do we.

To repeat the question: what does one expect these filmmakers to do? For those among them who come wreathed in morality because of their bravery in adversity, do we want them to be exemplars? Do we wish them to act as missionaries who will save us from our own grossness? At what point must an artist cry "Enough! All I want is a contract."?

And if we move these demands from the ethical to the aesthetic sphere, do we wish them to carry on with the Modernist project when we ourselves have abandoned it? And why are we at a loss to explain what happens when such filmmakers do not do what we feel they ought to? (One has heard such mutterings about, say, Polanski.)

Perhaps we should make fewer demands; or to put it another

way, perhaps we should let the film artists be themselves. As to what is lost and what is gained in the move from the Lenin Hills to Beverly Hills, well, life is a series of choices, whether for plumbers or filmmakers. And not all expatriate film artists may wish to share the Romantic view that they can work only from some position of permanent opposition. Whereas one can agree that not all of them can reach the dizzy heights reached by one of them, as described for us this morning by Gerald Peary, of having a backrub from three chorines—I take it simultaneously—nevertheless some may feel that, far from being in an exiled condition, home was never like this.[1]

A further observation occurs to me: an artist from a background marked by a powerful religious or political system might be tempted to recall it with a certain nostalgia, especially after exposure to California. I am reminded of Elem Klimov's observation: "We make vertical films; you make horizontal ones". Thus on the aesthetic level, such artists might very well feel that their expressive devices, their artistic bank balance, might be better protected inside the much-maligned narrative structures of the mainline film industries than they would be by joining forces with, say, those postmodernists who like to go on about "the crisis of confidence in the rationalism of the classical episteme".

What is this aesthetic bank balance? It will include, if one may generalize, an authenticity and variety of feelings evoked, a certain level of abstraction, a delight in and a mastery of certain cinematic tropes. How best to spend it or conserve it inside a marketing structure? I'm not at all confident of the outcome. I was struck by Vida Johnson's remark earlier, quoting Konchalovsky, about coming from a country where "feeling takes precedence over reason". It would suggest the extent of the shock experienced in encountering a Benthamite technologized culture such as this one. When Bertrand Russell visited the Soviet Union in the twenties, he came away lamenting that the Bolsheviks were taking a nation of artists and turning them into a nation of engineers. It would be unfortunate if here they found they had to metamorphose into sellers.

More optimistically, we may take sustenance from the formula suggested by Joyce, surely the exile par excellence: "Silence, exile and cunning". And, he might have added, the greatest of these is cunning. For whatever the loss and pain involved in the artistic diaspora under discussion here, these artists have surely not forgotten how to be cunning.

ENDNOTE

1. The reference here is to a remark made by Gerald Peary in the discussion following Session One, but not included in the transcript published here. [Ed.]

Discussion and Responses

Session Three

Vlada Petric addressed Peter Christensen:

If we agree that most East European filmmakers working in the West, particularly in the USA and Canada, have failed to create films artistically—and ideologically—equal to the best achievements they have made in their own countries, it then seems even more perplexing that they themselves are not at all disturbed by this fact. On the contrary, they often claim, some even insist, that it is not their intention.

In the few cases when their films do represent serious artistic accomplishments, a close examination of these films reveals that the aesthetic as well as spiritual core of these works derives from the "Old World." Andrei Tarkovsky proves this in the most blatant way: his *Nostalghia* (1983) and *The Sacrifice* (1986) are saturated with Russian atmosphere and a non-Western world view. Obviously, in art, spiritual quality, which is generated by the maker's psycho-emotional constitution, cannot be changed overnight, let alone replaced by a mood that is alien to the very nature of the artist. It is exactly this realization that prompts immigrating film directors to produce trivial films which exhibit their aesthetic mastery, entertainment effects, and genre properties. As a result, even when they succeed in producing satisfactory light comedies, attractive romances, or dynamic thrillers, their overall aesthetic level is extremely low. I emphasize this because we are dealing here with filmmakers who, once, were excellent artistic directors who not only knew how to express themselves creatively, but also succeeded in conveying complex socio-psychological problems in a highly cinematic manner.

The central issue of our discussion should, therefore, address the following question: why do the creative aspirations of the immigrating directors almost instantly turn into mediocrity and commercialism—

features that do not characterize their European careers? Why do
they agree to function against their intrinsic, intimate artistic drives?

Take, for example, Milos Forman, whose first film made in America,
Taking Off (1971) is still his best artistic achievement since he left
Czechoslovakia. There are indications that he tries to "forget" this
film, to dissociate himself from a work that was a financial flop,
hence becoming an obstacle in his—otherwise successful—endeavor
to reach the heights of Beverly Hills where he presently abides.
Most of his colleagues try to follow suit, producing purely entertainment movies which do not, however, make money, while others opt
for some kind of compromise by treating serious subjects in a conventional manner, which, by its nature, thwarts aesthetic issues.
Dusan Makavejev's most significant works, including *WR.:
Mysteries of Organism* (1971), were not financial hits, but his
Australian-made flick, *The Coca-Cola Kid* (1986) was, according to his
own admission, his first financial success, simply because the director finally decided to cater to popular taste. What can one say about
Andrei Konchalovsky's *Maria's Lovers* (1985) or Nikita Mikhalkov's
Dark Eyes (1987), typical examples of the films tailored according to
the Hollywood recipe? Even more pretentious and technically effective films, like Konchalovsky's *Runaway Train* (1986), as well as Ivan
Passer's *Cutter's Way* (1981), concerned with serious socio-political
issues, stopped short of achieving a significant cinematic impact,
much less artistic value.

Where *The Lightship* is concerned, the literary structure of the script
provided good material for an intimate psychological drama involv-
ing several characters "imprisoned" on a trade ship. Unfortunately,
Skolimowski, one of the most inventive of East European
filmmakers, totally abandoned his original, unconventional directorial style, especially his method of composing his shots, opting for
the conventional shot-reverse-shot technique of shooting lengthy
conversations in front of the camera. Thus he failed to transpose the
Conradian mood contained in Lenz's novel into a cinematic
equivalent, remaining "somewhere in between". Listening to the interpretation of *The Lightship* by my literary colleagues, and after
comparing them with my cinematic experience of the film, I must
conclude that the more they have read into the characters and the
narrative signification of the film text, the less they reflect the actual
structure of the film, demonstrating the analyst's imagination rather
than the film's cinematic/artistic complexity.

Alexander Batchan:

I'm always impressed by people who are able to present very good papers on very bad films such as *Anna*; I think the film is a nonentity; I don't think it launched a director's career (he is really a theatre director) and this is his first film. I don't think Agnieszka Holland was associated with the film quite the way Natasa describes: the idea was hers but she didn't write the script. At some stage she was busy in Europe and withdrew.

Natasa Durovicova:

My argument is not contingent upon Agnieszka Holland's participation in the film although I do hear her voice speaking through it. I'm willing to throw that out.

Alexander Batchan:

When you put Holland and the director, Bogajewicz, together they are quite different in terms of talent even though Holland's German films such as *Angry Harvest* are minor compared to the works she was doing in Poland when she was associated with Wajda. When I asked Bogajewicz at a press conference why Czyzewska the actress was not used herself in the film, no one could give me an adequate answer. Sally Kirkland did not seem to know much about her.

Natasa Durovicova:

I think this proves my point that the film uses authenticity for a certain cachet, as a kind of currency of exchange, and this is a currency of exchange associated with East Europeanness. On the one hand there is a moral cachet which allows them to tell the rest of the world "what life is really like", which becomes a cliché that forms part of a generic circuit making use of the notion of authenticity for popular mass consumption. It is then dismantled for popular consumption. The filmmakers were astute enough to gauge the possibility offered by this cliché and I would like to reserve judgement on the moral value of their recirculation of these familiar motifs.

Alexander Batchan:

There IS an audience for East European films even if it is just a small one (and maybe half of that audience is sitting here) This audience cannot support the release of these films in a major American city. There is no government support of course and the cost of producing and distributing films these days is so high that it is very difficult for any art film to exist. But the audience IS there.

Slawomir Grunberg:

I would argue with this because I think the task of the East European filmmaker coming here is not to get the small audience you are talking about, but to reach a larger audience on TV or in major movie theatres. That is a goal of anyone coming here to direct.

Paul Coates:

I would like to ask Natasa Durovicova where a film like *Anna* situates itself with regard to a term like "pastiche"; is it trying to create a world in which "pastiche" does not exist? Does it present itself as a kind of pastiche? Or does it fall short of pastiche; does it fall into pastiche because of the nature of the people making it?

Natasa Durovicova:

Sure, because we have to deal with the question of audiences: there is a stratum of the audience to whom the illusion is relevant and makes sense, and then there is the larger audience for whom Poriskova always plays the same role of wide-eyed beauty who radiantly says, "Well, this was my life"; then there is the generic audience which does not know the first or the second but is content.

Paul Coates"

Are there several levels of pastiche interlocking or do they cancel each other out?

Natasa Durovicova:

I don't think negation is applicable to the concept of pastiche.

The Films of Dusan Makavejev

Between East and West

Daniel J. Goulding
Oberlin College

From his earliest days as an amateur film maker (1953-1958) and as an award-winning documentarist (1958-1964),[1] Dusan Makavejev established himself as one of the most fertile and inventive of a younger generation of film makers, theorists and critics who spearheaded Yugoslavia's *new film* (*novi film*) movement of the sixties and early seventies.[2] Beginning in 1965, he made a series of creatively distinctive and witty feature films which won for him increasing international critical attention: *Man is not a Bird* (*Covek nije tica*, 1965), *Love Affair or the Diary of a Switchboard Operator* (*Ljubavni slucaj ili tragedija sluzbenice PTT*, 1967), *Innocence Unprotected* (*Nevinost bez zaštite*, 1968), and *WR: Mysteries of the Organism* (*WR: Mysterije organizma*, 1971).

During his Yugoslav period, Makavejev created increasingly complex and multilayered film collages which challenged the viewer to move freely within the films' open spaces and multiple imagistic associations.[3] The nexus of his thematic concerns also grew more complex and multidimensional in its implications. He remained throughout the period an ironic, irreverent and sophisticated gadfly who stung with wit and cunning, lifted the veil of public pomp to expose its empty interior, debunked the rituals of reification and cant, challenged officially sanctioned myths, exposed the obscenity of repressive power even when it was dressed in the illusory garb of sanctioned bureaucratic niceties, explored the actual and metaphorical realms of sexuality and eroticism, and celebrated the uniqueness and liberating spirit of the individual.

This paper advances the argument that Makavejev's film *WR: Mysteries of the Organism* serves as the fulcrum for an understanding of his complete work. It is a film which not only summarizes and expands upon his Yugoslav period, but also anticipates the thematic and stylistic preoccupations of his later films made in the West: *Sweet Movie*, 1974, produced in Canada; *Montenegro*, 1981, produced in Sweden; *The Coca-Cola Kid*, 1985, produced in Australia; and *Manifesto*, 1988, a U.S.-Yugoslav co-production.

In *WR: Mysteries of the Organism* Makavejev uses the psychoanalytic theories of Wilhelm Reich as a touchstone for wide-ranging political commentary and satire. The film is divided into two sections. The first intersperses a documentary account of Wilhelm Reich's life, work, persecution, and death in a Pennsylvania prison with examples of bioenergetic and primal scream therapies of contemporary Reichian practitioners along with various scenes and interviews reflecting contemporary America (circa 1969-1970). The second section is a fictional story set in Yugoslavia, which centres on Milena, a liberated young revolutionary whose attempt to spread the gospel of Reichian sexual freedom to a physically handsome but politically conditioned Russian skating star is finally rewarded with decapitation by his ice skates. Milena's roommate, Jagoda, practices Reichian sexual freedom with unusual devotion, pursuing the doctrine with unflagging enthusiasm in her sexual couplings with Ljuba "the Cock" and the Yugoslav "natural man" Radmilovic.

In the context of the film, both superpowers, the United States and the Soviet Union, are depicted as monuments to sexuality misdirected into power politics and militarism. The principal symbols of American repression are the right-wing excesses of the McCarthy era, in which pathologies of "Get the Commies" were combined with suppression of intellectual unorthodoxy and the contemporary (at the time the film was made) U.S. militarism in Vietnam.

Stalin is the pre-eminent symbol of Soviet repression. In the context of the film, he gradually absorbs Lenin and takes on his guise. The contemporary symbol of the repressive Stalinist-Leninist orthodoxy is represented in the politically conditioned Russian ice-skating champion Vladimir Ilyich (after Lenin's first name), whose well formed lips speak nothing but socialist clichés.

Yugoslavia represents a separate path to socialism, espousing a humanistic self-management socialist doctrine but not always living up to its claims. It is Milena's self-appointed task to enliven self-management and self-regulating socialism by preaching the doctrine of liberation through orgasm: "Only by liberating both love and labour can we create a self-regulating worker's society", and she admonishes the workers to "fuck merrily and without fear" (Makavejev, 31). Makavejev assumes an ironic and satirical attitude toward all forms of dogmatism and cant—including an affectionately satirical handling of Milena's naive and simplistic presentation of Reichian sexual politics which she manages to convert into political cant and demagoguery. He satirizes both conventional sexual taboos and mechanical and doctrinaire revolts against them (from Jackie Curtis's bisexuality to Betty Dodson's paintings of men and women masturbating). He adopts an ironic view of New Left anti-Vietnam protests by interspersing scenes of Tuli Kupferberg of the "Revolting Theater" prowling the New York streets, autoerotically caressing his rifle while the song he wrote for the Fugs plays on the soundtrack: "Kill, kill, kill for peace".

There are extended scenes of vigorous and joyful sexual intercourse in the film but, ironically, no orgasms. Scenes of sexual intercourse are separated by dissolves and inserts, which provide a structural filmic equivalent to Reich's belief that we live in an age of incomplete sexuality, in which sex has become subservient to politics, institutionalism, and dogma. This notion is further conveyed in the repetition of motifs in which arousal is followed by freezing. The most widely discussed example of this motif is the sequence in which the editor of *Screw* magazine, Jim Buckley, has his penis manipulated to erection by the sculptress, Nancy Godfrey, and a plaster cast is made of its erect state. This scene is followed by a film segment from *The Vow*, Chiaurelli's idealized portrayal of Stalin, in which Stalin proclaims, "Comrades, we have successfully completed the first stage of Communism" (130)—a juxtaposition which equates the powerful but repressive Stalin with a frozen phallus and emphasizes the frozen nature of the revolution under Stalinist centralized, hierarchical dogmatism.

The complex and ambivalent relationship between Yugoslavia and the Soviet Union is suggested in the relationship between Milena and the Russian ice skater Vladimir Ilyich. Milena sees Vladimir perform during a guest tour in Yugoslavia and falls instantly and romantically in love with him. Despite her views concerning complete sexual freedom, Milena approaches Vladimir awkwardly and with diffidence. In their first encounters, Vladimir speaks in socialist slogans and takes a condescending view toward Yugoslavia's separate path to socialism: "We Russians ... we do respect your efforts to find your own way. You are a proud and independent people. But we are confident you will learn from your own experience that our way is best!" Milena responds that "time will tell who's closest to the best", and Jagoda chimes in prophetically, "The closest kin will do you in" (105).

As Vladimir begins to relax in the free ambience of Milena's and Jagoda's apartment, he is inspired to observe, "Well, I've been to the East and I've been to the West, but it was never like this!" (127). On a romantic stroll with Milena along a snow-covered riverbank, Vladimir declares, "I like being here! I confess there's much I don't understand. But your people are wonderful" (135). They kiss romantically to the melancholy strings of the Hungarian Gypsy song "Like a Beautiful Dream." Vladimir at first yields to the sensual moment and then quickly reasserts his rigid, doctrinaire character in a speech which is a close paraphrase of Lenin's own words: "... nowadays if you stroke anybody's head, he'll bite off your hand! Now you have to hit them on the head mercilessly ...

though in principle we oppose all violence" (136).[4] Milena attempts to turn Vladimir back to a more sensual mood, but he slaps her, and she falls down. Vladimir is filled with remorse and asks her to forgive him. Milena begins to strike him repeatedly around the head and shoulders and makes an impassioned plea:

> You love all mankind, yet you're incapable of loving one individual: one single living creature. What is this love that makes you nearly knock my head off? You said I'm lovely as the Revolution. You gazed at me like a picture ... But "Revolution" musn't touch! ..
>
> Meanwhile you put your body at the service of Art! Your magic flood-lit figure serves the needs of the masses!
>
> A bunch of lies is what you're serving ... the People and the Party! A toy balloon is what it is ... not a revolution! A petty human lie dressed up as a great historical truth! Are you capable, you rotten louse, of serving the needs of the species by taking the one basic position for an ecstatic flight to the target ... like an arrow ... or a vigorously hurled ... spear? (139-140)

After this speech, Milena continues to strike Vladimir bitterly and unthinkingly until he stands up in front of her, tears in his eyes, and they kiss passionately. After prolonged and copious lovemaking (not shown in the film), Vladimir severs Milena's head from her body with his ice skates (also not shown), in an effort to reassert his authoritarian rigidity and doctrinaire purity.

The last two scenes of the film metaphorically pose the possibility, despite the past, of reconciliation. Milena's severed head, on a white tray in the autopsy room, speaks and bitterly equates Stalinist-Leninist orthodoxy with Fascism but expresses no shame concerning her own and Yugoslavia's Stalinist past:

> Cosmic rays streamed through our coupled bodies. We pulsated to the vibrations of the universe. But he couldn't bear it. He had to go one step further. Vladimir is a man of noble impetuousness, a man of high ambition, of immense energy ... He's romantic, ascetic, a genuine Red Fascist! Comrades! Even now I'm not ashamed of my Communist past! (142)

Filled with remorse—his rigid doctrinaire mask dissolved—

Vladimir wanders near a Gypsy camp in the snowy landscape. With his arms outstretched, he appeals to an unknown God in words written and sung by the Russian underground poet Bulat Okudjava:

> O Lord, my God, my green-eyed one,
> Before the earth stops turning
> And all our pain is done,
> Before this day is through
> And the fires are still burning
> Grant to each some little thing
> And remember, I'm here too. (144)

Awakened sensuality and tenderness have placed Vladimir in touch with his humanity and the hope of redemption. During the last lines of Vladimir's song, the film cuts to a shot of Milena's smiling head and then to a shot of a photograph of a smiling Reich, the author of this political miracle, and the film ends on an optimistic note.

In his film, Makavejev attempts, in an undogmatic way, to celebrate individual creativity, humor, spontaneity, sexual joy, and irony as mechanisms of counter-repression. He calls his film a dream machine for self-confrontation—Makavejev's own attempt to use humor, spontaneity, and irony to challenge received myths, cant, and institutional rigidities, open up new avenues of thought, and possibly provoke social change.

Following a structural motif in WR: Mysteries of the Organism, Makavejev's film itself excited widespread arousal in Yugoslavia but, after a complex struggle, was placed under a freeze, which lasted until less than two years ago when the film was re-released for domestic viewing and received an enthusiastic reception.

The relationship between Milena and Vladimir in WR is anticipated in the central love relationships depicted in his first two feature films, Man is not a Bird and Love Affair, though neither of the earlier relationships carries with it the same density and complexity of imagistic and metaphorical associations as those found in WR. In both of the earlier relationships, a relatively more liberated and sexually open female is paired with a socially, culturally or politically conditioned conservative male: the middle-aged Slovenian engineer, Jan Rudicki, and the vivacious young hairdresser, Rajka, in *Man is Not a Bird*; the culturally conservative sanitation inspector, Ahmed, and the sexually liberated switchboard operator, Isabella, in *Love Affair*.

Man is Not a Bird is set in the industrial town of Bor in eastern Siberia, where a large copper factory is undergoing modernization. A highly skilled and politically committed engineer from Slovenia, Jan Rudicki, is brought in to direct the installation of new machinery and speed up production. He is serious, stolid and devoted to his work. Rajka, the pretty daughter of the family from whom he rents a modest sleeping room, seduces the engineer and a love affair develops. Rudicki, however, is too preoccupied with meeting work deadlines to nurture his love affair with Rajka, and she eventually finds vibrant and joyful sexual satisfaction with a virile and ruggedly handsome young provincial dandy, Zarko.

When Rudicki has completed his work, a symphony orchestra is brought from Belgrade to celebrate the event. Before the concert, Rudicki receives a medal and commendation for his exceptional achievement. The orchestra plays Beethoven for the edification of the assembled workers. In the meantime, Zarko and Rajka are joyously consummating their mutual desires in the cab of his truck to the swelling chords of Beethoven's Fifth.

The most realistic and conventional of Makavejev's films, *Man is Not a Bird* nonetheless is filled with sharp satirical commentary. Throughout the film the smoothly articulated premises of rationalized socialist self-management objectives are subverted both by real factory conditions and by the exuberant, primitive and anarchic lifestyles and behaviour of the workers. At one point in the film, Rudicki's concentrated attention is distracted by an exuberant worker who swings precariously over the machines on a rope loudly announcing that he is a bird. Rudicki stolidly proclaims that "Man is not a bird", a statement which proves to be sadly prophetic in his own case. The workers also reject self-managed planned culture in favour of bawdy tavern torch singers, hypnotists, snake charmers and other circus performers, who symbolize life as an abundance of sensations and attractions.

The last scene of the film shows Rudicki in long shot, walking slowly across the grey expanse of the factory yard. He has been rewarded for his work but has lost the opportunity to open his life to spontaneity, tenderness, and joy and to the possibility of genuine individual creativity.

The ironic documentaristic vision of Makavejev's first feature film achieves greater complexity of expression in his internationally successful second film *Love Affair*. At the narrative level, the film portrays a warm and humorous love affair which turns suddenly dark and ends in bizarre tragedy.

Isabella, a lively, sensual, and free-spirited switchboard operator, who has enjoyed several affairs, meets a kind and serious young sanitary inspector, Ahmed. They end up in Isabella's apartment, where she takes the initiative in prompting their first tender and joyous sexual union. They live together and enjoy an uncomplicated period of idyllic sensuality and domesticity, in which trivialities and small, offbeat moments are infused with humor and warmth—she preparing delicious food, he bringing home a record player and having a new shower installed.

Ahmed is called out of the city by his work, and during his long absence Isabella has an affair with a young postal worker, and later learns that she is pregnant. Soon after Ahmed returns, the relationship turns sour when Isabella coldly refuses marriage and the entrapment it symbolizes for her. Deeply wounded, Ahmed gets drunk and determines to commit suicide by throwing himself into an antique Roman well. Isabella follows him, and in her struggle to prevent Ahmed from taking his life, she accidentally falls into the well and is drowned. Ahmed is later arrested and charged with her murder.

Contrasted to this sensual and tragic love affair are collage filmic interjections which portray a modern, rationalized, cool, and indifferent world. Makavejev wittily juxtaposes tender and erotic scenes between Isabella and Ahmed with kindly but pedantic lectures by an elderly and distinguished sexologist, Professor Kostic, concerning phallic adoration in early cultures, analysis of the nature of coitus and its representation in paintings, and a learned disquisition on the hen's egg as the perfect unit for the study of human reproduction. Scenes of the postmortem examination of Isabella's body are accompanied by lectures on detection and identification of corpses. The tragic and bizarre circumstances of Isabella's death are missed altogether by rationalized methods of police detection and a learned and beside-the-point criminologist's lecture on the psychology of murder.

Makavejev's film also suggests the polarities and tensions of Yugoslav reality in a period of rapid social change. Isabella is a member of the Hungarian minority in Yugoslavia, attempting to adopt a modern, liberated lifestyle free of Balkan male domination. She has financial independence and her own apartment in the city, and she freely chooses her lovers. Ahmed is a member of the Moslem Slav minority, representing the most traditional and conservative expression of a male-ordered and male-dominated social structure. His quiet formality and kindness mask deeper layers of fiery pride and passionate ferocity.

Isabella and Ahmed's relationship is paradigmatic of that found in *WR* and several of Makavejev's later films: a relationship in which sexual liberation and passion are followed by reaction and counter-repression (often violent), which, in turn, may be, and sometimes is, followed by remorse and the possibility of redemption. Moreover, Makavejev's experiments in *Love Affair* with discontinuous narrative development and film collage are further elaborated in his next film *Innocence Unprotected*, and culminate in his most sophisticated film of the Yugoslav period, *WR*.

Of his films made in the West, *Sweet Movie* most closely follows upon Makavejev's stylistic and thematic concerns in *WR*. Indeed *Sweet Movie* is, in many ways, a remake of *WR* painted in darker and more pessimistic hues and with even wilder and more surrealistic imagistic associations. Like *WR* it delivers an ironic and satiric double critique of the degeneration of communist ideals and practice in the East, and the trivialization of human values, excessive self-interest and consumer-oriented narcissism and commodity fetishism in the West. Any hope that *WR* might have held out for the subversive force of Reichian sexual politics is rather thoroughly pummelled and put to rest in *Sweet Movie*, a film in which sexual orgasm is associated with the last dying spasms of communist revolutionary mythology on the one hand, and burbles to expiration in a huge vat of chocolate featured in a TV commercial on the other.

In this, the most controversial and least distributed of Makavejev's feature films, there are two bizarre fictional stories which are continuously intercut with each other as well as with other insertions and filmed material—the most important of which is the Nazi documentary film of the exhumation and examination of the corpses of hundreds of Polish officers murdered by the Red Army in 1939 in Katyn forest.

The first fictional narrative concerns the sexual adventures and misadventures of a Canadian beauty who wins the title of Miss World 1984 for being judged the virgin with the most exquisitely formed hymen. Her prize is marriage to the wealthiest bachelor in the world, the billionaire Texan, Aristoteles Aplanalpe. He whisks her away in his plane and discourses expansively on his worldwide acquisitions, including a recent purchase of Niagara Falls which he plans to convert into "a fantastic quadraphonic extravaganza unaffected by weather conditions and in living colour" (something even Ted Turner or Donald Trump might envy). Before consummating the marriage, Aplanalpe engages in an elaborate cleansing ritual with rubbing alcohol to assure absolutely antiseptic conditions. Having completed these loving labours, he then removes his erect penis from his white shorts (which are decorated with cherries) and urinates on his expectant and prostrate bride—an unexpected perversity which invites from her an understandably prolonged scream of loathing and protest.

Despite her protests, she is then passed into the hands of the black superstud, Jeremiah Muscle, where she suffers even more varied forms of sexual degradation. Finally she escapes from Jeremiah's tender mercies and falls (this time willingly) into the arms of the superstar singing sensation, El Macho, who wins her over with his sequined eyelids and electronically hyped ersatz Spanish love ballads.

Somewhat later, she stumbles into the real-life Milky Way Commune, headed by Dr. Otto Muehl, whose radical therapy consists of inviting the participants to regress toward the womb so that they can recapture the freedom and joy of playing with their own and others' genitalia and with their food and body excretions. Miss World regresses to a fetal position, sleeps in a crib, is suckled by the black, large breasted Momma Communa, and, at one point, rather catatonically rubs a man's flaccid penis across her cheek.

Finally, Miss World's sexual odyssey ends all too sweetly in a huge pool of chocolate which is especially constructed for an elaborately produced TV commercial to sell candy. Her nude body is covered with liquid chocolate and she writhes seductively to orgasm before expiring by suffocation—as an excited cameraman zooms in for the final big closeup.

The second discontinuous narrative line involves vain attempts by the radical prostitute Anna Planeta (a decadent version of the Milena character in *WR*) to breathe some life into the moribund myths of the worldwide communist revolution. She captains a ramshackle ship called "Survival" with a huge figurehead of Marx gracing its prow. Limp strands of his beard drag in the water as the ship plies its way through the harbour and canals of Amsterdam. Anna stands proudly on the head of Marx as the old Italian revolutionary song, "The whole world is our country; our law is freedom", is heard on the sound track. Later she sings her theme song: "Is there life on earth? Is there life after birth?"

The interior of the ship is a shrine to the fallen heroes of the revolution; its martyrs and its assassins—huge fading collage photographs of Trotsky, Stalin, Lenin, the Kremlin leadership presiding over a parade in Red Square adorn the walls, and a clutter of other memorabilia recall the corpses of the past. Stuffed in the hold of the ship as well are bags of sugar, sweets and candy eggs which Anna uses, along with the sweets of her body, to lure passengers aboard.

An especially eager passenger is a young Russian sailor (Luv Balkunin) who comes aboard and makes love to Anna on the prow of the ship in broad daylight to the cheers of the shore's onlookers. Later they make love in a huge bed of sugar. Following the sailor's orgasm, Anna plunges a knife through the sugar into his gut and mixes the blood and sugar into a thick paste. The sailor at first laughs and welcomes his martyrdom—explicitly linking himself to the martyred sailor (Vakulinchuk) in Eisenstein's *Battleship Potemkin*—but then his head jerks backward, his mouth opens in a final death spasm and he resembles more nearly the frozen death mask of one of the corpses dug up in Katyn wood. Anna had remarked that the revolution "is full of corpses." The sailor had replied, "The whole world is full of corpses." Anna had earlier in the film added to the world's body count by luring four young boys to their martyrdom after first seducing them with candy and the allures of her body.

Anna's story ends when the Amsterdam police arrest her and carry her off half-naked, screaming, and kicking, while the bodies of the sailor and the four boys are laid out in plastic bags along the shore. In the concluding sequence of the film, images of the row of body bags are intercut with images of Miss World expiring in the vat of chocolate, and with the grisly (black and white) images of exhumed corpses from Katyn woods. The final cut of the film is from these corpses to the corpses of the young boys, also shot in black and white. As the camera holds on this final scene, the boys begin miraculously to stir and to emerge from their plastic entombment. The frame then freezes, colour bleeds back into the screen image, the final film credits are superimposed, and the film ends by evoking the possibility of regeneration and rebirth even in the midst of such widespread entropy and deformation of human values.

Sweet Movie, Makavejev's most pessimistic and controversial film, received practically no distribution—East or West. As a result, he found himself unable to find backing for another film until seven years later, when he made a modest comeback with his Swedish-produced film *Montenegro* (1981), followed four years later by *The Coca-Cola Kid* (1985), produced in Australia. In both of these films Makavejev abandoned his earlier experiments with discontinuous narrative structure and multiple levels of montage associations. He did not abandon, however, his predilection for bizarre plots, surrealistic images and sharp social and political satire. In both films the balance of his satirical critique shifts Westward: in *Montenegro*, he provides a witty examination of the crazy, neurotic, perverse and murderous urges that may lie just under the smooth, repressed and conformist surfaces of bourgeois life and values. In *The Coca-Cola Kid* he exposes the lunacy of market driven psychology and product fetishism—even when the product is as effervescent, egalitarian and sensually provocative as Coca-Cola! In both films, sexuality remains the ultimate force in Makavejev's subversive universe—messy, unpredictable and anarchic.[5]

In such a short paper, it has been possible only to suggest a few of the thematic and imagistic threads which have shuttled their way to and fro through Makavejev's central work *WR*. What is most apparent is Makavejev's consistently off-beat and surrealistic view of individual sexual dynamics and their connections with the larger cultural, societal and political order. The creative space he occupies intersects East and West, but belongs to neither—existing somewhere in the interstices and folds of a world whose major ideologies and political polarities he can neither accept nor reconcile. One can only hope that he maintains his unique stance and continues to celebrate the liberating power of individual creativity (including its quirky, eccentric and bizarrely atypical manifestations) against social conformity, institutional rigidity and the obscenities of repressive power—East or West.

ENDNOTES

1. His most interesting amateur films are *The Stamp* (*Pecat*), *Anthony's Broken Mirror* (*Antonijevo razbijeno ogledalo*) and *Don't Believe in Monuments* (*Spomenicima ne treba verovati*). His best known short films are *Smile '61* (*Osmeh '61*, 1961), *Down With Fences* (*Dole plotovi*, 1963), and *The Parade* (*Parada*, 1962).

2. For a definition and analysis of new film tendencies in Yugoslavia during the sixties and early seventies and the controversies surrounding their development, see Goulding, *Liberated Cinema: The Yugoslav Experience* (Bloomington: Indiana University Press, 1985) pp. 62-84. For commentary on Makavejev's films, see also, pp. 122-125; 137-142. Discussions in this article of *WR: Mysteries of the Organism, Man is Not a Bird*, and *Love Affair* are paraphrased closely from this book.

3. For an interesting discussion of Makavejev's experiments in film collage, see Herbert Eagle, "Collage in the Films of Dusan Makavejev," *Film Studies Annual*, vol. 1 (1976) pp. 20-37. See also his chapter "Yugoslav Marxist Humanism and the Films of Dusan Makavejev," in David Paul, ed., *Politics, Art and Commitment in the East European Cinema* (New York: St. Martin's Press, 1983) pp. 131-148.

4. For a complete text of Lenin's remarks from which this speech is derived, see "Let's Put the Life Back in Political Life", an interview with Dusan Makavejev, *Cineaste*, Vol. VI, no. 2 (1973), p. 18.

5. From published reviews I have read, this generalization would also apply to Makavejev's most recent film *Manifesto*, though I have not yet had the opportunity to see it.

WORK CITED

Makavejev, Dusan. *WR: Mysteries of the Organism.* New York: Avon Books, 1972.

Filmmaking in the Middle: From Belgrade To Beverly Hills

A Cautionary Tale

Andrew Horton
University of New Orleans

The world suddenly took note of Yugoslav cinema in 1985 when Emir Kusturica won the Golden Palm at Cannes for Best Film with *When Father Was Away On Business*. But the relationship of Yugoslav filmmakers to Hollywood in all its protean forms is another matter.

Of course second generation Yugoslavs Karl (Mladen Seklovich) Malden and Peter Bogdanovich have done well in Hollywood, and Oscar winning, Yugoslav born screenwriter Steve Tesich has little to complain about. Also there is London based producer George *Friday the 13th Part I-?* Zecevic whose Smart Egg Production Company commands respect in the horror genre circles. But what of those filmmakers who first made a name for themselves in Yugoslavia and who have later tried to work in or with the Hollywood system? That is the territory that will concern us in the discussion that follows. I wish to specifically make this Belgrade and Beverly Hills connection clear, for I am not treating the possibilities of Yugoslavs working in other Western European cinemas in this study. We begin over Turkish coffee in Hotel Moscow in Belgrade years ago, and pass on to double expressos on Wilshire Boulevard and on 83rd and 2nd Avenue in Manhattan more recently. What I wish to present is something of the "in between" experience of Yugoslav filmmakers working in or dealing with American cinema over the past decade or so. And I want to make this exploration in an "in between" manner, mixing personal experiences as a professional American screenwriter who has worked with Yugoslav filmmakers for the past nine years, together with some of the thoughts I've had on this subject as a film scholar/critic.[1]

When the Turkish coffee arrived that summer afternoon in Belgrade in 1980, I was talking with Srdjan Karanovic whom I had just met. I had already viewed with great pleasure his award winning films *The Fragrance of Wild Flowers*(1978) and *Petria's Wreath* (1980). For me much of the haunting power of these films and others which I had just seen including works by Sasha Petrovic, Goran Markovic, Goran Paskalevic, and Rajko Grlic, and Zika Pavlovic, had to do with how refreshingly different they seemed from Hollywood movies. In the United States, I had only had access to some of Makavejev's work as examples of Yugoslav cinema. Now a new cinematic vista opened before me. I had lived in Europe for over five years by then and could feel but not clearly articulate how these Yugoslav directors, each with his own vision, collectively, however, mapped out a section of world cinema that was distinctly its own and which no simple label such as "Balkan" or "Southern European" or "East European" (a label which certainly does not fit) did justice.

Karanovic with his usual good humor agreed. "And for that very uniqueness," he said, "Yugoslav cinema is condemned to the festival circuit rather than the suburban mall cinema chains." In part, of course, we could say that it's difficult for any foreign director to crack into the Hollywood system. But what we will pursue here are some of those difficulties I believe pertain especially to Yugoslav filmmakers who I feel are particularly caught "in the middle."

Karanovic ordered another round of coffee and began talking about American movies and a possible visit to the United States. That meeting ultimately led to several American visits and a happy screenwriting collaboration on three feature film scripts and a handful of treatments, including the completed film, *Something In Between* (1983).[2] The title, of course, captured much of what we felt about the "in between" nature of Yugoslavia today as a country and as a state of mind. "Neither East or West...in the middle!" says Marko, the Yugoslav playboy in the film trying to explain to Eve, the American girlfriend of his best friend, what Yugoslavia is all about.

The title proved prophetic for the film's production as well. Karanovic and Centar Films of Belgrade had hoped the project would be an American-Yugoslav co-production. Yet after a two week effort to locate an American co-investor in 1981—yes, he learned that fundraising often takes years for even well liked American projects—Karanovic and his Belgrade producer decided to go ahead without additional funding and *Something In Between* wound up as a Yugoslav film, with many festival awards, a wide international distribution including Canada, and a release deal with Cannon Films (which, alas, despite some 1988 *Variety* ads to the contrary, has yet to materialize).

Let us be more specific about the Belgrade to Beverly Hills situation.

Yet before going further, we should mention an obvious but useful point: if we speak of the contact between the Socialist countries and Hollywood, we necessarily start with the strong influence of anyone's accumulated lifetime of seeing Hollywood films. Borges wisely wrote in one of his film reviews, that "the greatest virtue of Russian films was their interruption of a steady diet from California."[3] Those working in film outside the United States can, in this sense, never be completely divorced from Hollywood. It's hard to imagine, therefore, a filmmaker anywhere, even, let's say, in Albania, who is not aware of and thus, to some degree, influenced by the classical Hollywood narrative form of story telling with all of its advantages and limitations. This is also to suggest that in part a Yugoslav director in Yugoslavia is necessarily aware of the difference between Hollywood norms and Yugoslav in pursuing his or her art.[4]

Our specific topic, however, concerns the actual working contact of recent Yugoslav directors with the Hollywood system either on American productions or on co-productions. And in this brief space let me offer four observations, keeping in mind, of course, the dangers of over-simplification.

1: Without something of a total commitment to working within the Hollywood system, success proves extremely elusive.

Question: "Why, except for the magical montages of Slavko Vorkapich (including *David Copperfield, Romeo and Juliet, The Good Earth, Boys Town* and *Mr. Smith Goes to Washington*) has no Yugoslav filmmaker made a lasting impression on Hollywood to the degree that other Middle and Eastern European and Soviet filmmakers such as Fritz Lang, Michael Curtiz, and Billy Wilder, to mention an earlier generation; or Roman Polanski, Milos Forman, and Andrei Konchalovsky in more recent Socialist dominated years?"[5]

If there were one simple answer then naturally every deserving young Yugoslav filmmaker who desired so, would be signing a contract with Vestron, New Line Cinema or Spielberg himself.

Yugoslav director Slobodan Sijan, however, recently provided me with a thoughtful remark over chicory coffee in New Orleans, where I live and work, which at least partially addresses this question. According to Sijan, "We Yugoslav filmmakers are different from the other European and Soviet directors in this one important point: while most of them came to the United States and to Hollywood to live, having closed the possibility of returning behind them, we have always felt that one of the advantages of being Yugoslav has been this in-between state of being able to go to Hollywood, but also to be free to go home, whenever we chose to. For this reason I think we never really try hard enough to understand the Hollywood mentality, psychology, spirit." (Surely the recent studies of the importance of East European Jews in setting up Hollywood is in part testimony to such an observation.)

Sijan openly sees himself as an example of what we could call the "Yugoslav syndrome." Having burst onto the international film scene with enthusiastic and warm honors and reviews for his debut comic feature, *Who Is Singing Over There?* (1981), he continued to explore comedy mixing what he felt to be a Balkan spirit with some strong Hollywood genre elements in a series of films including *The Marathon Family* (1982), *How I Was Systematically Destroyed By Idiots* (1983) and *Strangler Vs. Strangler* (1985). An admirer of American genre films, he then felt ready to attempt working on a Hollywood production. The project was with Cannon and ultimately was titled *The Barbarian* and was to be shot in Yugoslavia to cut production costs.

To make a very long story short, Sijan explained over a second cup of chicory coffee that with the benefit of several years distance from the project he could see a double bind that caused him to drop out from this, his first Hollywood effort. "Before I went to Hollywood," he commented, "I thought I understood American movies. And I thought my films, especially *Marathon Family*, were quite American. But looking at them now I realize how wrong I was, how little I really knew about American films from a practical level." The double bind was his lack of a Hollywood street wise education and his unwillingness to make all of the "compromises" or commitments he felt he was being asked to make, artistic and political, to get the job done.

Sijan's point is well taken. Surely those who have come to the United States to live have necessarily adopted a different attitude than those who are here "on assignment." This is not, of course, to say that every director who commits him or herself to living in Beverly Hills or Brooklyn will succeed. But it does mean that an "in between" mentality has often worked against the kind of commitment to Hollywood that success within the system appears to demand.

2. The importance of the status of the director in Yugoslavia makes it difficult for Yugoslav filmmakers to adapt to the producer-driven system of Hollywood.

I suspect that this observation is true of directors from other countries as well. But I have watched with admiration how much artistic control and production power is given directors in Yugoslavia. Only a handful of Hollywood directors could dream of reaching such a position. Part of the sheer pleasure I felt in working on *Something In Between* was how almost effortlessly what we wrote wound up on the screen with any changes made coming from Karanovic himself. No long story conferences with studio heads, no marking of a script as "the final third rewrite," and no anxious executive taking over the film in the editing room in order to rescue his vision from the director's (in fact an extra pleasure was that of being flown over to sit in on the editing of the final cut to have one last input into the project).

Thus for a Yugoslav director with a reputation to suddenly find him or herself in Hollywood "taking" meeting after meeting with producers, investors, hangers-on, and others, attempting to convince, please, cajole all of them in an act of brazen salesmanship clearly runs against the grain for most Yugoslav trained filmmakers. Spoiled? Not exactly. It's just that in terms of status, leaving Belgrade or Lubljana or Zagreb or Skopje for Beverly Hills is a bit like living out Orson Welles' remark that, "I started at the top and worked my way down to the bottom."

This attitudinal difference is both cultural and professional and definitely very real. One brief example. One well-known Yugoslav cinematographer was asked to apply for an assignment on an important American mini series being shot in part in Yugoslavia. The American producer asked him in the interview, "Are you the best?" The cinematographer was embarrassed and did not know what to say except, "Well, my credits and awards are listed on my resume." "Yeah," said the producer, "but I asked you are you the BEST?" The cinematographer blushed and pointed again to his resume. The interview ended and our Yugoslav candidate did not get the job.

In short, it is the need to hustle continually within the post-studio, pre-packaged Hollywood system that is extremely foreign to the Yugoslav training and temperament.

3: Much of the Yugoslav approach to film narrative is shaped by a non linear tradition of story telling quite opposed to Hollywood's plot driven system.

This past year has witnessed the critical and commercial success in the United States of a Yugoslav novel, Milorad Pavic's *Dictionary of the Khazars: A Lexicon Novel* (New York: Knopf, 1988) published in both male and female editions. The title, once again, is apt. This is a narrative that the author invites, in fact urges us to experience "as a dictionary," picking up and putting down at random and entering with any given "definition."

Such a playfully deconstructive approach to Western narrative should not strike the knowing reader as purely post-modern in the tradition of Kafka, Italo Calvino, and Milan Kundera, but as part of a long Yugoslav heritage of "subversive" literature composed under Occupation, be it of the Turks, Austro-Hungarians, Nazis or others. And, even more, a tradition that has thrived and survived in large part due to an impressive oral literature (think of the satirical Marko cycle of poems as well as the Battle of Kossovo cycles, all dating back hundreds of years). Even in theater, what we would call the "review," something akin to vaudeville, had a stronger following than the French or British tradition of the Well-Made Play.

It is little wonder, therefore, that the heady surrealistic cinematic collages of Makavejev, the feisty yet gut wrenching drama of a work such as Petrovic's *I Have Even Met Happy Gypsies,* and the wholly experimental dream essence of a new film such as debut filmmaker Slobodan Pesic's *The Harms Case* have not found favor with commercial American distributors interested in Aristotelian plot and Onassis like profits.

When Karanovic and I began to work on *Something In Between,* he showed an earlier version (written in collaboration with playwright Saki Marinovic) to me and others and got the same comment from everyone: "Interesting situation but there's no story." "Of course there's a story," he answered in frustration; to which others replied, "Yes, but not a Hollywood story." Shortly before he returned to Belgrade, over expresso coffee in Brooklyn, he said, "I saw *Gone With The Wind* on TV last night and guess what? It had a story!" It was an important moment and a telling comment, for it captures, I think, much of the confusion and what I can only describe as a mis-matching of talents when Yugoslav filmmakers meet the Hollywood system.

High concept—the ability to reduce a film to a few one syllable words—is foreign to the much more freewheeling and complex spirit of Yugoslav filmmakers. As I write, Emir Kusturica is teaching at Columbia University and waiting to hear how Columbia Pictures executives plan to market *Gypsy Caravan*, his recent film about Yugoslav gypsies filmed entirely in Gypsy. The film has already been accepted In Competition at Cannes but the studio heads have yet to see it. It is difficult to imagine being more in the middle than this: to have made a Yugoslav story for an American studio in a third language which must be subtitled, not dubbed. But such a complicated waiting game will not be new for Kusturica. While Cannon bought the rights to *When Father Was Away On Business*, they pulled it from a brief circulation in only a handful of cities, with no video distribution. Such a status, to be a Cannes winning filmmaker under a Hollywood distributorship but put on the shelf is, alas, far too frequent a tale to surprise veteran Hollywood observers.

4: The family-like atmosphere and size within much of the Yugoslav film industry (budgets, cooperation, inter-connectedness, etc.) make it difficult to adjust to the less personal and more finance driven American scale of production.

While differences certainly exist between filmmakers in Yugoslavia, there is, nevertheless, a degree of cooperation and a spirit of "family" that I have not found in Hollywood or New York. Filmmakers trade off scripts, help write each other's films, do bit parts in each other's works, even make post-production plans in a spirit of mutual support rather than competition. Once, for instance, in Belgrade, I listened to three filmmakers agree on whose film should be aimed for which festival so that "we don't all fight against each other for Cannes or Montreal or Berlin."

And yet the dream of a Hollywood on the Danube or a Belgrade on the Pacific persists. After all, wasn't *The Last Emperor* shot in China by an Italian director with a British, Chinese, American cast?

Maybe those Yugoslav directors who by-pass the usual Hollywood channels can claim the greatest sense of satisfaction.

This past summer I was offered the chance to do a rewrite on a Yugoslav script about American characters in a dramatic romance to be shot on the Dalmatian Coast with a Yugoslav director/-cinematographer, Bozidar Nikolic and American (Chicago) financing. *The Dark Side of the Sun* went through none of the usual delays of months and years. I wrote during the past summer, they shot in the Fall, and the film is ready for distribution next month. Distribution, of course, remains the unknown quantity in the formula. But what is important is that the film got made. Though the difficult part is yet ahead—how to sell the film—Nikolic avoided the often depressing delays and rejections that are frequently part of trying to enter the corporate oriented Hollywood system. He made a film the way he is used to making a film and was fortunate enough to find American dollars earned by Yugoslav-Americans to pay for it. Thus, at last, a more satisfactory example of filmmaking in the middle. And thus my cautionary rather than cynical note to this tale.

Another cup of expresso arrives at the Italian cafe that Karanovic frequents in Manhattan as he teaches at NYU and Brooklyn College on a Fulbright grant. It is December, 1988, and he has just been honored at the Kennedy Center by the AFI and the Yugoslav Embassy. We are recovering from the champagne and working on a new treatment which we wish to offer to American Playhouse. I go over some details and Karanovic puffs on his cigarette as he barks, "Not bad, Horton, but you need to find a stronger story."

We're still in the middle. But it seems to be where we are most comfortable!

ENDNOTES

1. For a consideration of contemporary Yugoslav cinema, see my following articles: "The Mouse That Wanted to F—K A Cow: Makavejev's Cinematic Carnival Laughter," *Comedy/Cinema/Theory*, edited by Andrew Horton (Berkeley: University of California Press, forthcoming 1990; "Oedipus Unresolved: Overt and Covert Narrative Discourse in Kusterica's *When Father Was Away on Business*," *Cinema Journal*, Vol. 27, No. 4 (Summer 1988), pp. 64-81 (reprinted in Serbo-Croatian in *filmograph* [Belgrade], Vol. XIII, No. 39-40 [Fall 1988], pp. 58-64); "Carnivalesque Parody: Bakhtin and Makavejev Considered," *Exquisite Corpse*, Vol. 5, No. 6-8 (July/August 1987) p. 422; "The Whole Story: Yugoslavia's Multi-Faceted Cinema," *World Cinema Since 1945*, edited by William Luhr (New York: Ungar, 1986); "The New Serbo-Creationism," *American Film*, Vol. XI, No. 4 (January/February 1986), pp. 24-30; "From Satire to Sympathy in Yugoslav Film Comedy," *East European Quarterly*, Vol. XX, No. 1 (Spring 1986), pp. 91-99 (Reprinted in the Slovenian journal *Ekran*, Vol. ii, Nos. 1/2 (Summer 1986), pp. 35-37; "Filmmaking in the Middle: An Interview with Srdjan Karanovic and Rayko Grlic," *New Orleans Review*, Vol. 12, No. 1 (Spring 1984), pp. 101-106; "Buses, Undertakers, and the Belgrade Strangler: Slobodan Sijan on Comedy," *New Orleans Review*, Vol. 12, No. 2 (Summer 1985) pp. 77-93; "Satire and Sympathy: A New Wave of Yugoslav Filmmakers," *Cineaste*, Vol. XI, No. 2 (1981), pp. 18-22 (translated and reprinted in the Yugoslav cultural journal, *Knjizhevne novine* [February 1982]). See also entries on Karanovic, Kusterica, Grlic, Sijan, Papic, Stiglic, Makavejev, Zafronovic, and Pavlovic in *Magill's Survey of Cinema: Foreign Films* (Pasadena: Salem Press, 1986).

2. The other screenplays include *Virginia* (with Saki Marinovic), an unusual "partisan" tale of a woman raised as a man in Southern Yugoslavia which Cannon Films has expressed interest in filming and *Upside Down*, an American located tale of "green card" marriages of convenience told as a romantic screwball comedy of our times which was a semi-finalist in the Sundance Institute competition in 1987.

3. Edgardo Cozarinsky, *Borges in/and/on Film*, translated Gloria Waldman and Ronald Crist (New York: Lumen Books, 1988) p. 27.

4. This applies even to works that appear quite strongly rooted in a particular culture. Emir Kusturica's Cannes Golden Palm winner, *When Father Was Away on Business* (1985), is undeniably "Yugoslav" and more particularly, "Bosnian" and yet, as Kusturica has stated in interviews, he is an admirer of John Ford, a tribute that might be traced to various influences in his shooting style (a preference for a stationary camera in many scenes) and even attitude/content (like *Grapes of Wrath* and other Ford films, Kusturica's two feature films released so far center on the importance of family).

5. I should note that Vlada Petric has made an enduring mark on American film

studies as a Yugoslav experimental filmmaker in the 1960s who turned Harvard professor and who has for over twenty years influenced students and colleagues alike, but I am focusing specifically on those who attempted a long term relationship with the Hollywood system.

Hollywood in Yugoslavia

Gerald Peary
Suffolk University

When I was in Belgrade for five months in 1986, studying Yugoslavian Film Comedy on a Fulbright Fellowship, no native could understand why I would so waste my time. "He must be crazy," Emir Kusterica (*Father is Away on Business*) said, when I met him briefly one evening at Belgrade's dining spot, The Writers' Club. But Yugoslavian film aficionados were soon pleased I was there, because I could answer pressing questions about what they deemed truly significant: Hollywood cinema.

"How do you pronounce the names of the directors, 'Frank Borzage'? 'Budd Boetticher'?" I was asked eagerly by film critics. They were hungry for accurate vocabulary about cult "auteurist" filmmakers in Andrew Sarris's book, *The American Cinema*, which is read as dogma in Yugoslavia. I was a guest at Belgrade's Faculty of Dramatic Arts for a showing of the 1960 Randolph Scott western, *Commanche Station*. That day, the "B" American director's name was said correctly for the first time by the proud Serbo-Croatian-speaking professor: Boetticher, pronounced exactly as for the famous series of travel guides.

In Yugoslavia, it's not only university professors and their students who are passionate about Hollywood cinema. The citizenry too cannot get enough of American studio pictures. Probably more than any other Eastern European country, Yugoslavia is Hollywood-saturated, and the citizenry look openly West, past puritanical socialist realism to unadulterated escapist American entertainment.

Hollywood is everywhere:

(A) On television. In 1986, not only was *Dynasty* broadcast every week but additionally, at odd hours, a seemingly arbitrary collection of Hollywood studio "B" movies also was televised. The most avid fans taped these films, and some possess a collection of several hundred American pictures, from Elvis Presley musicals to prime "film noirs".

(B) On VCR. There are several private stores now in Belgrade where customers line up and order foreign videos for the equivalent of $5 each in dinars. The videos are pirated, duplicated endlessly from tapes purchased in West Germany. The copying of videos happens in Belgrade with Yugoslavian government complicity, because officials claim half the profits. However, the profits that remain in private hands are truly extraordinary in a country where even college professors and medical doctors make $200 a month.

Which videos? Yugoslavians bragged to me that they saw Spielberg and Lucas science-fiction extravaganzas on video in Belgrade before such films opened theatrically in America.

(C) In the theatres. Several moviehouses in Belgrade show only American films, including one that specializes in soft-core pornography. Yugoslavia's byzantine economic system is at work here: private distributors supply films to the theatres, and nothing is as profitable as Hollywood features. In the first three months of 1986 in Belgrade, eight of the ten top-grossing films were American, led by *Beverly Hills Cop* and *Rocky III*. But Yugoslavs are so Hollywood-hungry that even marginal American genre films, those that play in the USA in small Southern towns and drive-ins, can succeed spectacularly in first-run Yugoslavian houses. *Lone Wolf McQuade* and *Up the River* were also among the Top Ten.

Yugoslavs, including many intellectuals, seem especially fond of the works of "auteurist" action directors such as John Milius, Walter Hill, Clint Eastwood, and John Carpenter. That many of their favourites are macho political conservatives seems of little concern. Only "liberal Americans", they say, fuss about such irrelevant matters.

The popularity of John Carpenter is a particularly curious phenomenon, as Yugoslavs rate the genre director of *Halloween*, *The Thing* remake, and *The Fog* at the very top of filmmaking. A typical opinion was that of Sonja Savic, the extremely popular Yugoslavian film actress of *Something in Between* and *Una, My Love*. Savic grew up watching American cinema, especially pictures with Marlene Dietrich and Marilyn Monroe. Of contemporary directors, Savic insisted when I interviewed her, "Carpenter is the best with women. I prefer Carpenter's actresses to those of Spielberg and Coppola."

(D) In the archives. The Yugoslavian Film Archive in "Film City" on the edge of Belgrade is one of the largest in the world, containing 42,000 films. Many of these are unclassified because of stringent budgets and impossibly short staffing. Nobody knows authoritatively what is in the collection, but presumably numerous ostensibly "lost" films from around the world will be discovered there some day.

Even with its dire problems, the Archive has managed to make available a significant selection of Hollywood films, always in 35mm, to Yugoslavian universities and cinemathèques. Again, the collection is arbitrary, consisting of whatever was given to the Archive by distributors and exhibitors during the last sixty or seventy years. (Fortunately, the films were hidden, buried in the ground, during Nazi occupation.) But the demand to see Hollywood cinema is so strong that the Archive's Hollywood selection is constantly in circulation.

For most Yugoslavs, this is the way they have learned, however haphazardly, about the history of the American cinema.

(E) In the cinemathèques. The "kinoteka" in Belgrade, which shows two films a day, is filled with students when American films are shown from the Archive, approximately three times a week. When I was in Belgrade, every Sunday for several months was a "John Ford night", and these showings were especially packed. Yugoslavian movie fans laugh aloud at the rowdy, macho humour of Ford movies, and they are not ashamed to enjoy Ford's sentimentality either. When I lectured on one of the Ford films shown, *Wings of Eagles*, I told the "kinoteka" audience that few in the United States knew of John Ford's artistry. Certainly not college students. My pronouncement was met by scepticism. Surely I was joking? Surely, John Ford in the USA was an institution?

A theory for Ford's amazing popularity in Yugoslavia: so many of the films are set in a kind of fairyland military, including the 1940s "cavalry trilogy". In Yugoslavia, where the draft is universal but where there never are wars, the male population relates directly to Ford's in-uniform world. (In Yugoslavia, being in the army is a big, harmless joke. Many men serve in army units in their own home town, and socialize still with their civilian friends.)

Soldiers, many of them ex-students, would show up to see Ford movies at the "kinoteka". I was once asked by a soldier to hurry up my lecture, because he was due back at the barracks! This perhaps explains the Yugoslavs' easy intimacy with Ford, while the same movies can seem strange and old-fashioned in America, where students often hate western films, sentimentality, and where the draft is long abolished.

(F) In film production. Yugoslavia is a haven for runaway, non-union English-language films, particularly with the American dollar's formidable strength against the Yugoslav dinar. Also, Yugoslavia can make good on its strategy to attract foreign productions: promising every kind of terrain and weather, from snow-covered Slovenian mountains to lush, blue Adriatic Ocean within hours of each other.

Jadran Films in Zagreb has been the most successful production company in luring foreigners. There is even a noticeable "Jadran look" to such films, often made-for-TV movies set during World War II including scenes in Nazi concentration camps. A Jadran-film is characterized by a murky, green-brown colour to the film stock, and high-cheekboned Slavic extras.

Among American films shot in Yugoslavia are: Orson Welles's *The Trial* (Kafka in Zagreb), *Sophie's Choice*, *Fiddler on the Roof*, Sam Peckinpah's *The Iron Cross*.

(G) As a cross-cultural factor in Yugoslavian epic filmmaking. There have been a series of large-budget Yugoslavian films, clumsy celebrations of the partisan effort in World War II, which utilize international casts. For example, Yul Brynner and Orson Welles appeared in *The Battle of Neretva* (1971), inexplicably, an Oscar nominee. Rod Taylor starred in *Partisans* (1975). Richard Burton played Tito in *Sutjeka* (1973), for which the movie set turned into a mutual admiration society. Off-screen photographs show Burton thrilled to be standing about with Marshall Tito, and Tito excited to be played by Richard Burton!

To date, there have been no literal adaptations of Hollywood films, but many recent Yugoslavian movies show at least casual American influence. *The Balkan Express* and *The Small Train Robbery* are period comedy capers made with *Butch Cassidy and the Sundance Kid* before the mind of the filmmakers. In *Tigar*, a gentle comedy about a Yugoslavian boxer, the pugilist has a poster of *Rocky* on his wall.

Yugoslavian experimental filmmakers, also influenced by American models, often combine pop collage with American rock or jazz soundtracks. There is a resemblance to Kenneth Anger's style of "Hollywood underground".

However, it is only with the feature films of Slobodan Sijan, from *Who's Singing Over There?* to *Strangler vs. Strangler*, that a major Yugoslavian filmmaker has announced, both in interviews and in the body of his work, a strong allegiance to Hollywood cinema. Sijan edited the first book anthology in Serbo-Croatian dedicated to the cinema of John Ford. The Ford influence permeates *Who's Singing Over There?*, beginning with a band of disparate characters riding a bus through the countryside. In Ford's *Stagecoach* and

Wagonmaster, there are similar characters on similar journeys.

Other Sijan films show the influence of "auteurs" Howard Hawks and Fritz Lang. It was no surprise that, when Sijan was awarded a Fulbright to the United States, he chose to spend his months living around Los Angeles, observing the Hollywood studio life first-hand. He has declared often that this is where he feels comfortable.

Back in Yugoslavia, Sijan's passionate defense of American cinema has been extremely influential. He is a director whom many young film students and critics revere. If he adores Hollywood, they will too.

Sijan has found the perfect ally for his Hollywood aesthetic in a Faculty of the Arts screenwriting professor named Nabojsa Paikic, who wrote the screenplay for Sijan's *Strangler vs. Strangler*. More than anyone in Belgrade, Paikic proselytizes for American "auteurist" cinema and genre films. He is a self-styled provocateur, who sees himself on the kind of fierce, iconoclastic mission of François Truffaut and the early *Cahiers du Cinéma* crowd. As a film critic, he praises the directors he loves and attacks those he loathes, and with complete abandon. He uses his professorship at the Faculty of Dramatic Arts as a podium for his combatative aesthetics. More often than not, Paikic is at war, his foes including his own colleagues at the university.

Some of Paikic's enemies have declared that Paikic, so adoring Hollywood, hates Yugoslavian cinema. Untrue. In fact, Paikic is extremely knowledgeable about Yugoslavian film history. But his master plan is to rewrite this official history along "auteurist" lines. That means discovering the works of personal directors whose films have been denigrated, or forgotten. That means something far more controversial, debunking many traditional favourites.

Paikic has begun his project by, in unpublished work, assigning all Yugoslavian directors to exactly the categories used by Andrew Sarris in his book, *The American Cinema*. At the top of Paikic's chart is a small "Pantheon", which includes two of Paikic's talented friends, Zica Pavlovic and Sijan. *The Far Side of Paradise* includes, among many directors, Dusan Makavejev. But many of Yugoslavia's most honoured filmmakers, including Sasha Petrovic and members of the so-called "Czech school" (the directors who studied in Prague: Karanovic, Kusterica, Markovic, Grlic, Paskaljevic, Zafranovic) are placed in undesirable categories: "less than meets the eye", "lightly likeable", or "strained seriousness".

To Paikic's credit, a reshuffling of the Yugoslav canon is desperately needed. All official histories of the cinema, including those written by Americans, reward the same films and filmmakers. But not Paikic's unofficial history: he manages to lead his students to marvellous Yugoslav films which have been passed over. Also, frankly, some of the sanctified names deserve debunking, including Petrovic and Paskaljevic.

But Paikic can be quite unfair in his polemics. In his blanket condemnation of the Czech school, Paikic is blind to the cinematic virtues of even the most personal films of Srjan Karanovic. As for Kusterica's *When Father Was Away on Business*, Paikic obstinately refused to see it!

Paikic's critics, those bruised by his attacks, point out his rightist "cowboy" politics—both Paikic and Sijan were proud supporters of Reagan, not the actor but the politician! And they accuse Paikic, a transplant from Bosnia to Belgrade, of acute provincialism. It can't be denied: Nebojsa Paikic, Yugoslavia's foremost booster of Hollywood cinema, has never been outside of Yugoslavia's boundaries in his whole life!

Discussion and Responses

Session Four

Vlada Petric, as discussant:

The fate and behavior of the East European filmmakers who have emigrated to the West is not significantly unlike the careers of other "immigrant" directors throughout the history of American cinema, including such masters as Jean Renoir, Victor Sjöström, Moritz Stiller, Fritz Lang, even Michelangelo Antonioni and Hector Babenco. Slavko Vorkapich and Robert Florey entered the history of American silent film not as makers of commercial movies (which they extensively and successively produced both in the silent and sound eras), but as creators of the famous experimental short feature *Life and Death of 9413, A Hollywood Extra* (1928). All of Eisenstein's projects associated with Hollywood, however, ended up using American (not Hollywood) funds to shoot documentary footage for the epic *Que Viva Mexico* (1931-32), which was never completed by himself. After a lengthy dilemma, Eisenstein realized that accepting Hollywood conditions would mean a total negation of his artistic integrity.

The same situation continues to this day: the only way to be admitted to the big American studios is to abandon artistic considerations. As an alternative, there exists "underground" and non-mainstream film production which does not guarantee financial gain for the makers. And this is not why most of the East European directors came to the USA: they had ample opportunity to practice this in their native countries. Yet, it is obvious that if any contemporary filmmakers are to be mentioned as contributors to American cinema, they will emerge from non-commercial production, as exemplified by Jim Jarmush's *Stranger Than Paradise* (1985), Percy Adlon's *Bagdad Cafe* (1988), and Slava Tsukerman's *Liquid Sky* (1983)—the kind of filmmaking the leading emigré directors try to avoid at all costs, regardless of their ability to succeed in it. They are equally scared of the fate of their American colleagues, like Terrence Malick, who after his masterpiece *Days of Heaven* (1978), was deprived of the possibility to make the kind of films he is deeply interested in. This is a paradox characteristic of the film world where money controls art; it is also a tragedy for the American film as an art form.

The second discussant, John Mosier, added these ideas:

I have been struck by the extraordinary number of misconceptions of East European cinema and Eastern Europe generally.

1. In Daniel Goulding's talk on Makavejev, I was struck by the thought that in three or four cases such as his, the work done outside their native country is at least as good as the work done inside it. I don't support the theory that their work necessarily represents a vast falling off into the world of Mammon.

2. The second point, which Andrew Horton brought up regarding Yugoslavia as "something in the middle", is a good metaphor to use in a slightly different sense. Geographically or culturally it likely is in the middle, but between Prague and Moscow. Yugoslavia has set a pattern which we will likely see followed in other countries in the next two decades.

We should also keep in mind the other European filmmakers like Bunuel and Malle who have worked outside their own countries.

3. America should send American academics into other countries to give American audiences an idea of the climate in Eastern Europe. We must understand their intellectual climate or opinion and their perceptions of American culture and literature.

Graham Petrie, as unofficial third respondent, had this to say:

1. A good question: What is Eastern Europe?

2. The problems faced by Yugoslavian filmmakers are not always the same as those faced by other Eastern Europeans. There is perhaps a link between the Yugoslavs and the Hungarians and between the Czechs and the Poles.

As Catherine Portuges pointed out when talking about Márta Mészéros, Hungarians and Yugoslavs can go home if they don't make it abroad, but Czechs and Poles did not have that choice, at least in the 1960s and 1970s.

As Paul Coates pointed out, the least successful films made by Polish directors abroad have been made by Vajda and Zanussi, who can go back to Warsaw anytime they like. Polanski and Skolimowski and the Czechs did not have that choice; they had to stay and try to make it in the West.

3. Regarding the love of Hollywood amongst the younger filmmakers; this is true in Hungary as well as in Yugoslavia, where some of the new directors seem to want to reject their own tradition of cultural and political examination that they have been brought up with and now want to make Hollywood-style movies. Yet when they go abroad, for example, Pál Gábor or Károly Makk of the older generation, who are respected figures in Hungary and have tried to make films in America, they find they are relatively unknown figures who cannot expect the automatic prestige which they would get at home.

The solution for the younger filmmakers, as for the Yugoslav directors whom Horton described, is not to try to get into the mainstream of Hollywood filmmaking, which could take them years. Instead, like György Szomjas and Péter Gothar, they've tried the same strategy as the Yugoslav directors: to go there with a small budget and to try to work independently and reflect an alien consciousness in an entertaining and offbeat way.

Andrew Horton, in referring to Vlada Petric's discussion, pointed out:

Picking up on Vlada Peric's point, as to why East European directors should even bother to try to understand the Hollywood mentality, you have the case of György Szomjas who comes to America and for $100,000 makes his own film which is a total reflection of his own personality. He does not compromise. He is happy and realizes he can do it again. With $100,000 you have a lot of freedom; with $18 million you don't.

Vida Johnson:

Taking up Vlada Petric's point that we have not talked enough about the artistic and cinematic qualities of these films. I'd like to concentrate on Makavejev who has made significant films both in Yugoslavia and abroad. Daniel Goulding in his presentation did not give an evaluation regarding whether or not he agreed with the

basic premise of this conference: that most of these filmmakers go
downhill when they work abroad. I've heard John Mosier argue
against it and Vlada Petric argue for it. Let's use Makavejev to discuss whether there is this downhill progression or not.

Daniel Goulding:

I'm more interested in understanding Makavejev's imagistic associations rather than arguing whether he has gone uphill or downhill.
The whole question of his artistic merit is of a lower order to me. It
is a matter of choice and taste.

There is obviously a great shift after *Sweet Movie* when he abandons
the modernist practice of looking at multi-layered imagistic associations. It would be easy to say that he abandons it because he realizes he has to make some concessions to a narrative line. *Montenegro*
has a single story; to me he is still a satirist and a maverick and dealing with surrealist preoccupations. It is insightful; he still resists
being put into a slot and that is one of the things I most admire
about him.

I was disappointed in *The Coca-Cola Kid* but there he might have
been responding to a shift in the whole aesthetic of world cinema
rather than just making compromises. *Montenegro*, even though it
does have a simpler story line, retains his irreverent spirit. There is
not a downhill move; it is rather a shift in aesthetic and thematic
perspectives that needs understanding.

Bart Testa:

There are three periods for Makavejev: the Yugoslav period, the
period of *Sweet Movie* and *WR*, and then the more recent one. For
most critics his reputation collapses with *Sweet Movie*. There is Dan
Goulding's view that his films move towards the achievement of
WR and *Sweet Movie*; there is the other view that he is no longer a
humanist filmmaker after *Sweet Movie*. His characters become cartoons and he becomes a filmmaker concerned with what he calls
meta-montage in *WR* and *Sweet Movie*. He pulls away from improvisation and becomes concerned with formal and montage
strategies. He becomes concerned with the frame.

I see him as a counter-genre filmmaker and I would argue that
Sweet Movie is a critique of Eisenstein. As a counter-genre filmmaker
we can see shifting formal operations in his films and as a con-
tinuity in his work it all depends on what genre he is working

against in each film. If we go through his films purely on formal grounds we would notice that he changes and that he falls off the tracks with *The Coca-Cola Kid*.

Daniel Goulding:

There is in *Sweet Movie* a counter to *WR*. It has something to do with fundamental preoccupations; it is pessimistic and lacks the joy of the earlier work. It is a film about entropy and disillusionment. In *WR* sex is used anti-entropically. I think *Sweet Movie* is a very grim image of where we have gone. That is the way I read it anyway.

Vlada Petric:

I am appalled at Daniel Goulding's statement as a critic, writer and teacher that the artistic value of a film is of secondary importance.

Secondly, what happened with Makavejev is that the narrative structure does shift and becomes trivial. It is not necessary for a good film to subvert the narrative structure; lots of bad films do that too. On the other hand there is Hitchcock who makes great narrative films. The question is this: to what extent does the narrative deserve to be studied on a serious artistic level? Makavejev has failed to reach the Hitchcock level of the narrative level he has chosen in *The Coca-Cola Kid*, and in that respect he has gone downward.

Patterns of Spirituality in Tarkovsky's Later Films

Alexandra Heidi Karriker
The University of Oklahoma

I. Introduction

The work of Andrei Tarkovsky sets a unique standard for self expression in Soviet cinema before the Gorbachev administration's policies of 'glasnost' (openness) and 'perestroika' (restructuring). Introspective, symbolic and intensely spiritual, Tarkovsky's films diverge from the majority of post-Stalin canvases, such as the situation comedies, panoramas of war, or period tableaux lionizing party doctrine. It is not the case that Tarkovsky is the only Soviet director of merit to emerge since 1953. However, in comparison with the majority of the popular and acclaimed directors of the past thirty years, like Shukshin, Riazanov and Mikhalkov, Tarkovsky is the most subjective, the most metaphysical. And his work portrayed these attributes at a time when disregard for the tenets of socialist realism was tantamount to oblivion. Since Tarkovsky's works are more surreal than realistic, and more introspective than objective, his films cut against the grain of established Soviet policies. That he dared to remain elusive, philosophical and lyrical in an era of increasing pragmatism sets him apart from others of his generation.

In the use of imagery and narrative, as well as in poetics, Tarkovsky's films display an artistry which could not be squelched, even under the direst circumstances, as when his finished work was mercilessly cut or left on the shelf. It is a wonder that Tarkovsky's daring, risk-taking films were screened at all in the USSR. Only in the past few years, under Gorbachev's reconstruction campaigns, have his films and those of other notable directors like Romm, German and Shepitko become available for general viewing.

When Tarkovsky felt that he would no longer be allowed to make films in the Soviet Union, he decided to remain in the West. His grievances notwithstanding, it appears that Tarkovsky was in a privileged position while he was in the USSR, because he was not prevented from making films, even after *Andrei Rublev* was shelved and *Mirror* relegated to the third category of limited release to art houses.[1] If one considers the situations of the iconoclastic Paradzhanov (who was persecuted and incarcerated) or Askol'dov (whose film career virtually came to an end after he made his only film, *Commissar*), Tarkovsky's position seems preferable. Obviously, he was respected (or at least tolerated) in his native land as a filmmaker, and he was even permitted to travel abroad.[2] Recently, there have been Soviet retrospectives of Tarkovsky's work, and archival research on his films is no longer considered suspect. It is a pity that he was not lauded before his untimely death in December 1986, which came on the eve of a renascence of Soviet film, with the election of Elem Klimov as secretary of the Cinematographer's Union, and the distribution of several long-suppressed films, including Klimov's *Come and See*, German's *Road Control*, and Romm's *Ordinary Fascism*.

Would Tarkovsky have fared better in the West? Questions of funding, profitability and commercialism in the "profligate" capitalist environment soon seem no more enticing than guarding personalized ideals under socialism. Other experience suggests that Hollywood might have welcomed his talents, but not his vision. One may gain insights from the career of Andrei Konchalovsky, whose films *Runaway Train* and *Shy People*, which were made in the United States, met with critical but not commercial success.[3]

Are *Nostalghia* and *The Sacrifice*, which Tarkovsky completed in
the West, significantly different from his other films, or are his
poetical and theoretical concerns quite constant? All Tarkovsky's
films bear his unmistakable visual signature, and the last two
accentuate philosophical concepts of importance to him throughout his career.

II. Stylistic Traits

Andrei Tarkovsky is a strong visionary. He stated in 1982: "We-
've reached a time when we must declare open warfare on mediocrity, grayness and lack of expressiveness, and make creative
inquiry a rule in the cinema."[4] Tarkovsky's films bear witness to
his philosophy, which runs counter to official ideology. His films
The Steamroller and the Violin (1960), *Ivan's Childhood* (1962), *Andrei
Rublev* (1966), *Solaris* (1972), *Mirror* (1974), *Stalker* (1979), *Nostalghia*
(1983), and *The Sacrifice* (1986), reflect Tarkovsky's highly idio-
syncratic approach to cinema. Their narrative structures are multi-
layered, interweaving as they do memory, premonition, and imaginative musings into an intricate web. Flashbacks and flashfor-
wards occur alongside newsreel clippings, as in *Mirror*; reveries
intersperse the narratives, as in *Ivan's Childhood* or *Nostalghia*. A
given character can be played by several actors or actresses, or one
person assumes more than one role, as occurs in *Mirror*. Preferring
black and white film to color for its greater expressiveness, Tarkovsky at times tints the film, to give the impression of sepia
photographs. He employs color for dazzling effect, as at the end of
Andrei Rublev, when the fifteenth century iconographer's hand-
iwork fills the screen in vibrant color, in contrast to the stark
narrative, or in *Stalker*, where the wild green grass in the Zone gives
a fleeting feeling of paradise.

The sound tracks of Tarkovsky's films pulsate with the sounds
of birds, trains, and trickling water. Tarkovsky's filmic mosaics are
multi-dimensional; sparse in dialogue, they resound with lines of

poetry, as in *Mirror*, in which the verses of Arseny Tarkovsky, the director's father, provide a correlation to the stream-of-consciousness meanderings of the autobiographical persona. In *Stalker*, poetry functions variously to reinforce the protagonist's admonitions to his impertinent companions, to summarize the wife's confession, and perhaps to verbalize what the mutant daughter is reading.

Tarkovsky is an anomaly: in an age in which speed, special effects and action-packed drama lure hordes to the screen, Tarkovsky prefers a cinematic discursiveness that lingers over separate images, which reveal a shifting sense of reality. The paintings of Leonardo, Dürer, and Breughel, and Rublev's icons gain prominence in his films. Linked thematically with the narratives, these paintings underscore the permanence of art and beauty. Quotations from Nietzsche and Shakespeare, passages from the Bible, and references to Dostoevsky appear alongside visual accolades to Mizoguchi, Kurosawa and Bergman, directors whom Tarkovsky admired. In *Nostalghia* the inspiration of Fellini and Antonioni is felt, and in *The Sacrifice* the debt to Bergman goes beyond the use of his veteran cameraman or actors (Sven Nykvist, Erland Josephson and Allan Edwall) to encompass the setting, coloring, and orchestration.

But *The Sacrifice* is Tarkovsky's film, and Bergman himself was in awe of him. He stated, "Tarkovskij is for me the greatest, the one who invented a new language, true to the nature of film, as it captures life as a reflection, life as a dream."[5] According to Roger Ebert, "He is the greatest Russian filmmaker since Sergei Eisenstein and yet he stands outside the Soviet tradition of materialism and dares to say that he is spiritual, that he can 'still be summoned by an Inner Voice.' These days, it takes more courage for an artist to admit his spiritual beliefs than to deny them."[6] This praise notwithstanding, Tarkovsky has had his detractors as well. Regarded as "elitist" in the USSR, his films also receive negative criticism in the West, where they are maligned as too long, too slow and soporific. Undoubtedly, Tarkovsky has taken an unpopular approach to cinema, as for example, his portrayal of time as non-linear, non-chronological and discontinuous and his use of ellipsis and Aesopian language, which have long been seen as a means of circumventing the inexorable censor. His minimal sets and baffling story lines may have more in common with David Lynch's *Eraserhead* or Robert Altman's *Images* than with his countryman Nikita Mikhalkov's *Unfinished Piece for Player Piano*.

III. Spiritual Quests: Forms and Functions

Tarkovsky's world view is spiritual, as he avows:

> In my latest films and maybe in my future ones, I present just one issue, I want to show that there is something in the world that is quite discernibly wrong. This is the disharmony between man's spiritual and his material existence... To me, man is essentially a spiritual being and the meaning of his life consists of developing this. If he fails to do so, society deteriorates... I try to speak of what is most important, to show things that are not necessarily linked logically. I am seeking a way of showing subjective logic — thoughts, dreams, memory.[7]

In these pronouncements Tarkovsky provides a clue to both a central theme and its depiction in his films. In them, faith openly manifests itself; at times ponderous, at times subdued, it is ever-present. Metaphysical values are paramount for Tarkovsky. Striving for the incorporeal, his spirituality paradoxically dwells not on the celestial, but on the natural, on the earthy, and it encompasses a world view based on animism. Educated man has the most trouble embracing faith, for he must divest himself of all the superfluous elements in his life, as Alexander does in *The Sacrifice*, or he must rid himself of factors he perceives as negative, as Andrei does in *Nostalghia*. Some of Tarkovsky's characters pursue transcendence and remain humane, even in a dehumanized milieu, as the Stalker does in the Zone, or as the scientists do in the space station of *Solaris*. But belief is elusive and memory deceptive, and the individual often remains skeptical.

The search for self among the shards of childhood recollections accompanies the spiritual probings of Tarkovsky's characters, who are ravaged by feelings of remorse for aborted relationships or failed ideals, as in *Solaris, Mirror, Nostalghia,* or *The Sacrifice.* They are tormented by a need to reassess their lives and to expatiate their sense of guilt toward loved ones (Kris Kelvin in *Solaris,* Domenico and Andrei in *Nostalghia*) or toward society (Andrei Rublev and the Stalker).

Cyclical patterns of imagery, most often emanating from the natural world, are relevant to the characters' spiritual considerations because they function as cinematic equivalents of their inward journeys. The recurrent sequences of fire and flames, of rain inside buildings, of rivulets of water flowing over abandoned objects, and of reeds shimmering in pools suggest visual analogues for the characters' deepest feelings, which they usually are incapable of verbalizing. These repeated images can provide a solace for their torments, as in the Zone of *Stalker,* or they can function as stabilizing factors to ward off insanity, as on the space station in *Solaris,* where sheets of paper are torn and hung to approximate the soothing sound of fluttering leaves. The ties to earth and to natural phenomena nourish the scientists in space, and Stalker, too, receives sustenance from the thriving greenery of the Zone, which supports animal life, for it provides at least a fleeting and superficial link with the good earth, as it was before the devastation.

The large segments of silence on the audio tracks delineate another trait of Tarkovsky's films. Soundless sequences alternate with refrains of classical music and folksongs (both Eastern and Western) and poetry, often in voice-over narration. These highly selective audials underscore the self-absorption of Tarkovsky's characters.

At first, it appears that *The Sacrifice* deviates from the general pattern established by the earlier films in this regard, for there seems to be an inversion of the long periods of contemplative stillness with an abundance of chattering. This is, of course, in keeping with the protagonist's vocation. Alexander is a retired actor who refers to Hamlet's "Words, words, words", to imply the ineffectiveness of speech. Moreover, he promises to God to become silent and to sacrifice his most prized possessions, if only Apocalypse can be averted. But somehow the efficacy of prayer is questioned in this film, for Otto, the postman, urges Alexander to make love to Maria, the humble servant/witch. Otto signifies the devil, or his courier, for his sinuous ways, his inexplicable fainting spell, and his ancient map of Europe suggest emblems of black magic. His birthday present is juxtaposed with that of Viktor, who gives Alexander a book of icons, representations of faith. But it is not Viktor who is a paragon of virtue or even a role model; he is conducting affairs with both Alexander's wife and his daughter. Without allegiance to either, he resolves to go to Australia.[8]

The motif of speechlessness is pervasive in Tarkovsky's films. Andrei Rublev also takes the vow of silence, but in reaction to and in defiance of the violence and horror surrounding him. The teenager at the start of *Mirror* is cured of stuttering, and it is a tribute to Tarkovsky's realism that he used footage of a genuine stutterer and a real physician, who healed him through hypnosis.[9] The boy states solemnly and clearly that he can speak, and this pronouncement echoes subtextually through the other films as the characters attempt to take stock of their lives and to assert their beliefs. But more often than not, words in themselves are inadequate, and actions must supplant them, as in *Nostalghia*, when Domenico instills the need in Andrei to carry out the candle ritual, or in *The Sacrifice*, when Otto spurs on Alexander's deeds.

The miracle of speech and the power of silence run through *Stalker* as well. Engulfed in words, Writer, an introspective man, delves deeper and deeper into his own personality, peeling away the layers of false aspirations, as he stumbles out of his intoxicated bravura, emerges resigned, and refuses to reveal his intimate desires. After all, he muses, "How can I say that I really don't want what I don't want?" Professor, the pragmatic man, who brings sandwiches and a thermos into the Zone, and finds a bomb to blow it up, is much more silent. In his own way he is as cynical as the Writer; he feels that the Room must cease to exist, for it is inevitable that some group will put it to evil use.

The children in Tarkovsky's films are generally quiet and pensive. Ivan, in the dream sequences, is filled with love and wonder at the natural world, but as a scout he does not mince words and commands authority and respect. Stalker's child, who is lame and mute, has a quietude about her which suggests a spiritual link with God. The child in *Nostalghia* patiently listens to Andrei's recitation of a poem in Russian and to his drunken harangue about the numbers of shoes Italians buy.

Domenico's son asks his father if this is the end of the world, when he and his mother are rescued after seven years of captivity. Gossen or "Little Man," Alexander's son in *The Sacrifice*, who is recovering from a throat operation and is forbidden to speak, serenely listens to his father's rambling anecdotes, absorbing all the morals he presents. The following morning, Little Man initiates the ritual of watering the Japanese tree planted the day before. He speaks for the first time in the film, echoing his father, "In the Beginning was the Word. Why, Daddy?" The values of father are passed down to son in this film, for Gossen (with Otto's help) has made Alexander a diminutive replica of the house for a birthday present. Prescient of the impending conflagration, he reserves a small vestige of one of his father's most beloved possessions. The children in these films display a sagacity beyond their years.

They do not resort to their elders' babble, and when they do speak, it is gravely and intelligently.

IV. *Stalker*: Memories of Future Anguish

Tarkovsky's 1979 film *Stalker* seems uncharacteristically linear at first: a paid guide, at great risk to himself, takes Writer and Professor into the Zone, a restricted, contaminated area of an unnamed country beyond the border. Inside, there is purported to be a Room in which one's most secret wishes are granted. All three men leave the Zone without having entered the Room, and Stalker doubts that he will return. Such oversimplification, of course, not only distorts the narrative, but denies the medium of film. *Stalker* is a remarkable visual achievement, and the haunted, tormented face of Alexander Kaidanovsky, who plays Stalker, is unforgettable in its expressiveness and power.

The choice of the non-Russian term "stalker" for the title of the film suggests both the alien aspects of the character and the allegorical facets of the text. This is of course reinforced by the generic designations of the other protagonists.[10] In English, the name "Stalker" comprises the images of stealth and haughtiness. There is a negative connotation in its association with the spread of pestilence or famine. The narrative point of view underscores its title, as the camera furtively follows the characters in their clandestine approach toward the intangible quarry.

Philosophical, religious and political subtexts permeate the film. At its center are debates between pragmatism and anti-materialism, belief and skepticism, freedom and confinement, hope and resignation. There is a suggestion that the pursuit of happiness is connected with martyrdom, and when the Writer dons a wreath of thorns, the faithful Stalker is dismayed and offended. The wife's love/hate relationship with her husband alludes to a Dostoevskian acceptance of suffering and a craving for the pleasure it gives.

In contrast to the weighty issues, the language is very colloquial. The Writer especially resorts to slang and coarse expressions. His speech befits his questioning, scoffing, and at times blasphemous attitude toward what he interprets to be the platitudes or falsehoods of his companions. The timbre of the voices is quite similar, and often the speaker cannot readily be determined in the dusky shadows, which are so pervasive. This leads to confused identity, which is abetted by the bald or close-cropped heads of the men and their similar dark clothing.[11]

As the film opens, credits are run in color over a monotone scene of a stark and dismal bar, with a single patron drinking coffee. Cacophonous music fills the soundtrack, and a written text identifies the Zone as an area in which a meteorite fell or which marked a visitation from outer space. The viewer is led through a barren, dilapidated room to the bed where a man, woman and child are lying. Slowly, slowly the camera tracks the bed and the sleepers' faces and follows the man as he gets up. The sense of mystery increases with the duration of the shots, which are unedited and last a long time, much longer than in other feature films. The uncanny atmosphere is heightened by the nearly silent audio track: only the quiet, inherent sounds of the setting infringe upon it: a passing train, glasses clinking on the table.

The stillness is shattered by the wife's hysterical outburst when she realizes that her husband is going into the Zone again. She entreats him not to leave, for if he is imprisoned once more their sickly daughter might die. "I am imprisoned everywhere," he responds tersely, and his demeanor, clothing and haircut attest to his recent convict status. The wife's attitude is reversed at the end of the film, as she soothes the trembling, emotionally drained man by saying, "I'll go with you to the Zone," to which her husband retorts, "You can't. What if you fail, too?" Even though Stalker feels he has faltered in his mission, the film does not end on a note of despair.

In the final sequences, the wife acknowledges him as a holy fool, or *blazhennyj*, which designates a feeble-minded individual who frequently has physical defects as well. In Russian tradition, such persons often are portrayed as spiritual leaders or mystics who fight against the established mores of a society which conceals corruption and duplicity. They function as the conscience of the people. Blazhennye or *jurodivye*, God's fools, seek out evil and disclose it. Only after iniquity has been unveiled can it be combatted.

The handcar ride into the Zone bombards the viewer with conflicting sensations. The monotonous terrain and the slow, measured clanking of the wheels have a lulling effect, which in turn is dispelled by the men's disquieting, backward glances. The characters' actions increase the sense of dread in the audience. Viewed from the back or in profile, the men are silent, hunted.

When they reach the Zone, Stalker exclaims, "Well, we're home now." He falls face down into the lush, long grass, renewing his bonds with Nature in a ritualistic kissing of the earth. But its greenery is deceptive, for the flowers which grow there have no fragrance. Objects, such as a bombed-out car, with its dead occupants unaffected by putrefaction, stand as stalwart monuments to the mysterious properties of the area.

The spiritual quest is significant in *Stalker*, but the guide's role as seer is undermined by his fear of the Zone's powers and its perils. Anxious and cowering, he appears to take extraordinary measures to avoid its hazards, but the other two men clearly disobey his instructions and are not punished, as Stalker forewarns. He has few attributes of leadership, and he never goes first, but sends one of the others to test the ground. Although verbally he continually professes belief in the Zone's powers, his facial expressions, gestures and demeanor bespeak apprehension, anxiety, and terror. His superstitious behavioral rituals are dogmatic, but the Zone defies even these attempts to master it. It eludes him once again, and consequently his own faith is shaken.

Stalker's assertions reach a feverish pitch and culminate in a passionate rendition of Arseny Tarkovsky's poem "Vot i leto proshlo" (Now summer is gone). The verse expresses man's dissatisfaction with intangibles such as fortune, luck and security; these are not enough to bring happiness to the poetic persona. The poem suggests that all desires are illusory, for what could be more welcome than warm sunshine, a five-petalled leaf, or a day washed clean as glass? Moreover, it directly relates to the men's aim for going into the Zone. The poet implies that if all the benefits of nature are not enough for man, then he will never be happy.[12]

This fervent feeling is echoed by the faint strains of Ravel's "Bolero", which is heard over the rumbling of a train which marks the scene change to the other side of the Zone. Even though only a few bars of "Bolero" are heard, the steady rhythm of the musical piece, which increases in intensity and volume up to the tempestuous climax, correlates well with the shrilly escalating sounds of the approaching train.

Because Stalker can choose whom he will accompany into the Zone, the Writer feels he exploits human misery in determining who is to live and who shall die. Stalker plaintively denies that guides can enter the Zone with mercenary motives. He cites the tale of Porcupine, who ostensibly wished for one thing, but received another. His subconscious desire for wealth overwhelmed his request for forgiveness for his brother's death.

Bunker Number 4, where the Room is located, is a bombed-out dump, with pools of radioactive waste and undulations of the ground which suggest quicksand. It is hardly a haven for weary travelers or a sanctuary for pilgrims. At its threshold the men scrutinize their reasons for entering and decide against it. All three of them return from the Zone with greater cognizance of their personal needs, passions, and limitations.

Although his wife believes that their daughter was born lame because of Stalker's occupation, which damaged his genes by the radioactive waste, she does not regret marrying him, even though her life with him has not been easy. "It would be worse if there were no sorrow, then there would be no happiness either, there would be no hope," she concludes.

After their return to the bleak wasteland on this side of the Zone, Stalker carries Monkey (Martyshka), the daughter, on his shoulders past a factory emitting foul smoke, but the trio pays no attention to its poisonous fumes. The daughter seems almost an extension of Stalker in this scene. The love of the parents for their mutant child is evident in their tender gestures toward her. And it is love in the final analysis which saves Stalker from self-abnegation.

At the end of the journey, Stalker returns in abject disillusionment, but the devotion and self-sacrifice of his wife restore him. Perhaps his clandestine wish was granted, a subconscious desire which he himself may not have acknowledged, namely, for his clairvoyance to be passed on to his child.

The final sequence of the film begins with the bleeding over of the soundtrack with a recitation, in the mother's voice-over narration, of Tiutchev's love poem, "Liubliu glaza tvoi, moi drug" (How I love your eyes, my friend).[13] The child puts away the book she has been reading and stares at two glasses and a jar. Slowly the glasses begin to move along the table, until one of them falls off as the muffled sounds of Beethoven's "Ode to Joy" are heard over the whistle and rumble of a train. A curious peace suffuses her face as she lays it on the edge of the table. The dog's whining reinforces the mystical aspects of this scene. The Stalker's child exhibits the gift of telekinesis, which confirms the attribute of *blazhennost'* in her as well. The audio-visual aspects of film, melding so beautifully in this scene, poignantly display Tarkovsky's masterly art of composition.

Dogs, horses and birds consistently appear in Tarkovsky's films.[14] The black dog in *Stalker* might have been a threatening wolf, for its first howl, heard off camera, is menacing to Professor and Writer in the Zone. But it moves with a playful canter, and it becomes a guardian, a companion for the men. When the wife asks if anyone wants the dog, Writer answers that he has five of them at home. The wife's happy response to the statement indicates that she recognizes a man who loves animals as good and humane. Writer returns from the Zone more at peace with himself, having achieved a modicum of self-knowledge, if not faith. The Professor, too, reassesses his need to adhere to scientific precepts. When the phone in the bunker proves to be working, he calls his chief to inform him that he has found the bomb and will use it, even though he is warned that this will ruin his career as a scientist. Although he has stood up to his supervisor's authority, he nevertheless fails to detonate the bomb.

Loosely based on Arkady and Boris Strugatsky's science fiction novel, *Roadside Picnic*, which is set in Canada, the film departs from the printed work in several telling ways. The Zone is entered in the book for the sake of analytical experiments, and scientists strive to obtain samples from within. Tarkovsky shifts the emphasis from the retrieval of material objects to a philosophical journey of self-discovery. He himself said that in his film, "the Zone is not a territory, but on the contrary, a trial, which one either passes or fails. Everything depends on self-dignity, on how far one is able to distinguish between the important and the transitory."[15]

The deletion of humor from the script of *Stalker* is in keeping with its allegorical nature, which is underscored by the ubiquitous designations for the characters. The film can be interpreted as a political fable of imprisonment, as a religious parable of the quest for a miracle, as a secular search for happiness, as a family drama of the near collapse of a marriage. As with any allegory, the readings are multifold.

V. *Nostalghia*: Rituals and Icons

Nostalghia was a joint Soviet and Italian venture, but about 90% of the film was shot in Italy. It continues an exploration of issues raised in Tarkovsky's earlier films, such as the search for faith, unfulfilled aspirations, problems of male/female relationships, nostalgia for home, country, and family, (which combines a desire to return physically to a house as well as spiritually to *rodina* and maritally or sexually to one's wife.) The characters, too, do not differ markedly from the others who are driven by a quest.

Ostensibly researching the life of Sosnovsky, an 18th century Russian composer who was sent to Italy, Andrei Gorchakov is fed up with the beautiful vistas of the Italian countryside, and says he does not want anything else just for himself. Nervous, moody, and detached, he is filled with longing for his homeland. He has visions of his wife and family and becomes more and more self-absorbed as the film progresses. Only one desire gives purpose to his life, and that is to carry a lighted candle across the pool of St. Catherine of Siena, at the urging of Domenico, a local madman who kept his family imprisoned for seven years because he feared the imminent end of the world. His preoccupation with Domenico leads to an identification with him. An eerie dream-like scene in a deserted street, in which Andrei reaches out to close the mirrored door of a wardrobe and his hand is met on the other side by that of

Domenico, confirms the *doppelgänger* motif. After Domenico, unknown to Andrei, commits self-immolation in Rome, Andrei succeeds (but only on the third try) in his ritual expiation for the deeds of the madman, who himself had been prevented from carrying it out.

The anguish of the madman is pitiable and touching, but that of Andrei is not. Andrei feels that culture cannot be understood by people of other countries, and he advises Eugenia to throw away the book of Arseny Tarkovsky's poems that she is reading in translation. Because Andrei's opinions are narrow and spiteful, the viewer cannot sympathize with him. The way he is presented on the screen enforces this aversion. Frequently, Andrei is viewed from the back or in profile, and even upside down (as are Ivan and the Stalker). This positioning obscures facial expressions and conceals emotions, in a reversal of the Bergmanesque full-face closeups which Bruce Kawin has called "Mindscreen".[16] "People don't like to reveal their innermost thoughts," Stalker says, and Tarkovsky's positioning of his characters enables them to retain the austere privacy of their opinions and feelings. Andrei's demeanor is matched by his attire: waking or sleeping, he is dressed in an overcoat, protected from external sensations in its cocoon-like covering. He is another Chekhovian "man in a shell."

Eugenia is much more sensitive. She's undoubtedly attracted to Andrei and is frustrated in his lack of interest in her sexuality. At one point Andrei tells her how pretty she looks, but the glimmer of hope in her eyes fades as he continues talking about Domenico. She uses her charms to arouse him, both in provocative gestures and in revealing dress, but to no avail. Her frenzied baring of her breast is a cry for love, certainly it is enacted to elicit a response from him, but he just says, "s uma soshla" (she's crazy) and leaves. She follows him into the hall and accosts him with the fact that he should go back to the wife he almost betrayed. After he whirls around and grabs her, he ends up with a bloody nose.

Clearly, the idea of an extra-marital affair is on Andrei's mind, since he dreams not only of his *dacha*, dog, and pregnant wife,

Maria, but also of Eugenia. In an annunciation of astounding radiance, Eugenia is approached by Maria, who gently smooths back the wisps of hair around her face and whispers in her ear.[17] Early on in the film, the sacristan in the chapel told Eugenia that woman is here to bear children and to raise them with patience and suffering. When he inquires if she intends to ask for children or to be spared them, Eugenia answers that she is just looking. Her detached, intellectual stance prevents her from kneeling, and, indirectly, it hinders her belief as well. She asks the sacristan why women have more faith, and when he reverses the question, she answers that she has never understood these things. Apparently, an intellectual approach to faith leads nowhere. But her lack of devotion does not prevent the mysterious dispersion of birds out of the statue of the Madonna heavy with child.

When she returns to Rome, Eugenia dresses more sedately. Her demeanor is more reserved. Her hair is up, as it is in the dream, and she is wearing a more traditional, business-like suit, rather than the flowing, voluminous garment she had on in Bagno Vignoni. When she calls Andrei about Domenico, Eugenia makes a point of informing him about her friend, Vittorio, with whom she is going away to India. Silent and somber, Vittorio appears as unloving, or at least as unresponsive as Andrei.

Any discussion of Tarkovsky's films which ignores the visuals has the possibility of striking false, because the pictures, stills, and sets are so beautifully composed. Tarkovsky would shudder if one said "contrived", since he speaks against directors who try exceedingly hard to elicit lyricism and emotion.[18] Nevertheless, the final shot in *Nostalghia*, of the *dacha* embedded within the walls of a ruined cathedral is precisely so memorable because it is arranged. In this dream-like vision, alien cultures can unite, and there can be a peaceful resolution of all the soul-searching and anguish. As snow begins to fall, tranquillity descends. The length of the shot emphasizes the permanence of the vision; it certainly is an unforgettable image in film.

VI. Conclusion

Tarkovsky's philosophical and artistic concerns have remained constant in emigration, as have his major themes and their exposition. But the underlying sexuality of the female characters has become more pronounced, as evidenced by Eugenia in *Nostalghia*. In *The Sacrifice*, Adelaide's hysterical outburst takes the form of orgiastic abandonment in the face of doom.

Doubting, searching, reminiscing, Tarkovsky's characters examine themselves and their motives for action and achieve a wary equilibrium, more often than not on unstable ground. A quest for the spiritual exhausts them. Stalker asks, "What do you have against praying?" Alexander prays, but he reinforces his vow to God by coupling with a witch. Which of the two, then, was responsible for averting Apocalypse? Faith carries with it the potentiality of miracles, and Tarkovsky's last three films certainly speak to this potential, but the viewer has to be mesmerized by the encomium as much as the supplicant. In *The Sacrifice*, the way is paved for miracles with the anecdote of the photograph of the mother in contemporary dress and her dead son seen alive in uniform. The Christian ritual washing of hands in the film combines with pagan passion to invert Biblical rites and lend an aura of spirituality not bounded by conventional doctrine.

Notwithstanding the power of the message, it is the visual icons which form an indelible memory of Tarkovsky's films, and these have improved with age, like fine wine.

ENDNOTES

1. See Herbert Marshall, "Andrei Tarkovsky's *Mirror*," *Sight & Sound*, Vol. 45, No. 2, Spring 1976.

2. The critical literature on Tarkovsky is growing, and the following merit special

attention: Mark Le Fanu, *The Cinema of Andrei Tarkovsky,* (BFI Publishers, London, 1987); Lee Atwell, *"Solaris:* A Soviet Science Fiction Masterpiece," *The Film Journal,* vol. 2, No. 3, issue 6, 22-25; Ian Christie, "Against Interpretation: An Interview with Andrei Tarkovsky," *Framework,* 14, Spring, 1981, 48-49; Michael Dempsey, "Lost Harmony" Tarkovsky's *Mirror* and *The Stalker," Film Quarterly,* vol. XXXV/I, Fall, 1981, 12-17; Viktor Dyomin, "Andrei Tarkovsky," *Soviet Film,* 3, 1983, 18-19, 26. Peter Green, "The Nostalgia of *The Stalker," Sight & Sound,* vol. 54, No. 1, Winter 1984/85, 50-54; Jay Leyda, *Kino: A History of the Russian and Soviet Film,* 3rd ed. (Princeton, NJ: Princeton University Press, 1983); Albert Leong, "Socialist Realism in Tarkovsky's *Andrei Rublev," Studies in Comparative Communism,* vol. XVII, Nos. 3 & 4 Fall/Winter, 1984, 227-233; Mira Liehm and Antonin J. Liehm, *The Most Important Art: Eastern European Film after 1945.* (Berkeley, CA: University of California Press, 1977); Herbert Marshall, "Andrei Tarkovsky's *Mirror," Sight & Sound,* Vol. 45, No. 2, Spring 1976 and *Masters of the Soviet Cinema — Crippled Creative Biographies.* (London: Routledge and Kegan Paul, 1983); Ivor Montague, "Man and Experience: Tarkovsky's World," *Sight & Sound,* Vol. 42, No. 2, 1973, 89-93; Maria Ratschewa, "The Messianic Power of Pictures: The Films of Andrei Tarkovsky," *Cinéaste,* vol. 13, No. 1, 1983, 27-29; Andrei Tarkovsky, "Between Two Worlds," (Introduction by J. Hoberman), *American Film,* vol. 9, November, 1983, No. 14, 75-77 and *Sculpting in Time: Reflections on the Cinema.* (London: Bodley Head, 1986); Jeanne Vronskaya, *Young Soviet Film Makers.* (London: Allen and Unwin, 1972); V.N. Zhdan, ed., *Kino Segodnja.* (Moscow: Izdatelstvo Iskusstvo, 1971).

3. Konchalovsky's captivating films certainly have more accessibility than those of Tarkovsky, since they have well-developed narratives, and enough sex and violence to entice the jaded American movie audience. Spectacular camera work, fine acting, and a sense of place (attributes of *Runaway Train* and *Shy People*) are of less concern to the predominantly young American audiences.

4. Interview by Tony Mitchell, *Sight & Sound,* Winter, 1982-3, pp. 54-56.

5. Ingmar Bergman, Swedish Film Institute pamphlet, *The Sacrifice,* unpaginated.

6. Roger Ebert, New York Films release, *The Sacrifice,* Fall 1986, unpaginated.

7. *The Economist,* July 14, 1984, p. 88.

8. Suggestive at first of a vacillating and ineffectual Chekhovian character, Viktor demonstrates more Dostoevskian aspects in his shocking resolve to go to Australia. He carries a revolver in his doctor's bag, and there is the suggestion that he is planning to kill himself, in the manner of another degenerate womanizer, Svidrigailov, for whom suicide was synonymous with "going to America." Disgusted with Alexander's family, he reproaches them in a scene replete with hatred and denigration.

9. In the name of realism, Tarkovsky set fire to a cow when he was filming *Andrei Rublev,* and when the film of the burning house in *The Sacrifice* was damaged, Tarkovsky had the house built anew and the scene reshot.

10. Of interest is the fact that no one has a typical name in the film. The wife is not addressed by name, the daughter only by nickname, "Martyshka" (Monkey). Writer cannot remember the name of the woman who brings him to the bar, and she

does not tell him, since she is overwhelmed by being face to face with a real "Stalker." Writer refers to Stalker as Big Snake to suggest an insidious tempter. Stalker makes a point of not introducing the men to each other and refers to the scientist as Professor. He also tells the tale of "Dikobraz" (Porcupine), who wished for one thing and had a more secret desire granted.

11. The Professor seems to retain his identity longest, for he is much taller than the other two, and his hat is a distinguishing characteristic, but when it falls off, baring him of protective covering, he too begins his journey of self-discovery.

12. The original and a translation of the poem are provided in Andrey Tarkovsky, *Sculpting in Time, Reflections on the Cinema.* Translated by Kitty Hunter-Blair. Alfred A. Knopf, New York, 1987, pp. 191 and 252.

13. *Sculpting in Time.*, pp. 197 and 253.

14. In *The Sacrifice* chickens appear in the house and are shooed away by Marta, who is naked. Sheep cross in front of Maria's house when Alexander goes there at Otto's bidding. These animals, which are used in divination and necromancy, accentuate the pagan ritualistic aspects of Alexander's sacrifice.

15. As cited in Ratschewa, p. 29.

16. Tarkovsky's preference for back, side or upside-down shots of his characters is not limited to Andrei Gorchakov or to this film. His camera angles are innovative and function to delineate the characters in a visually metaphoric manner.

17. Mark Le Fanu mistakenly identifies her as the "annunciatory angel chastely kissing his wife on the cheek.", p. 117.

18. For example, he gives a negative opinion of Larissa Shepitko's film, *Ascent*, in *Sculpting in Time*, p. 152.

"Hideousness and Beauty":

A Reading of Tarkovsky's *The Sacrifice*

Jim Leach
Brock University

A ndrei Tarkovsky made his last two films outside Russia. The effect of working in foreign contexts must have been of great significance for a director who stressed the importance of "the theme of roots" in his previous films.[1] The experience of exile is central to *Nostalghia* (1983) which was made in Italy and which, according to the director, is concerned with "the impossibility of importing or exporting culture, of appropriating another people's culture".[2] The experience of Italy is here filtered through the consciousness of the Russian protagonist; in *The Sacrifice* (1986), made in Sweden, the central consciousness belongs to a native Swede and his spiritual crisis is presented in terms which clearly relate the film to the Swedish cultural tradition, most notably to the work of Strindberg and Bergman. Yet, for Tarkovsky, exile is not just a matter of a person's "remoteness from his country" but also represents "a global yearning for the wholeness of existence" (204). In this sense, all his films deal with the experience of exile, and *The Sacrifice* is no exception.

Tarkovsky has pointed out that his Russian roots link him to "those traditions in Russian culture which have their beginnings in the work of Dostoevsky" but whose "development in modern Russia is patently incomplete" (193). The frustration and dislocation of the internal exile, cut off from the cultural tradition with which he identifies himself, underlies Tarkovsky's description of *Andrei Rublev* (1966) as a film dealing with "the impossibility of creating when the desires and hopes of the people and the aspiration of the artist to express his soul and his character are neglected".[3] However, as Tarkovsky makes abundantly clear in *Sculpting in Time*, his "reflections on the cinema" which appeared in the same year as *The Sacrifice*, the gap between artist and audience in the absence of a common cultural tradition is the characteristic experience of the materialistic modern world.

The disorientation experienced by the exile can also be related to the "strangeness" which is part of the spectator's experience of Tarkovsky's films. Tarkovsky has rejected allegorical interpretations of his films, insisting that the images "mean nothing more than the images which they are".[4] Yet the quest for transcendent meaning is central to Tarkovsky's theory of art:

> The artistic image is always a metonym, where one thing is substituted for another, the smaller for the greater. To tell of what is living, the artist uses something dead; to speak of the infinite, he shows the finite. (38)

Tarkovsky defines art as "a means of assimilating the world" but, in the face of the human desire to "become one with" an ideal that lies outside the self, art must also bear witness to "the unattainability of that becoming one, the inadequacy of his own 'I'" which is "the perpetual source of man's dissatisfaction and pain" (37). The artist can only offer images that hint at the possibility of a spiritual "home" which neither artist nor spectator can see.[5]

Tarkovsky's films thus place the spectator in the position of the exile. The activity of the camera during the long takes, one of the hallmarks of Tarkovsky's style, has been effectively described by Marcel Jean: "Tarkovsky's camera searches, scrutinizes, wanders, but never succeeds in finding the detail which will give a meaning to the whole".[6] The search involves the spectator in the quest for meaning which motivates the central characters, while the refusal of a single symbolic or allegorical meaning activates the "nostalgia" for a "lost harmony" which Michael Dempsey has seen as central to Tarkovsky's vision.[7] Whether this harmony ever actually existed or is a purely imaginary construct, whether the search for it offers the possibility of a solution to the problems of the contemporary world or is simply a delusion which only serves to intensify these problems, these are questions which the films cannot answer but which the spectator must deal with on the basis of the experience of each film.

In the case of *The Sacrifice*, these questions centre on the response to Alexander's final sacrificial act, the burning down of his house as an offering to God who has miraculously caused the threat of nuclear war to disappear. Peter Green describes this sacrifice as "the liberating act of a man . . .who sees an opportunity of becoming an instrument of human redemption" and suggests that any difficulties we may have in dealing with the implications of his actions stem from our conditioning by the "modern world" in which "Alexander's readiness to sacrifice seems something of an anachronism".[8] This interpretation is supported by Tarkovsky who writes that:

> In the face of disaster on that global scale, the one issue that has to be raised, it seems to me, is the question of man's personal responsibility, and his willingness for sacrifice, without which he ceases to be a spiritual being in any real sense. (220)

Mark Le Fanu, however, stresses the effect of Alexander's "sacrifice" on his family, whose home is burned down without their knowledge or consent.[9] The point is that any spiritual significance that the sacrifice may have, as well as its relationship to the ending of the nuclear threat, cannot be visibly represented, while the physical and mental suffering caused by Alexander's actions is clearly visible (and is, in fact, foregrounded in the high-angle long take in which the family struggle through the puddles in the barren landscape as they confront the burning building and try to cope with Alexander's apparently mad behaviour).[10]

This problem of representation is central to Tarkovsky's treatment of art in *The Sacrifice*. He rejected theories of representation, like Eisenstein's montage theory and the structuralist approach, which treat cinema as a "system of signs" rather than a "direct, emotional, sensuous response" to the wholeness of the natural world (176). Yet the problem of representing this wholeness is heightened by the fragmentation which is an inescapable effect of modern cultural experience. Tarkovsky suggests that modern artists do not want to "make any sacrifice" so that their art has lost contact with a "higher and communal idea", and while his films demonstrate the need for an art which will have communal meaning, the "difficulties" in arriving at a common understanding of the meaning of these films stress the gap between this ideal and the actual experience of artist and spectator (38). *Sculpting in Time* suggests that this gap may be built into the cinematic apparatus, the product of modern technology, which has made possible an art form capable of a fuller representation of the natural world than any previous medium but which has been heavily implicated in the establishment of the "rhythms of modern life".[11] This ambivalence about cinema's relation to more traditional systems of representation is basic to the viewing experience offered by *The Sacrifice*.

As in many of his earlier films, Tarkovsky draws attention to this problem by providing allusions to other, more stable, systems of representation which testify to the possibility of the artwork as embodiment of a rich communal (and spiritual) experience. These allusions begin in the very first shot which sets up the tension between art and life (and the implication of the cinematic apparatus in its representation). As the credits appear, we are confronted with a detail from the centre of Leonardo da Vinci's *Adoration of the Kings* in which Christ's hand reaches out to the "offering" made by one of the kings. Bach's *St. Matthew Passion* is heard on the soundtrack but, shortly before the end of the credits, the sounds of seagulls are superimposed. The music ends and is replaced by the sound of waves breaking. After the final credit, the camera slowly moves up the tree in the painting and comes to rest on the leaves at the top. The replacement of the music by natural sounds and the ability of the camera to explore within the painting assert the power of the cinematic apparatus but also suggest the way in which this film will use its power to investigate problems of illusion and representation which are central to the relationship between art and life (and the film will never quite allow us to forget that this problematic includes the apparatus and, by extension, ourselves as spectators).

The image of the painted leaves is followed by a shot of Alexander planting a large branch in the ground beside the sea (accounting for the sounds in the last shot). His attempt to create a living tree out of a dead branch obviously connects to the tree in Leonardo's painting, while his attempt to communicate his aim to his son (silent, as we later discover, because of a throat operation) links the boy to the Christ child in the painting. Alexander introduces the ideas of faith (he tells a fable about a monk who succeeded in getting a branch to blossom), art and nature (he compares the planted branch to Japanese ikebana), and the need for system (the monk's achievement proves, he argues, that "a system, a method, has its virtues").

Otto, the mailman who arrives on his bicycle during this extremely long sequence-shot, describes Alexander as a journalist and critic who lectures on aesthetics at the university. In the following sequence, we learn that Alexander was once an actor, and he recounts how he decided to leave the stage because he could no longer accept the actor's need to "dissolve" his own identity in that of his character. He finds the whole process "sinful, feminine and weak"; Adelaide, his wife, comments on his equation of "feminine" and "sinful" and suggests that he quit simply to spite her. This moment in the film requires an extremely complex response. On the one hand, Alexander has sacrificed the material success which his acting had brought him; on the other, his unwillingness to sacrifice himself to the demands of the role suggests that Alexander is related to the modern artist described in *Sculpting in Time*. And then there is the question of the effect of his decision on Adelaide, who claims that he seduced her with his acting, lured her from

London, and then abandoned her.

The ambiguous implications of Alexander's renunciation of acting can also be related to his spiritual state. He has earlier described his relationship with God as "non-existent", and the whole film can be seen as a search for aesthetic and spiritual meaning which, in the modern context, may lead to madness rather than illumination. Yet its immediate context in the film also requires that we relate this discussion of acting to the concern with art and representation. The sequence has begun with a striking effect which foregrounds the gap between contemporary and traditional values as well as the role of the cinema in presenting this gap to us. At the end of the previous sequence, Alexander has collapsed, and there follows the first of the "visions" (shot in black-and-white) in which the camera moves above an overturned car across a deserted and desolate street, strewn with garbage, and comes to rest on an image of high-rise buildings reflected in glass. The image fades to darkness, and the next shot shows a hand turning over the pages of a book on icons. The beauty, colour and flatness of the icons contrast with the lack of colour and fragmented space of the previous shot and with the succeeding sequence in Alexander's house in which colour has been virtually eliminated and in which the deep-space of the rooms is often emphasized.

As the hand turns the pages of the book, Alexander's voice is heard speaking of the refinement, wisdom and spirituality of the icons. He refers to their "childish innocence" and feels that they are "like a prayer". Just as he says, "and all this has been lost. . .", there is a cut to a long-shot of a man standing at the window on the other side of a long room. Alexander finishes his sentence, — ". . .and we can't even pray any longer", and Viktor, the family doctor and friend, turns away from the window complaining that he has "lost control" of his day. Alexander then enters with the icon book, thanks Viktor for the present, and takes his place at the window. The simple contrast between lost harmony and modern anxiety is complicated by the fact that it is Viktor, the scientist, who has given Alexander the book of beautiful images achieved in the past, while his experience of these images cannot prevent Alexander from taking Viktor's place at the window.

The contemplation of the icons leads into Alexander's account of his decision to stop acting. As the celebration of his birthday continues, the problem of art and representation is developed in three incidents, all associated with Otto. The attempt to "frame" experience within the confines of art is raised by the seventeenth-century map of the world which Otto gives to Alexander as a birthday present. The map is admired for its aesthetic qualities, but it also represents how people saw the world at that time. The implication is that the world-view created a way of seeing that could still "frame" experience aesthetically. This has little to do with "truth", but Alexander suspects that modern maps have nothing to do with truth either. The gift also raises the question of the relationship of the material and the spiritual in art, since Otto insists that the map is an "original" and that all gifts must involve a "sacrifice" on the part of the giver. The map is thus contrasted with the icons and the Leonardo *Adoration* (shortly to be seen in Alexander's room) which are reproductions. Alexander obviously could not afford the originals, but ironically the inexpensive reproductions are made possible only by modern technology and are, in any case, indistinguishable from originals as they are reproduced by Tarkovsky's camera.

The relationship of the traditional and the modern, the spiritual and the material, also appears in Otto's story of the photograph of a woman that, when developed, included the image of her long-dead son. This unexplained phenomenon suggests that even the indexicality of photography, deriving from a technological base which it shares with cinema, cannot exclude the irrational world which art has traditionally explored. Otto's collection of unexplained phenomena is in itself an attempt to contain the unknown (he has 284 examples) and can be related to Alexander's belief in the possibilities of developing a system as well as to Tarkovsky's view of the film director as a "collector" of the "myriad well-loved details. . . which constitute life" (140). Otto's description of his collection prepares for the uncertainty which will build up around Alexander's later experiences, but it cannot provide the sense of harmonious order which traditional forms of art have been felt to provide.

Otto's third intervention is perhaps the most disturbing. The Leonardo *Adoration* is shot at an angle so that the leaves of a tree outside are reflected in the glass (the camera giving life to the painted image of the tree on which it lingered in the first shot). Otto asks Alexander what the "sinister" picture is and, when he is told, declares that he has always been terrified of Leonardo. The cause of Otto's terror is not identified. It may have to do with what Peter Green has called the "fearful aspects" of the painting: "the awe-filled countenances of the shepherds in the foreground, and . . . the animated scenes in the background and the wild, primeval character of the horses."[12] It could also have to do with the complex composition of the Leonardo and its use of perspective in comparison with the two-dimensional simplicity of the icons. Perhaps Renaissance systems of representation which map three-dimensional on to two-dimensional space, and which some theorists have seen as built into the cinematic apparatus, already contain the seeds of thee dislocation of modern art? Tarkovsky, in fact, writes of his admiration for Carpaccio, whose painting "solves the moral problems which beset people of the Renaissance, dazzled as they were by a reality filled with objects, with people, with matter" (49) and relates the spiritual content of Russian icons to their "denial of Renaissance perspective" (82). In any case, Otto's response makes clear that any spiritual experience expressed in a work of art is dependent on the needs and fears of the spectator.[13]

The role of the spectator also needs to be taken into account in dealing with Alexander's presentation of his reasons for giving up acting. As he tries to explain the feelings which led to his decision, we remain aware that this statement is being made by an actor playing the role of Alexander.[14] The foregrounding of the problem of "acting" complicates our response to such later developments as Otto's sudden, unexplained collapse and Adelaide's hysterical outburst after the news that nuclear war is imminent. Both of these actions are presented in long shot, the detached viewpoint under-lining the awkwardness of the first and the embarrassment of the second. The problem of "acting" is not just a matter of Alexander's past, before he became a lecturer in aesthetics, but also of our aesthetic engagement with Tarkovsky's film.

The instability of the representational systems at work in the film contributes to our difficulty in evaluating the status of the nuclear threat and thus the value of Alexander's sacrifice. The sequence in which the outbreak of war is introduced begins with the conversa-tion between Otto and Alexander in front of the reproduction of the *Adoration*. After Otto has left, Alexander turns toward the camera, a strange noise (perhaps a foghorn) which has been heard during the last few shots modulates into Japanese music while, at the same time, a male voice is heard speaking of the need for a nation-wide effort in the face of an emergency.[15] The absence of non-diegetic music from the film, except for the beginning and end, calls attention to the Japanese music which apparently underscores Alexander's pensive mood, but which is rendered diagetic when he goes to a cupboard containing audio equipment (with needles indicating volume levels) and turns the music off. He then finds the others in front of the television, which is identified as the source of the official voice. The initial hesitation over the diegetic status of the music and the voice foregrounds technology as a means of providing access to traditional art (as with the Leonardo reproduc-tion) and as a source of modern anxiety, while it also prepares for the dream-like quality of the subsequent action in which Alexander vows to give up everything if God will avert the impending dis-aster and (at Otto's behest) sleeps with Maria who, as a witch, can use her powers to make things right.

When he awakes on his couch after his encounter with Maria, the Japanese music is again playing and seems to signal, along with the light from a table lamp, the restoration of power and thus the success of his dealings with the "witch"— except that we remem-ber that he earlier switched the machine off. Since we have not seen Alexander return from Maria's house, there is a strong sense that he is waking from a dream, but it is extremely difficult to pin down where the dream began. The return of the music might suggest that the shot of Alexander turning it off was included in the dream, but another "explanation" is given when his daughter casually mentions that she had turned it on again while he was sleeping. This prosaic explanation forces us to question the status of the inexplicable actions we have just witnessed and thus to question the necessity for Alexander to fulfil his vow by burning down his house. Yet it cannot completely erase the uncertainty caused by the presence of the music and thus we cannot completely deny our participation in Alexander's "madness".

The crisis of representation in the film draws us into the world of the "fantastic" where natural explanations seem insufficient but cannot be ruled out.[16] In the opening sequence, Alexander has told his son that "there is no such thing as death, only the fear of death". The hesitation over whether the nuclear threat is real or, wholly or partially, dreamed suggests that there is also no such thing as nuclear war, only the fear of nuclear war. The question of whether the signs of nuclear war that lead to Alexander's sacrifice are real or imagined becomes irrelevant; the film explores the psychic consequences of living (as we all do) in a world under the constant threat of universal catastrophe. Yet this threat is presented as an intensification of the fear of death with which art has traditionally helped people come to terms. In fact, in Tarkovsky's original conception, the threat was to have come from cancer rather than nuclear war.[17] In making *The Sacrifice*, Tarkovsky, already suffering from the cancer that would shortly kill him, created a film which testifies to his belief that "hideousness and beauty are contained within each other", but which also questions whether the pressures of the modern world can provide the basis for an art which will resolve this "prodigious paradox" by producing "that wholeness in which harmony and tension are unified" (38). The ultimate paradox, however, is that Tarkovsky, dying, in exile, and alienated from a culture whose technology has apparently divorced it from the traditional values of art and nature, has achieved, working in the technological art of film, a rich and complex work which succeeds in becoming the aesthetic whole which its own discourse on representation has suggested may no longer be possible.

ENDNOTES

1. Andrey Tarkovsky, *Sculpting in Time: Reflections on the Cinema*, trans. Kitty Hunter-Blair (London: The Bodley Head, 1986), p. 193; all quotations from Tarkovsky are taken from this source, unless otherwise noted, and will be indicated by page references in the text.

2. Tony Mitchell, 'Tarkovsky in Italy', *Sight and Sound*, Winter 1982/83, 54.

3. Tarkovsky, quoted in Tony Mitchell, 'Andrei Tarkovsky and *Nostalghia*', *Film Criticism*, vol. 8, no. 3, Spring 1984, 3.

4. Ian Christie, 'Against Interpretation: An Interview with Andrei Tarkovsky', *Framework*, 14, 1981, 49.

5. The significance of the idea of "home" in Tarkovsky's films has been explored by Peter Green in 'The Nostalgia of the Stalker', *Sight and Sound*, Winter 1984/85, 50-2.

6. Marcel Jean, 'Andrei Tarkovsky' Le plan incandescent', *Sequences*, 127, December 1986, 36 (my translation).

7. Michael Dempsey, 'Lost Harmony: Tarkovsky's *The Mirror* and *The Stalker*', *Film Quarterly*, Fall 1981, 13.

8. Peter Green, 'Apocalypse and Sacrifice', *Sight and Sound*, Spring 1987, 111, 117.

9. Mark Le Fanu, *The Cinema of Andrei Tarkovsky* (London: British Film Institute, 1987), p. 125.

10. Compare Tarkovsky's discussion of the final shot in *Nostalghia* (the Russian hut within the Italian cathedral) which may express the "division" within the protagonist or "his new wholeness in which the Tuscan hills and the Russian countryside come together indissolubly"; *Sculpting in Time*, p. 216.

11. *Sculpting in Time*, p. 83; see also the comment that "the methods by which the cinema affects audiences can be used far more easily and rapidly for their moral decomposition, for the destruction of their spiritual defences, than the means of the old, traditional art forms", p. 187.

12. Green, 'Apocalypse', 113.

13. See also Tarkovsky's comment on the portrait of a woman, attributed to Leonardo, which he used in *The Mirror* (1975): "There is something inexpressively beautiful about her and at the same time repulsive, fiendish"; *Sculpting in Time*, p.

108.

14. Perhaps the discussion of acting here needs to be related to Tarkovsky's distinction between theatre and film; whereas theatre codifies by selecting a detail to "make us aware of an entire phenomenon", film "reproduces a phenomenon in its details", *Sculpting in Time*, p. 154. Does this difference eliminate the potential irony of Alexander attempting to explain his renunciation of stage acting even while we are responding to Erland Josephson playing Alexander in Tarkovsky's film?

15. The mysterious sounds that recur on the soundtrack of *The Sacrifice* clearly relate to Tarkovsky's discussion of the "enormously rich possibilities of electronic music for cinema", *Sculpting in Time*, p. 162.

16. See Tzvetan Todorov, *The Fantastic: A Structural Approach to a Literary Genre*, trans. Richard Howard (Cleveland: Press of Case Western Reserve University, 1973). Many other aspects of Tarkovsky's style support a "fantastic" reading of *The Sacrifice*: for example, at the end of the discussion of the *Adoration*, Otto leaves, without explanation, over the balcony of Alexander's upstairs room. A ladder is later seen standing beside this balcony and Alexander twice leaves this way, but the geography of the house becomes extremely unpredictable in the last half of the film.

17. See Green, 'Apocalypse', 113-114. Tarkovsky himself points out that Bergman uses war in *Shame* (1968) as a "catalyst for the cruel, anti-human elements in people" and that Karin's illness performs the same function in *Through a Glass Darkly* (1961), *Sculpting in Time*, p.147.

A Nostalgic Vision of Tarkovsky's *Nostalgia*

Anna Makolkina
University of Toronto

I will begin this presentation on a confessional note, i.e. I am not a film critic, but a literary one. Nonetheless, an interpretation of a cinematographic text may be undertaken from a literary point of view as well. Literature or "verbal art" which appeals to all of one's senses, including the visual sense, has always been a potential cinema. Thus, I intend to approach the film as a text.

A title of any literary text has always served as the first encounter between the text and its readers. Peter Nesselroth claims that a "text is framed by its title."[1] This may be particularly valid in case of a film-title whose semiotic function is much more vital to the cinematographic text and its screen life. A successful title may prolong it, while an inappropriately chosen film-title may virtually "kill" a film.

A film-title must possess the seductive power to draw the film-viewers, be its own advertisement, an introduction to the coming performance and a cryptic *annonce*. A vivid, powerful, imaginative and intriguing film-title is a sign of the possible cinematographic success which is conventionally measured by mass viewing or mass reading of the cinematographic text.

And such is the title chosen by Andrei Tarkovsky for his film. *Nostalgia* seduced international audiences, including even those whose familiarity with the Soviet "socialist surrealist", "Solzhenit-syn of the cinema", "cinematographic Christian and mystic",[2] was rather perfunctory. This provocative and subversive title of a modern film drew numerous Russian emigrés, of various ages, tastes, political views and of varying cultural and artistic preparation. For many of them, it was a shocking disappointment, since Tarkovsky introduced a new meaning to the familiar concept which they were unable to grasp. Many viewers would leave the screening of *Nostalgia* after the first twenty minutes, perhaps, deceived by the "wrong" title. Why did some of the viewers respond to the film in such a way?

My contention is that Tarkovsky had selected an appropriate sign of attraction for his *Nostalgia*, but he greatly disappointed some of the viewers who could not recognize the familiar concept behind it. The associations conventionally implied by the sign NOSTALGIA are those of homesickness. The word, which derives its meaning from the Greek *nostros* and *algia*, is universally understood as this painful longing about one's native land. Tarkovsky, a modern artist, expands the familiar semantic universe. His *nostalgia* as a word has another meaning. His film-text is a modern text which may be read and interpreted by a reader who is accustomed to decoding the message.

The paradox of Tarkovsky's concept of *nostalgia* lies in the expansion of the notion of *home*. For Tarkovsky, home is not only one's native land, not only Russia, but it is the lost world of noble human beliefs, illusions, abandoned beauty and longing for impossible happiness. This *semiotic polyvalence* of *Nostalgia* presents difficulty for some viewers who expected the familiar cathartic séance of reliving the past. They may have expected to re-experience the pain of return, the journey to the ancestral or abandoned past. These expectations were not met by the subversive modern cinematographic text *Nostalgia*.

Harvey Kaplan, a psychologist, writing on the state of nostalgia in his work *The Psychopathology of Nostalgia*, defines the commonly known "nostalgia" as a "universal affect, which entails the recognition and acceptance of the past that may never return" (465).[3] He distinguishes two states of nostalgia, i.e. the normal and pathological. The psychologist maintains that "in pathological nostalgia, there is a longing for the past without the acceptance that it is over" (465). In this sense, Tarkovsky's phenomenon of nostalgia introduced in his film-text *Nostalgia* does not fall into the category of abnormal nostalgia. His psychological state is normal. Tarkovsky does accept the loss of the past, but the tragedy of his nostalgia lies in the realization of the cultural, moral and intellectual loss of the past, *his* past, as the artist sees it.

His is not the longing for Home in the conventional sense. Tarkovsky's Home is the World of Western and Eastern Civilization, Humanity at large. And his, Tarkovsky's universe of nostalgia is at the foreground of his cinematographic text, while the familiar, the expected world of homesickness and the old Mother-Russia motif is unusually at the background.[4] This *semiotic inversion*[5] or the reversal of the semantic levels of the key concept— Nostalgia— is at the root of Tarkovsky's modern poeticity. Like any modern author, Tarkovsky turns upside down the traditional semantic worlds, plays with the change of the semantic planes, introducing unfamiliar visual, auditory and intellectual stimuli.

In his search for an original voice and genre, he subverts the classical genre of sentimental drama, on which the traditional experience of nostalgia is based. Instead of the expected tale about the Russian exile in Italy, instead of the promised spiritual abyss in Dostoevsky's style, the modern viewer deals with the film-text which is constructed in the best traditions of Kafka and Beckett, Fellini and Lena Wertmuller.

Once interviewed about the film *Nostalgia*, Tarkovsky said that he intended to recreate the psychological state, typically Russian, in the line of Dostoevsky.[6] Nonetheless, the intentions of an artist and one's actual artistic product may be often in conflict. Barthélemy Amengual[7] quotes Tarkovsky on another occasion: "Notre vie est une métaphore dès le début et jusqu'à la fin. Tous ce qui nous entoure est métaphore" (165).

His own pronouncement is the best characterization of his film. Tarkovsky's *Nostalgia* may be perceived as a metaphor of our

Present which is the state of longing for the Lost Mythical Order, Harmony and Meaning.

His *Nostalgia* could be perceived as the irrepressible desire to restore something, the Other, be it Beauty or Nature or Man. As in his other films, Tarkovsky turns to the Old Beliefs for the solution of the present crisis. The candlelight motif which is so much favored by Tarkovsky in his Andrei Rublev[8] and other cinematographic texts, is dominant in this later film as well. It is remarkable that the candlelight in the film *Nostalgia* is carried by Gorchakov, who may be seen as a nostalgic romantic image— a poet who saves humanity from darkness. Tarkovsky's pagan-Christian mysticism of *Andrei Rublev* gives way to the restored romantic myth of a Poet-God and Poet-saviour.[9] Tarkovsky's Gorchakov, with a candle in his hand, reconstructs the Carlylean Hero who carries the torch of enlightenment to the future generations in the land of Dante where the Eternal light burns and Hero-Poet reigns forever . . .[10]

The *theme of fragmented world* is dominant in the film, disclosing this additional semantic universe of Tarkovsky's *Nostalgia*. The author of the cinematographic text summarizes the longing for unity and harmony in this disconnected world where not only a Poet or Artist is an alien, but any other being as well. The scene with the madman setting himself on fire supports the notion of an indifferent, hostile world where people no longer feel and think, but function as the programmed parts of the modern monstrosity called the "advanced technological world". The presumably mistaken course of modern civilization is reinforced by the motif "strada sbagliata" (the wrong route) which the characters repeat in several film episodes. The verbal image of the wrong route is accompanied by the visual scene of the dead-end street to emphasize the mood of the utterance.

Tarkovsky's state of nostalgia is much more of a severe depression caused by the state of affairs in the so-called civilized western world. It is phenomenal that he experiences his low spiritual state in the land of Art and Beauty, country of Dante and Michelangelo, an Italy which is no longer regarded as the land of aesthetic ecstasy. Unlike Gogol or Viacheslav Ivanov, who would have liked to die in Italy amidst the sun, music and colour, who worshipped Italy and everything Italian,[11] Tarkovsky's Gorchakov sarcastically asks: "Perché cosi molto scarpe?" (Why so many shoes?) At this point he demonstratively looks at his own shoes and states that they had lasted him for eight years already. Gorchakov regrets that the land of Dante and Michelangelo, Leonardo da Vinci and Verdi turned to the art of shoe production. Modern art, modern artistic products, new tastes and canons of taste all seem to depress Gorchakov-Tarkovsky, the two voices which are fused into one single voice, deeply sad and nostalgic in a new sense.

It is only at the end of the film that viewers may find the familiar image of "nostalgia"-homesickness. This nostalgia of the last scenes in *Nostalgia* returns the viewers to the native conceptual ground, i.e. a Russian artist finds himself depressed and homesick in Italy. This is a paradoxical message as well, but it is expected as a part of the Russian nationalist myth. In the light of this patriotic myth no Russian may be happy outside his/her motherland, and even sunny Italy, the magic land of art, beauty and eternal pleasure of being, may not fulfil the spiritual needs of the self-imposed exile. "Why did I do it?" Gorchakov asks while in a state of his normal, familiar nostalgia. This question -signal of nostalgia- may be interpreted as "Why did I emigrate?" This conventional nostalgia was acknowledged by the critics as a natural reaction, an autobiographical trauma, aggravated by Tarkovsky's own inability to return to the Russia of 1983.[12]

The specific Russian motif and quality of nostalgia is nothing more than a tragedy created by a despotic human act. A purely national unique tragedy, i.e. the inability to return to one's country of birth, is tied to the universal human despotism, i.e. cruelty of which any Man is capable. Nonetheless, with the intuitive sixth sense of a genuine artist, Tarkovsky moves the Russian nostalgic drama to the periphery of the cinematographic text. The cruel Russian law is demonstrated as a part and parcel of the human universe— the creation of all beings.

What Tarkovsky's nostalgic drama may actually mean is longing for harmony and love and understanding which neither Soviet Russia nor modern Italy may offer to a thinking and sensitive soul. Tarkovsky asks in despair or in a state of "normal nostalgia":

"Quel mondo?" (What kind of a world is it?)

"Que fare con liberta?" (What to do with liberty?)

In search of meaning, his Gorchakov returns again to the dead end street—"strada sbagliata".

The staged state of nostalgia in Tarkovsky's *Nostalgia* can be substituted for mourning, as psychologist Kaplan suggests.[13] He also names the state of nostalgia as a "screen affect." In Tarkovsky's case, it is the state of mourning. In his film *Nostalgia*, he mourns his own life and the life of Humanity. His cinematographic text called *Nostalgia* bears the impact of death anxiety. Seeking a cure for his anxiety and ante-mortal depression, Gorchakov-Tarkovsky introduces the episode with the little Angela whom he asks: "Lei contenta?" (Are you contented?)

What does her very weak "Si..." (Yes) signify? Does it reconcile Gorchakov with his own self and "il mondo"- the World...?

ENDNOTES

1. Peter Nesselroth, "Literary Identity and Contextual Difference" in Mario Valdes and Owen Miller, eds. *Identity of the Literary Text* . Toronto: U of Toronto P, 1985: 41-54.

2. Barthélemy Amengual, "Andrei Tarkovsky après sept films" in Michel Estève, ed. *Andrei Tarkovsky. Etudes Cinématographiques*, nos. 135-138. Paris: Lettres Modernes, 1983: 157-179.

3. Harvey Kaplan, "The Psychopathology of Nostalgia" in *The Psychoanalytic Review*, v.74, no. 4, Winter 1987, 465-487.

4. The notions of foregrounding and selection are borrowed from the works of Russian formalists and are now widely used in the modern literary criticism, e.g.

Hayden White, *Tropics of Discourse* . Baltimore, Md.: Johns Hopkins U P, 1978: 112.

5. The term reveals the principle of selective focalization by the author, i.e. foregrounding and displacement of chosen signs, and it successfully describes the actual process of such selection.

6. Marcel Martin, "Andrei Tarkovsky ou la recherche de l'absolu," in Estève, ed., 147-157; Achille Frezzato, *Tarkovskij il castoro cinema*. Florence: La Nuova Italia, 1977.

7. See above no. 2.

8. Maja J. Turowskaja, *Andrej Tarkovskij*. Bonn: Auflage, 1981.

9. The concept of Poet-God may be found in all Western literary traditions during the reign of Romanticism. Soviet artistic discourse is largely based on the Romantic mythic ground that incorporates nineteenth century Western Romanticism.

10. The most revealing source on the special Poet's mission is Thomas Carlyle's *On Heroes and Hero-Worship*.

11. Gogol's reverence for Italy has been acknowledged by most of his biographers, who use his letters of the Rome period—1836-1848.

12. Amengual clearly states it in his "Andrei Tarkovsky après sept films". See above no. 2.

13. See Kaplan.

14. Kaplan, 468.

Discussion and Responses

Session Five

Vida Johnson, as discussant, commented on the unity of Tarkovsky's work in the Soviet Union and abroad:

In contrast to some of the other directors discussed he presents a single vision. This may be a virtue as well a downfall. Tarkovsky is either loved or hated; he is either admired or found tedious and overrated. He moves on various levels in *Stalker* and Heidi Karriker perhaps underrates his humour. We should also be aware of the richness of the slang and colloquial language of the film.

I disagree with Heidi Karriker's characterization of Andrei in *Nostalgia* as "nationalistic, chauvinistic, and callous". He does not come across as negative and it is characteristic of Tarkovsky's films that we don't always know who the good guys or bad guys are.

For Tarkovsky the world is constructed in grays rather than in blacks and whites and this is reflected in his characters. Andrei is someone who is torn like Tarkovsky himself between love of his country and a longing for a world which does not and cannot exist.

The observation that there is an increase in sexuality in his later films and the similarity in the two hysterical fits by the women in *The Sacrifice* and *Stalker* suggests that his films do not change all that much from his Russian to his Western films. I would like to argue for a universality in both thematic and cinematic terms.

Vida Johnson congratulated Jim Leach on his paper but pointed out that:

According to Tarkovsky's collaborators on *The Sacrifice,* he did not know of his illness while he was actually shooting the film and the sense of sadness in the film perhaps reflects his own position as the ultimate exile. It is not really meaningful to talk about him as an emigré; he was always an internal emigré both in the Soviet Union and abroad.

During her research Dr. Johnson had asked the younger Russian filmmakers: what did Tarkovsky contribute? "He discovered for us the visual language of film. One of the most impressive things about Tarkovsky is the nature of his imagery; whatever meaning one wishes to read into it."

Graham Petrie:

He is a symbol of the intransigient filmmaker; he was lucky enough to be able to work with almost complete freedom in Italy and Sweden. One wonders what would have happened to him had he tried to make a film in America. He apparently thought this could be possible. But even in Sweden with its tradition of tolerance towards independent, single-minded filmmakers, even there he had problems. According to Anna-Lena Wibom, the producer of *The Sacrifice*, who admired him very much, he had no sense of the reality of what was possible. Especially in the matter of extras and crowd scenes, where he reluctantly had to make do with far fewer than he had initially demanded. When Ms Wibom was asked if she would work with him again in Sweden, she said "no", for two reasons. 1. Her mandate was for Swedish films and 2. Tarkovsky could only have survived if he had learned to scale his ambitions down to what was economically feasible as Bergman had done. She doubted that he could have done this kind of thing in the long term.

This leads into something else: one might consider the question as to whether Makavajev, who seems to have retained his outrageous style and themes while working in Sweden and Australia, could have adapted to the free enterprise system in the United States.

Gerald Peary questioned Anna Makolkina's "allegedly scientific" theory that Russian emigrés leave *Nostalgia* after twenty minutes because they have a different definition of it from that presented in the film:

This is just my guesswork, but it seems probable that audiences leave after twenty minutes because they are looking for a conventional narrative and the film does not give them that. Your claims of scientific objectivity in understanding audience reactions are in fact purely subjective.

Anna Makolkina:

I don't claim to be a scientist and it is impossible to be scientific in terms of artistic interpretation. The meaning of "nostalgia" in any language is universal. It is also a universal word linguistically. As a semiotician I am dealing primarily with universals first and themes which are held in common rather than differences. The paradox in Tarkovsky's cinematic text is that he subverts the language. He creates a new language and new meanings. We should be prepared to analyse these new languages and these new signs.

Paul Coates:

I was struck by the harmony among the various panelists in analyzing Tarkovsky's themes of lost harmony and I would like to strike a dissonant note. It was said earlier that you either love or hate Tarkovsky as a whole and we all know from Heidegger and the auteurists that an artist is always making the same work. That statement represses the dialectic that exists between work and oeuvre. Certain artists on reaching a certain point or a certain work in their career seem to have objectified their concerns to such a degree that all they can do thereafter is repeat themselves. I would be inclined to argue that this would be the case with Tarkovsky after *Mirror*. It is an extraordinary masterwork.

It is quite clear by the time of *Nostalgia* that something has begun to go seriously wrong. I don't think it is because of exile; it is something that begins to happen in *Stalker*; it may be even have happened because of what happened to *Stalker* itself. The ruined negative in the first version may have led Tarkovsky to believe that there was a blight on the whole enterprise. I don't know.

Something begins to go wrong in *Stalker* and it begins to go wrong because he has in a sense almost ceased to be an artist and is becoming a preacher. He is giving up images and begins to rely almost exclusively on words. You can see this in *Sculpting in Time* and in the misunderstanding of his own work which Tarkovsky perpetrates in his book. He virtually disowns *Solaris* and implies nothing of interest can be done with the science fiction genre in spite of the fact that *Solaris* is clearly a very great work indeed.

Although there may be thematic concerns linking his work from beginning to end it is worth considering, nevertheless, that the work may move towards one particular moment which crystallizes these concerns and that this may happen early in autobiographical artists such as Scorsese with *Mean Streets*. For Tarkovsky this happened with *Mirror*. However, a society categorizes people as artists, and so directors carry on working and carry on doing what they'd been doing up to that point, despite the fact that they have no clear *raison d'être* any longer for doing it. This is not a particularly Soviet or East European exile concern, as the example of Scorsese makes clear, but one that relates to the notion of self-expression and what happens to the artist when he or she has expressed him or herself and nevertheless continues to be defined, particularly on the basis of the success of that expression, as an artist.

Heidi Karriker:

Tarkovsky's death means that we have a finite body of work to analyze. Although Paul Coates' remarks are perceptive, I do find that there is a thread. I find that his quests were the same at the end although they were perhaps more morbid than they were at the beginning.

Jim Leach:

The point I would most agree with is the reference to *Sculpting in Time*. The position Tarkovsky takes there is fascinating, but much less complex than what comes through in the films themselves.

The issue of language in the later films needs to be cleared up, particularly in *The Sacrifice* where, leaning towards Bergman, he uses words much more extensively than he has in the past. *Andrei Rublev* also undercuts the words, as Heidi pointed out, and there is a strong tension between language and silence, even in that film.

Anna Makolkina to Paul Coates:

Do you insist on the prevalence of language in *Nostalgia*?

Paul Coates:

I was using language as a symptom of what goes wrong and I wouldn't see it as the only cause of this.

Anna Makolkina:

Do you see it as a conflict between the verbal and the auditory signals?

Paul Coates:

I see it as a question of rationalization, which is often verbal rather than visual, and Tarkovsky is trying to rationalize his position from some point in *Stalker* onwards.

Anna Makolkina:

No one can analyze exactly what goes wrong because the perception of a work of art is strictly subjective. We can try to establish what goes right and what we understand in common and agree on, otherwise there would be no discussion and no common ground. In *Nostalgia* the common ground would be the sense that there is something different in this film. The theme of nostalgia itself and the depiction of the state of nostalgia requires much more of a dialogue. There is a sense of equilibrium in this state and there is a harmony and a balance between the visual and the auditory.

Vida Johnson:

There seems to be a general agreement, even amongst people who love Tarkovsky, that his best films are *Andrei Rublev* and *Mirror*. I don't think he has lost his visual touch in *Stalker* although there are problems with the Dostoevskian discussion among the characters outside the Room.

Paul Coates:

That is the point I have a problem with too.

Vida Johnson:

The dialogue without the images can sound trite. The conditions of filming in the West clearly affected the films themselves. For instance he did not always speak the same language as his actors did. Another, he simply did not get the kind of devotion from the people making the sets, did not get the same attention to detail. He required the detail.

John Mosier:

I would agree with Paul Coates that there is a sense of repetitiousness, a falling off, in the last three films. Tarkovsky's failure to adapt to Swedish filming techniques lead me to wonder: could a director like Tarkovsky have continued to operate within the Soviet Union even at a later point? I dislike the formulation that the great artist is unable to adapt to a commercial system.

Bart Testa:

Despite Tarkovsky's own denials in *Sculpting in Time*, is cinema an art of signs or not?

Jim Leach:

I would say it is. Tarkovsky rejected structuralism and Eisenstein's work, but his actual practice in his films is more complex than the rather dogmatic position he takes in his book. A work of art has to be a system of signs. The point of *The Sacrifice* is that art fails and MUST fail to live up to the ideal he puts forward in his book. In exploring that failure he produces something profound and interesting. In *The Sacrifice*, by introducing levels unexplored before, he pushes further his analysis of the medium simply by increasing the number of codes at work within the film.

Reflections on Makavejev

The Art Film and Transgression

Bart Testa
Innis College, University of Toronto

I. A Preliminary Remark regarding National Films and Commercial Cinema

The broad question raised by several papers at the McMaster University conference on Soviet and Eastern European film directors working the West, and debated at length in the concluding round-table, orbited around the problematic relationship between national film practices in European Socialist countries and the international style of commercial cinema centered on Hollywood. The point of the question is what happens when filmmakers from Eastern Europe emigrate to the West and try to resume the practice of their art.

Schematizing the conference discussions in a simple way, I think this question faced in two directions, one descriptive and the other critical. The descriptive question concerns the account to be given of the changes film directors undergo when they move from the national film culture in which directors were trained, financially and institutionally supported and, to some degree, repressed, over to the international commercial film industry in which market-driven apparatuses of film finance, production and distribution define the conditions of filmmaking. In coarse outline, the directors' common trajectory, from Socialist, state-sponsored film cultures to Capitalist film industries, suggests a general structure into which these parts might be fitted. However, blocked-out stereotypes like "national film culture" and "commercial film industry" need much filling in and, soon, refinement breaks them down into segments, sub-segments and particles with their own historiographic issues.

Nonetheless, when those at the McMaster conference made a working distinction between national film culture and international commercial film industries, they were marking out a valuable heuristic difference. However, the critical face of the question was made more difficult because of the sharpness of that difference. The critical question was put this way: Does the work of an Eastern European director decline when he or she enters the Western industry? The answer, made most insistently by Vlada Petric at the conference, is that such work does go into decline because the *aesthetic* integrity of the director is necessarily compromised by the necessity of submitting his/her art to the codes of narrativity prevailing in Western commercial cinema. Although at any moment that narrativity is undergoing development, conventionalization of narrative filmic practices is continuous and so narrativity seems to operate in the West as a prisonhouse of film language within which the film artist must toil. In Petric's highly prescriptive and deductive argument, the emigré director is defeated aesthetically before he or she has begun filmmaking in the West.

No counter-argument was made to Dr. Petric. There was no critical defence of films made in the West as superior to those directors had made in their home film cultures. Conference participants agreed that Eastern European film cultures are committed to the "art film" that arises out of national cultural traditions while directors in the West have to work within genres and conventional narrative codes. For me, the most arresting reply to Dr. Petric, made at the concluding round table discussion, was to say that Eastern European cinemas now need to transform their filmmaking to make them conform to the commercial practices of the West.

The present paper consists of reflections on the first emigré period of the Yugoslav director Dusan Makavejev, which began in 1973. Parts of this paper were prepared prior to the McMaster Conference but were rewritten in response to the stimulating discussions there. These reflections treat a relatively minor issue suggested by the broad question raised at the conference: the state of critical discourse on the "art film" during the mid-seventies when Makavejev's *Sweet Movie* (1974) first circulated.

Although the director had shot a significant portion of *WR: Mysteries of the Organism* (1971) in the United States, Makavejev's emigré career was initiated with *Sweet Movie*. Both works are firmly entrenched within the so-called "Black Cinema" moment of progressive Yugoslav filmmaking, so at first it seemed that the director could continue, even expand his national-artistic project in the West. However, the critical and commercial scandal of *Sweet Movie* stalled the director's career and it was only resumed in 1981, with *Montenegro*, a film far less daring in the disjunctiveness of the montage with which director was assocated in the early seventies and far less intellectually aggressive. It also was well received. Critics seemed glad Makavejev was back and the art-house/festival audience caught on to the film as a bizarre sex comedy. Makavejev's experience could suggest a test case of a film director who moves to the West, tries to carry on his ambitious artistic project, fails and, after a delay, retreats into a more conventional narrative cinema and recuperates his career.

As a step toward making such a test, I attempt a discussion, first, on the context of the negative reception of *Sweet Movie*, which I think can illustrate a crisis of the "art film" concept emergent in seventies film culture that is still with us and still affects definitions of "non-commercial" national filmmaking. Second, by focussing on *Sweet Movie* as a latter-day Surrealist film engaged in the revival of montage valorized under a Brechtian banner, I want to suggest that its aggressiveness punctures "art-film" decorum.

II. The Sins of *Sweet Movie*

Before *Sweet Movie* circulated in 1974-1975, Makavejev was hailed as a film artist among the most impressive of the post-New
Wave generation. After *Sweet Movie*, Makavejev was dismissed as
a charlatan, even a pornographer. Richard Roud, director of the
New York Film Festival and editor of *Cinema: A Critical Dictionary*,
called Makavejev a vulgar opportunist, arguing that there was
always this side to the filmmaker, but with *Sweet Movie*, that side
has taken over.[1] To cite a another dismissal, Robert Phillip Kolker,
in *The Altering Eye, Contemporary International Cinema*, declares,

> In the early seventies, the Yugoslav filmmaker Dusan Makavejev
> received some recognition for his lunatic investigations of sexuality
> and politics in films that mixed documentary and fiction, acted se-
> quences and archival footage in aformal collage that brought some
> of Godard's techniques to a curious dead end. [2]

Something had gone very wrong with *Sweet Movie*. It eclipsed
Makavejev as effectively in the later seventies as its predecessor,
WR: Mysteries of the Organism had spotlighted him at the start of
the decade. If we step back a moment, to the days of "some
recognition", we encounter Makavejev's name in the list of directors that Ian Cameron drew up in preparing his hopefully entitled
anthology *Second Wave*.[3] As its title indicates, Cameron's book
sought to discern in the cinema at the end of the sixties a new
generation that would, in the next decade, continue the amibitious
developments of the *nouvelle vague*. By the end of the seventies,
progressive film culture settled for Germany's *Das Neue Kino*,
which replayed the first New Wave a decade after it in a conscious
register of secondariness, as the films of Rainer Werner Fassbinder
and Wim Wenders make abundantly clear. If today we were to
attempt an anthology similar to Cameron's *Second Wave*, we would
encounter serious problems of both historiographical and critical
kinds. These problems involve the twin notions of film movements
and the art film.

The historical assumption behind the notion of a "second wave" is that "film movements" were fated to unify in a coherent thrust in world cinema. This role of film movements arose from the fact that they form a central concept with which film critics thought about the development of post-War world cinema. The national outburst of a *cinéma des auteurs* in country after country in the decades following the Second World War seemed crucial to the vitality of film art. The first to formulate the ambitions of film movements was André Bazin. His realist "evolutionary" film aesthetics were intimately linked to Italian Neorealism and Bazin's writings on this movement virtually invented the modern film movement idea.[4] Bazin's influential concept rested on a paradox. Film movements are national, and indeed nationalistic. They seek to restore the nation's filmmaking by turning in a new way to the realities of national life and national culture. At the same time, film movments emerge out of the fundamental *telos* of cinema and are, therefore, world-cinema developments. National films that focus on a specific time and place also make an aesthetic leap forward for cinema as a whole.

Why? Because the intervention that arises from the artistic will to reclaim cultural and social home turf is conceived, first, as a revolt against the dominant institution of cinema, the commercial "classical" narrative film whose capital is Hollywood; and second, as an evolutionary advance in the art of film *per se*, toward realism, initially in social terms, later mainly in cultural terms. Neorealism, the *nouvelle vague*, *Cinema Novo* and the new cinemas of Eastern Europe are all appropriated under this critical programme as evidence of the continuing seriousness of film.

Formulated as both an aesthetics and a politics of film, the film movement, then, has served progressive film culture, since the fifties, as a cinematic counter-discourse of international proportions that was seen to have energized cinema and promised the eventual overthrow of the hegemonic Hollywoodized commercial film industry. In the sixties especially, the film movement was seen to break with conventions, to go where commercial cinema was too cowardly to go, was too bound up with dominant ideology to go, was too formally conservative to go.

As a critical construct, the concept of the film movement was bound up with the notion of critique and we should recognize, in the light cast by essays like Annette Michelson's "Film and the Radical Aspiration",[5] that critique in the sense used by those writing ambitously on modern film was conceived within the setting of a humanist modernism rooted in Enlightenment critiques of doctrine and ideology. Moreover, the film movement came to be seen as always coincident with notions of authorship, expressivity, organicity, political and social critique and a variety of realisms both naive and critical.

Within the critical construct of the film movement I am sketching here, this critique is also copasetic with Romantic concepts of art as organic expression. Its crucial manifestation is the "art film". The art film mounts a critique of the myths and values of mass culture and false consciousness from its position of the open and authentic artistic vision, the vision of the auteur, first in concert with the liberating national film movement, where the critique draws its strength from national traditions and aspirations, and later, through the individuated auteur's sensibility. Realism undergoes a parallel transfiguration once artistic sensibility and not a social realism is the focus of interest, as the standard critical histories of Italian film attest. As with other values of aesthetic modernism, however, the art film remains, despite this transformation of types of realism, the true defender of the integrity of film art against the kitsch of non-art cinema, Hollywood and its international imitators.

Kolker's *The Altering Eye* is at the other end of the critical tradition that Bazin instigated. Indeed, Kolker starts with a Bazinian recapitulation of Neorealism as the first post-War film movement. As a whole, his book constructs a critical history of post-War cinema on the Bazinian premise: in terms of its resistances, critiques and interventions against Hollywood; and in terms of the aesthetic trajectory of film style through which the cinema defines its integrity. But, by the end of the book, Kolker rather sadly abandons any real hope for the overthrow of Hollywood or for the sort of political-aesthetic art of the future the modern cinema should have engendered. National movements and strong auteurs successively take position against the empire of Hollywood narrative cinema. But the history of their rises and falls is a history of repeated "dead ends". Kolker's depressive evaluations of Antonioni, Bertolucci, Godard and others are not as summary as his dismissal of Makavejev, but the logic of his argument is the same. He attenuates advanced cinema prospects for any liberating critique. Indeed, critique becomes endlessly prefatory, as Godard and Straub in the sixties, and Schroeter and Fassbinder in the seventies show. Some directors turn from this prefatory work back to conventional film-making, as Brazil's Cinema Novo directors, recent German films, the current French cinema, and the later films of Bernardo Bertolucci illustrate.

Kolker's account conforms to a critical orthodoxy of the "art film" and the now-classic history of film movements pervasive in academic film studies (and this was reflected at the McMaster conference). This account can be brought under questioning but I believe that Kolker is a critic in a long line of film history and criticism and he is quite representative of the position already well formed in the mid-seventies when Makavejev's *Sweet Movie* appears.

The "second wave" was perhaps the last piece of the "art film" construct and perhaps the most adventurous. But that was part of the problem brewing in progressive film culture in the aftermath of the sixties. The de-codification of narrative cinema undertaken by Godard and then developed by Oshima, Straub and Rocha and others, together with the search for new forms both in the service of critique and national/auteurist expression had reached a crisis. Godard was the exemplary filmmaker (as he is for Kolker) and Makavejev was one of the intriguing followers.

Then Godard abandoned his auteurist status and the art-film mode to practice semiotic counter-cinema in his Dziga Vertov period. His rejection at the hands of former supporters like Richard Roud[6] parallels the dismantling of the humanist apparatus of film criticism. Two things then happened: a re-theorized film criticism took up semiotics in the cinema, as exemplified by *Screen*, and rejected the art film to take up ideological analysis of Hollywood classical cinema; and, in the film journalism-film festival consensus, the idea of the art-film regressed, a process marked by the success of *Das Neue Kino*, and, a decade later, by the success of a cinema-retro instanced by *Diva*.

In one obvious sense, both Godard, with *Wind from the East* (1969) and Makavejev, with *WR: Myteries of the Organism*, had already broken with the art film construct that had provided their work with a context. By foregrounding ideology and rhetoric, these and other filmmakers were pushing against the concept of "film as art", conceived as auteurist expressivity and realist organicity of form. Within an emergent semiotics of the cinema, Godard was recuperable as a politicized formalist, but, with *WR* and *Sweet Movie*, Makavejev did something that Godard did not do. Makavejev transgressed the "decorum" of the art film.

A self-avowed humanist art-film critic, Robin Wood, writing on *WR*, suggests how notions of organicity and expressivity constitute the art-film's decorum. Wood has two problems with *WR*. First, he believes Makavejev emphasizes the "ludicrous excesses" of Wilhelm Reich's later years and scants the psychoanalyst's unification of Marx and Freud in the twenties and thirties. Second, Wood argues *WR* displaces what he calls the "exploratory 'realist' narrative" style that Makavejev had perfected with *Switchboard Operator* (1967) and instead uses "stylized, mostly comic charade".[7]

Wood's description is right on both points. Makavejev believes that Reich betrayed his early work when he abandoned Marxism and took up the Orgone Box. The director views the later Reich as someone who fell into what he calls (and despises) "spirituality". The parodic aspect of the film's portrait of Reich indicates Makavejev's thinking at the time. In his lectures during the mid-seventies, Makavejev traced a history of Marxist cultural theory in search of what he called "anti-metaphysics". He fixed upon Freudianism, Formalism and Surrealism. He shaped a syncretistic thinking into an opposition between "spirituality" and "anti-metaphysics". This opposition structures the textual work of both *WR* and *Sweet Movie*. A student of the Belgrade school of Surrealism in the fifties, Makavejev later came to the view that the traditions of Marxsm should be clustered around a Surrealist sensibility that could, be systematically subversive and still systematic. As a latter-day Surrealist, Makavejev dispensed with ideas of art, affirmed the powers of non-art cinema (the Hollywood musical and the porno film, for example, as fantasy machines) and broke with humanism in cinema.

Wood's complaint that Makavejev becomes schematic is implicitly a complaint about the director's abandonment of a humanist style. This style, characterized by realist film language and naturalistic acting, is always closely connected to, often isomorphic with art-film values of aesthetic integration, emotional wholeness, and auteurist self-revelation. At the level of style Makavejev effectively, if not purposively, effaces the art film when he overthrows the decorum of a humanistic style. This is the heart of Wood's criticism: *WR* does not engage the empathy of viewers, nor an appreciation of the film's "art". *Sweet Movie* goes even further in sinning against these basic critical values of the art film. Its cruel humour, extreme sexuality, heterogenous stylistics and often awkward bluntness constitute an open provocation against these critical values.

Makavejev moves toward the possibilities of a transgressive cinema that serves a concept of therapy, not art, one in which hilarity and outrage, juxtapositions of horror and erotic delight become favorite strategies. The object of Makavejev's provocations is "spirituality". In his conception, it comes in two potent political forms: the obsessive-compulsive/aggressive erotic behavior that Norman O. Brown names "the excremental vision" in the West; and the eroticized revolutionary sacrifices that the director associates with Stalinist culture. In the first of these Makavejev would find the object of his caricatures the West's commodification of sexuality, and in the second, the erotics of a revolutionary death cult. *Sweet Movie* is a site on which Makavejev attempts to collide these forms of "spirituality" and in that collision he explodes humanism and art-film aesthetics into a highly rhetorical, intellectualized Surrealism that sometimes looks and behaves like Brechtian cinema.

III. Brechtian Cinema, Provincial Surrealism and *Sweet Movie*'s Style

Martin Walsh's *The Brechtian Aspect of Radical Cinema* is one of the few studies to emerge from semiotics to treat films that formerly were examined in the art film context. Walsh enlists Makavejev's later films in an emergent new Brechtian cinema. He argues that the form of a Brechtian film will dislocate the smooth progression of part of a film narrative toward catharsis. It will do so in order to construct the work "vertically" through an ensemble of effects that engender that intellectual activity which Brecht sometimes called "abstraction."[9]

Walsh opens up comparison between Brecht's epic theatre and the "epic retardation" characteristic of Eisenstein's montage in *Battleship Potemkin* (1925) and *October* (1928). Walsh interprets some famous passages—like the bridge-raising sequence and Karensky's climb up the steps in *October*—as "paradigmatic" moments in "historical demonstration". He believes these moments arise from a specific cinematic origin, namely, montage disjunction, which serves as the base-line of Brechtian cinema. It is through montage, Walsh believes, that the cinema activates its specific capacity for alienation effects. However, Eisenstein's particular stylistics are not prescriptive and the possible radical projects open to Brechtian cinema become numerous. It was Walsh's intention to provide a full analysis of these projects but this was interrupted by his untimely death in 1977. Yet the thesis he sought to develop remains suggestive. Of Makavejev Walsh writes that he moves "toward a provocative subversion of our normative concepts of reality, both textually and behaviorally," and he included him, on the strength of *WR* and *Sweet Movie*, in the new Brechtian cinema.[10] Walsh does say more, specifically that Makavejev's montage of diverse film materials—documentary, archival oddities, cinéma-vérité and Brechtian dramatic tableaux (such as the courtyard sequence in *WR*)—cracks the "illusion of reality."

Interestingly it is not essential for Walsh that Makavejev deploys such canonical Brechtian usages. For Walsh, what matters is the project of an intellectual cinema that provokes in the spectator a critical state of reception through disjunctive formal strategies. The importance of Makavejev's films in the early seventies lies in the director's montage methods and the break they occasion with an organic form and humanist-empathetic style of filmmaking. So, what Walsh sees as virtues, critics like Wood see as Makavejev's sins against the art film.[11] This dichotomy in critical values manifests the ongoing crisis of the art film, of film movements and indeed of the idea of contemporary cinema.

Here, however, we come to a turn. *Sweet Movie* is notorious for its dislocation of "realist illusion", not because of its formal usages but because of its sexual transgressions. The infamous "Milky Way" segment of the film, in which Otto Muehl's therapeutic commune engages in enthusiastic rituals of regression into pissing, shitting and vomiting, is the most glaring example. Makavejev does not conceive of "anti-illusionism" in the formal terms that Walsh indicates, but in Surrealist terms, as tactics of transgression against taste, art and sexual codes. In his lectures Makavejev interprets even Eisenstein himself, not in terms of the montage aesthetic, but in terms of an erotics arising from Makavejev's own Surrealist suspicions—about the black/gold/red color scheme of *Ivan the Terrible, II*, and especially about the myth of revolutionary sacrifice in *Battleship Potemkin*, suspicions prominently put into practice in *Sweet Movie*, a film that is partly a re-reading of *Potemkin* itself.

Makavejev has explained that he was interested in combining Eisenstein and Surrealism. Makavejev's Surrealism differs from both the classic Parisian and the Hispanic schools. The distinct tradition of Surrealist art of the Belgrade school is to embrace the subversive possibilities of anti-art as a liberation enacted in the already revolutionary situation of Titoist Communism. So, whereas Parisian Surrealism positioned itself as a transgression against capitalist culture and its aesthetic sentimentalism, Belgrade Surrealism confronted the waning culture of Stalinism. The Yugoslav Surrealists sought to be liberated from "left fascism". They placed extraordinary emphasis on the body and greatly simplified notions of the psyche, in place of the discursiveness of classical Freudianism that underlay French Surrealism's literary emphasis. For them, Surrealism was no longer the linguistic cultivation of the marvellous but a therapy engaging the emotions and the body directly in the liberation of the material self from ideological repression.

Sweet Movie explores the possibilities of such a liberation, though this is expressed in a Brechtian parodic-yet-tragic register. The film is structured on two parallel stories but the montage joins between their interleavered segments complexify that parallelism. Miss Canada (Carole Laure) undergoes the trials women in the West endure, while the sailor Lev Bakunin (Pierre Clementi)—also addressed by his "collective" name as Potemkin after Eisenstein's famous battleship—descends into the psyche of the East. What Miss Canada endures is a picaresque tour through the excremental sexual aggression of Capital. It begins with a TV show where she must not only win a beauty contest but pass an inspection as a virgin conducted by her future mother-in-law. The millionaire marital prize (John Vernon) is an obsessive compulsive who washes Miss Canada thoroughly with alcohol after taking her to bed where he promptly pisses on her with his literally golden cock. Unsatisfied, he turns her over to his henchman, Jeremiah Muscle, for disposal and she winds up in a flightbag travelling through the chutes at Air Canada's terminal before flying off to Paris. There, she winds up on the Eiffel Tower where El Macho, a matador/pop singer (Sami Frey), interrupts shooting a tourist commercial to have sex with her, but the two wind up like stuck dogs and have to be separated in a restaurant kitchen.

This story is constituted as a sort of catalogue of images concatenated as a series purity/shit/gold/phallic aggression/commodization of sex. The vehicle Makavejev devises is a crude parody of a TV beauty contest, richman lifestyle, and several broad allusions, in the Paris section especially, to *Un chien andalou* and *L'age d'or*. Miss Canada finally arrives at the memorial extreme of sexual culture in the West—Germany. The notorious Muehl section of the film takes us to a utopia of regression: here Reichian theory finds a most extreme application. In a setting which is curiously medieval (and the shooting shifts from a fixed-camera high-key brazenness to an almost gloomy, hand-held *cinéma-vérité* style), the commune works directly on the body, ritualizing therapy as hysterical action. We recognize the sequences as real curiosities: a German, yet another German, rejection of the Enlightenment enacted through yet another regressive enthusiasm.

There is more to this association than its curiosity, more to the meaning of the segment than mere outrage. When Makavejev shifts styles, he detaches Miss Canada's tale from the parodic progression to a documentary mode. Actually, the film grinds to a halt here, for the documentary force of the passage, which is disproportionately long and extremely powerful in its vulgarity and humanity, collapses this parallel narrative under its spectacle. The patently artificial sections before this are just cartoons; this section is relentlessly brutal and even its theatricalism (as one of the Milky Way members chops his huge, false penis with a cleaver) bluntly violates taboos. Moreover, Makavejev interrupts the section with archival footage of "baby gymnastics" shot during the Nazi era. The montage specifies the commune historically: its members are the babies of the Nazi regime. Recalling Reich's theory of the "armoured body" and the fascist personality, these images of babies are the sign of the fascist body literally being made. So, Makavejev would have us understand that the Milky Way group are undoing their own infancy, undoing an historically specific fascist formation of the armoured body. Placed in a direct concatenation with the Capitalist media culture, these therapy sequen ces elaborate on the typology of the excremental as the root eroticism of the West. After this, Miss Canada disappears from the film until its coda when she appears in a vat of chocolate squirming to death as the cameras roll to record her for a TV commercial.

Potemkin's parallel story is prepared for by archival footage of the exhumation of Polish officers who were murdered by Stalinist troops and dumped in mass graves during the Second World War. Potemkin arrives in Amsterdam and is greeted by Captain Anna Planeta piloting the ship *Survival* through the city's canals, its prow boasting a face of Karl Marx that sheds one big tear. Potemkin hardly comes aboard before he enjoys some great "proletarian" sex with his hostess, the beginning of a tryst that ends when she savagely and erotically stabs him to death in a bed of sugar and sex. Then, too, as Planeta tells him, *Survival* is a ship full of corpses, the dead of the revolution, of Marxist history.

The "baby gymnastics" and the Polish footage, placed as hinges between the two narratives, are set out as equivalents from two different but parallel histories of the repressed. Potemkin cries out: "Fascination! Forward! Optimistic Tragedy!" And when he is murdered, he dies in an ecstasy that is not just sexual, but liturgical: he dies as a revolutionary sacrifice. He has another revealing line, "I felt so jealous when Vakulinchuk died," delivered just as Planeta bites viciously into his neck, the immediate prelude to his murder. The love/death in the sugar bed is another figure of regression, and one which is historical but this time not an undoing. Potemkin regresses into the masochism of the revolutionary martyr. His name is a tip-off, for he is the heir to the primal hero-victim of the revolution, Eisenstein's Vakulinchuk, the agitator aboard the *Potemkin* who falls to his death in the rigging in a Pieta.

Makavejev follows this sexual murder with a shot of people gathered around an organ singing a revolutionary anthem and follows this with people dancing to the music. Then, suddenly, he cuts to a shot of a single boot, the transition to long-take hand-held shots of a riot that accompanies the arrest of the murderess. What Makavejev has done is to reconstruct, by parody, the Soviet cinema's primal imagery of revolutionary sacrifice in *Battleship Potem-kin*—the death of Vakulinchuk, followed by the dyptich Odessa Steps sequence, where the people gather to mourn and to celebrate solidarity with the revolution, and are cut down by tzarist marines. The shot of the boot serves the same function in Makavejev's reconstruction as the intertitle "Suddenly" does in the Eisenstein original: to divide the sequence into two opposing parts. The ensuing riot is his version of the Odessa Steps slaughter, using the style and rhythms of late sixties TV news reporting in place of the constructive editing of the original.

Makavejev's treatment of the Potemkin-Planeta narrative makes that story the Communist parallel to the Miss Canada picaresque and both stories unfold the erotics of two kinds of anti-human politics of the body and systems of representation, the Capitalist-excremental and the Communist-heroic. However, Makavejev does not really succeed in combining Surrealism and intellectual montage. While a few work well, the juxtapositions of material are often awkward and the style of the film woefully uneven in realiza-tion. There are several reasons for this. In *Sweet Movie*, Makavejev overreaches his capacity as a stylist and so the intellectual concep-tion is not matched by its execution. The montage that Makavejev attempts is underdeveloped: he tries to juxtapose materials while also leaving the materials assembled intact. Eisenstein's classic caution that the realism of the cinematic image is obstinate and does easily surrender to montage assembly is ignored at a dir-ector's peril and Makavejev fails to devise a style that can give the film the aural-visual unity-in-diversity it requires. What he rather grandly terms his "meta-montage" and described operationally in his lectures fails to function either rhythmically (in Eisenstein's sense of a montage of the images' internal compositions) or textual-ly (the connative and allusionistic field is broken up and too jagged). The partial success of *Sweet Movie* lies in its articular parody (like the *Potemkin* section discussed above) that allow us to grasp its textual intention. The problem with *Sweet Movie* as a montage film is that its transgressions are not relentless enough, so that the system of "meta-montage" never becomes the engine of outrage.

ENDNOTES

1. Richard Roud, afterword to Robin Wood's piece "Dusan Makavejev" in *Cinema: a Critical Dictionary*, Volume Two. London: Secker and Warburg, 1980, p. 657.

2.Robert Phillip Kolker, *The Altering Eye: Contemporary International Cinema*. London: Oxford U P, 1983, p. 325. In a footnote on p. 326, Kolker admits to never having seen *Sweet Movie* but goes on to add, "By all accounts it continues his inquiry into sexual liberation more graphically, moving further into pornography, as he does with his more recent *Montenegro*." The ease with which Kolker, usually a meticulous critic, writes "by all accounts" underscores the prevasive dismissal of the director among art-film critics after the mid-seventies.

3. *Second Wave*, edited by Ian Cameron. New York: Praeger, 1970, see pp. 7-33 for Robin Wood's essay on Makavejev. The other directors discussed in the anthology are Skolimowski, Oshima, Guerra, Rocha, Lefebvre and Straub. A similar, but smaller galaxy of filmmakers is gathered by James Roy MacBean in the second part of his *Film and Revolution*. Bloomington: Indiana U P, 1975. MacBean's early chapters are devoted to Godard and he makes obvious the way Godard "after '68" forms the context for his consideration of the "second wave." The third part of his book is his critical rejection of semiotics of the cinema

4. André Bazin, *What Is Cinema?* Volume Two, edited and translated by Hugh Grey Berkeley: U of California P, 1971, see especially "An Aesthetic of Reality: Cinematic Realism and the Italian School of Liberation", pp. 16-40.

5. Annette Michelson, "Film and the Radical Aspiration", *Film Culture Reader*, edited by P. Adams Sitney. New York: Praeger, 1970, pp. 404-422.

6. Richard Roud, *Jean-Luc Godard*. Bloomington: Indiana U P, 1970, chapter 6.

7. Robin Wood, "Dusan Makavejev", in *Cinema: a Critical Dictionary*, pp. 656-657. Wood's very positive essay in the Cameron anthology concentrates on *Switchboard Operator* and the piece in Roud reprises that material before discussing *WR*, a film not made by the time of the earlier essay. Wood does not discuss *Sweet Movie* and has never seen the film.

8. Dusan Makavejev, "New Forms in Film", a gradate course of lectures at New York University, Cinema Studies Department, Summer, 1975. I have drawn extensively on notes from these classroom lectures. While interviews with the director fromthis period substantially agree with his lectures, they are far less informative, particularly with regard to historical background. I should add that the response

to *Sweet Movie* in this academic setting during the summer of 1975 was even more negative than the criticism cited and alluded to in this paper.

9. Martin Walsh, *The Brechtian Aspect of Radical Cinema* . London: The British Film Institute, 1981, see the chapter "The Complex Seer: Brecht and the Film", pp. 5-21. This anthology of Walsh's writings was published four years after his death.

10. In "Draft Outline: The Brechtian Aspect of Radical Cinema," *Brechtian Aspect*, pp. 129-131. Walsh intended to devote an entire chapter to Makavejev, to be called "Subversive Cinema" and he wanted to follow it with a chapter on Straub, "Ascetic Cinema". O fthese later chapters only the work on Straub was developed to any extent and the writing on Makavejev consists of a suggestive fragment.

11. Also see MacBean's chapter in *Film and Revolution* on *WR* in which he rejects the art-film Reichianism of Visconti, Petri and Bertolucci in favor of Makavejev.

NOTES ON PARTICIPANTS

ALEXANDER BATCHAN is a film critic working on his Ph.D. in Cinema/Russian Studies at Columbia University. His articles and interviews have appeared in *Cineaste, Columbia Film Review, Film Comment, Slavic and East European Journal* and *Russian History.*

PETER G. CHRISTENSEN teaches at Marquette University in Milwaukee. He has published articles on Soviet Cinema in *Soviet and East European Arts* and *Soviet and East European Drama, Theatre and Film.*

PAUL COATES lived and studied in Poland for several years and now teaches at McGill University in Montreal. He has written *The Story of the Lost Reflection: The Alienation of the Image in Western and Polish Cinema* (Verso, 1985) and other books on literature and film.

NATASA DUROVICOVA is Assistant Professor of Communication Studies at the University of Iowa. She has published in *Wide Angle, Quarterly Review of Film Studies* and elsewhere.

RUTH DWYER teaches Film at McMaster University, Hamilton, Ontario. She is completing a Ph.D. thesis at the University of Toronto on the films of Malcolm St. Clair.

DANIEL GOULDING is Professor of Film Studies and Theater, and Program Chair at Oberlin College, Ohio. His books include *Liberated Cinema: The Yugoslav Experience* (Indiana University Press, 1985) and, as editor and contributor, *Post New Wave Cinema in the Soviet Union and Eastern Europe* (Indiana University Press, 1988).

SLAWOMIR GRUNBERG graduated from the Polish Film School in Lodz in 1981. He has made several video documentaries in the United States, including *USAIDS — Small Town Dilemma* (1988) and *When the Family Gets AIDS* (1988).

ANDREW HORTON is a film critic and scriptwriter who teaches at the University of New Orleans. His filmed scripts include

Something in Between (directed by Srdjan Karanovic) and his books include *The Films of George Roy Hill* (Columbia University Press, 1984) and, as editor and contributor, *Modern European Filmmakers and the Art of Adaptation* (Ungar, 1981) and *Comedy/Cinema/Theory* (forthcoming from the University of California Press).

VIDA JOHNSON is director of the Program in Russian at Tufts University. She has written articles and delivered conference papers on contemporary Soviet Cinema and is working on a book on Andrei Tarkovsky with Graham Petrie.

HEIDI KARRIKER teaches at the University of Oklahoma. She has published articles in *Canadian-American Slavic Studies, World Literature Today* and *Russian Language Journal* and is working on a book on Andrei Tarkovsky.

GEORGE LELLIS holds the Chair of Drama and Communications at Coker College, Hartsville, South Carolina. He is the author of *Bertolt Brecht, Cahiers du Cinéma and Contemporary Film Theory* (UMI Research, 1982), *Film: Form and Function* (Houghton Mifflin, 1981), and *The Film Career of Buster Keaton* (G.K. Hall, 1977), both of the latter with George Wead.

JAMES LEACH teaches Film at Brock University, St. Catharines, Ontario. He is the author of *A Possible Cinema: the Films of Alain Tanner* (Scarecrow Press, 1984).

PATRICK McFADDEN teaches Soviet and East European Cinema at Carleton University in Ottawa. He was a founding editor of the magazine *Take One*, has published articles in *Film Society Review*, and is a frequent broadcaster on film on CBC Radio.

ANNA MAKOLKINA is a Northrop Frye Fellow at the University of Toronto. She has published articles and delivered conference papers on aspects of Russian and Slavic literature.

JOHN MOSIER teaches in the English Department at Loyola University in New Orleans and is Editor of *The New Orleans Review*.

GERALD PEARY is an Associate Professor of Communications and Journalism at Suffolk University, Boston, and a contributing editor of *American Film*. He writes on cinema for the Los Angeles

Times and the Toronto Globe and Mail.

VLADA PETRIC is Curator of the Harvard Film Archive. He has edited *Films and Dreams: An Approach to Bergman* (Redgrave Publishing, 1981) and has recently published *Constructivism in Film: The Man with a Movie Camera* (Cambridge University Press, 1987)

GRAHAM PETRIE teaches Film at McMaster University, Hamilton, Ontario. He has published *The Cinema of François Truffaut* (Zwemmer's, 1970), *History Must Answer to Man: The Contemporary Hungarian Cinema* (Corvina Press, Budapest, 1979) and *Hollywood Destinies: European Directors in America, 1922-1931* (Routledge & Kegan Paul, 1985).

CATHERINE PORTUGES is Director of the Program in Film Studies at the University of Massachusetts, Amherst, Massachusetts. She is working on a book on the films of Márta Mészáros.

BART TESTA teaches Cinema Studies at Innis College, University of Toronto and Semiotics and Visual Art at Victoria College. He has published articles in *The Canadian Journal of Social and Political Theory* and has contributed to the volumes *Words and Moving Images* (Media Texte), *Dialogue* (Media Texte), *Making the Invisible Visible* (Scarecrow Press) and to the catalogue for the travelling exhibition *Spirit in the Landscape* (Art Gallery of Ontario).

JOHN TWOMEY teaches Film at Ryerson Polytechnical Institute at Toronto and is a past chairman of their School of Radio and Television Arts. He created the Soloviov Design Exhibition, which is now in the hands of the artist's widow.